RENZO PIANO BUILDING WORKSHOP

Phaidon Press Limited
Regent's Wharf
All Saints Street
London N1 9PA

First published 1997
Reprinted in paperback 2000

© 1997 Phaidon Press Limited

ISBN 0 7148 3933 7

A CIP catalogue record for this book is
available from the British Library

Frontispiece illustration: Cy Twombly
Gallery, Houston, USA.

Printed in Hong Kong

RENZO PIANO BUILDING WORKSHOP

Complete works

Volume three

Peter Buchanan

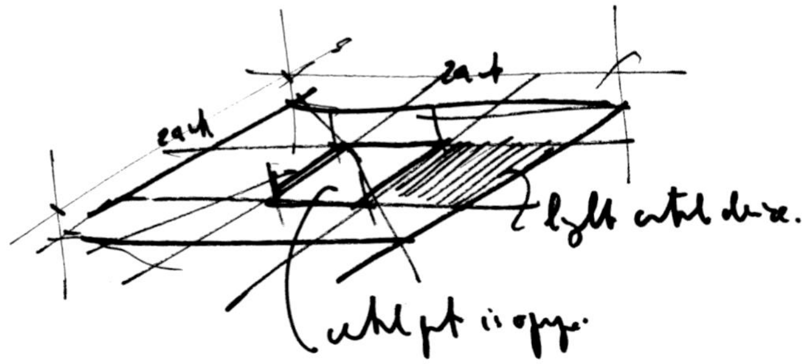

Contents

From Pompidou to Kansai   **6**

Lingotto Factory Renovation   **40**

Tate Gallery at Bankside   **54**

Cy Twombly Gallery   **56**

Cité Internationale de Lyon   **74**

Île Seguin and Bas Meudon   **98**

Rome Auditoria   **102**

Grand Stade   **114**

Saitama Arena   **120**

Kansai International Airport Terminal   **128**

Renzo Piano Biography   **230**

Acknowledgements   **231**

Bibliography   **233**

Index   **236**

Photographic Credits   **239**

6

The completion of the Kansai International Airport, a building far bigger than the Pompidou Centre, and as much if not more of an architectural milestone, together with the ongoing comprehensive refurbishment of the Pompidou Centre make this an appropriate moment to take stock and reflect upon Renzo Piano's career to date. It is also an opportunity to ponder the wider significance of his architecture for today and the future.

Perhaps the most overwhelming impression to emerge from any publication of Piano's work is of its extraordinary heterogeneity. This is even more striking when looking at the work in all three volumes of the Complete Works; although the common themes also emerge clearly. These include a predilection for a sense of lightness, particularly for light-weight construction assembled from components specially developed for each project. These constitute what Piano calls the 'pieces', the elements that are utterly intrinsic to the identity of the design. Other long-pursued preferences include structure exposed internally, bringing daylight in through the roof, reconciling technology and nature, and more recently for terracotta cladding and complex curves sheathed in repetitive metal panels.

Yet despite these recurrent themes, and the recognizably common spirit and sensibility shaping them, the heterogeneity arises because the designs are exceptionally unburdened by any dogmatically narrow, theoretical approach or predictable personal design

From Pompidou to Kansai and back again

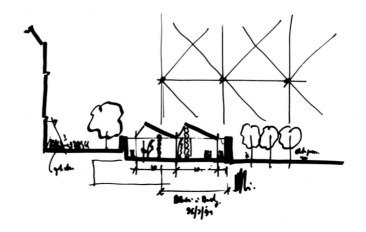

8

1

2

idiom. Instead they are shaped to an exceptional degree by programme, place and the times. Unique to each project, these inevitably result in very different designs. Moreover, these same factors determine another key feature of Piano's work which is always different, further contributing to its heterogeneity: the precise and carefully judged balance between the use of imported, leading-edge technologies and of local, traditional materials and crafts (or updated versions of these). In this way Piano seeks to draw on both what is still vital and valid in the local culture and what is most effective and apt in our now global civilization, the universalizing tendencies of which he resists with this fusion of the local as well as by developing conspicuous components, the 'pieces', unique to each project. This surely is one of the most important and topical quests an architect can pursue today, and it is this which makes Piano's work so different from the logotype, brand-image designs of other star architects, as well as that of those who blindly follow the so-called 'technological imperative' of using the latest technology.

But then, what is especially evident when looking at the major themes addressed by each of Piano's works, since and including the Pompidou Centre, is just how topical they have been. As well as being shaped by the factors already mentioned, the Building Workshop's architecture is also a product of Piano's ever-evolving approach, and those of his key collaborators. These not only reflect the times, but have also developed with the accumulated experience and maturity of each person. As Piano's career has progressed, his *œuvre* reveals a constant broadening of concerns, expanding from an initial few, purely objective ones, to a wide range of both objective and subjective issues.

Especially in contrast with current projects, the early works of the Studio Piano era (Volume One p 46) were very narrowly focused. Although lightness, translucency and economy of means are aesthetic as well as technical issues, these designs deliberately, and almost exclusively concentrated on very objective issues, such as achieving maximum spans and volumes of enclosure with the minimum of weight and material. These achievements (consistent with Buckminster Fuller's then influential ideas of the necessity of doing more with less) can be assessed objectively because they are entirely quantifiable.

From this very narrow focus (with which he originally honed his design approach, technical expertise, aesthetic predilection and the elements of an ever-expanding vocabulary) Piano has steadily extended the range of concerns addressed by his architecture. He has never foregone his concern with meeting objective technical challenges and criteria, but these have expanded from concerns with structure and assembly into an ever-widening spectrum of issues, including acoustics and how these can be adjusted, ideal environmental conditions, and the energy efficiencies gained in using an increasing range of passive

3

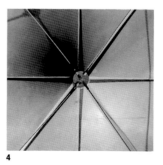

4

5

Previous page

Pompidou Centre: oblique view of escalator
tube suspended outside west elevation.
Beyond is IRCAM Extension.

Details of early works by Studio Piano
assembled from repetitive lightweight units.
1 Reinforced Polyester Space Frame, Genoa,
1964–65.
2 Woodwork Shop, Genoa, 1965.
3 Mobile Structure for Sulphur Extraction,
Pomezia, Rome, 1966.
4 Italian Industry Pavilion, Expo 1970, Osaka,
1969–70.

Early works by Studio Piano.
5 Shell Structural System for the Fourteenth
Milan Triennale, 1967.
6 Office-workshop for Studio Piano, Genoa,
1968–69 showing structural and servicing
elements.

means to ensure these conditions. These are
now overlaid with a proliferating range of
far-from-objective cultural issues (such as
local history and notions of urbanity), and
even highly subjective ones (such as the
appropriate atmosphere and the formal and
material allusions that trigger personal and
collective memories). And always important
is the inspiration of, and search for, ever new
ways of not just harmonizing with nature but
actually emulating it.

There are several major milestones that
chart the expanding range of concerns in
Piano's career. These include the UNESCO
Neighbourhood Workshop, IBM Travelling
Pavilion, the Menil Collection, San Nicola
Stadium, rue de Meaux Housing, UNESCO
Laboratory-workshop and so on (every
reader's list will differ slightly). But the
Pompidou Centre and Kansai International
Airport stand out from all of these because of
their size and familiarity to millions, and most
especially because they are truly seminal statements about two quite different eras. In time,
Kansai is bound to be seen as being as important to the architecture of the 1990s (and no
doubt even more so to that of coming decades)
as was the Pompidou to that of the 1970s.

The major work from Piano's partnership
with Richard Rogers, the Pompidou Centre,
opened a new era in Piano's work: it introduced new concerns and ways of working,
and initiated an international dimension to
his career. His first work truly concerned with
people, it was designed to be explored and

enjoyed by the throngs who now swarm both
outside and through the building. It also
introduced Piano to a collaborative way of
working, conceiving of and developing the
design, not just with Rogers, but in an intense
collaboration with a large team of independent consultants as well as with the architects
working for Piano & Rogers. All of these people, in differing degrees, made their contribution to this collaborative adventure, which
has been Piano's way of working ever since.

Moreover, this was, as Piano has described
it, 'an international adventure', not just
because it introduced him to the world stage
that he has operated on ever since, nor
because the building's components were
made in various parts of Europe, but also
because members of the architectural and
consulting teams came together from around
the globe. Certain key contributors, who first
worked with Piano on the Pompidou Centre,
have continued to work with him: his associates, Shunji Ishida, Noriaki Okabe and
Bernard Plattner, and the Ove Arup &
Partners' engineers, Peter Rice (structures)
and Tom Barker (services).

This international dimension has been a
distinctive aspect of the Building Workshop
ever since. Not only has the multinational
make-up of its members and consultants
continued, but it is the only architectural
practice in the world it would be misleading
to classify in terms of the countries in which it
originated and is now based. The Building
Workshop is hardly Italian or French; and its

9

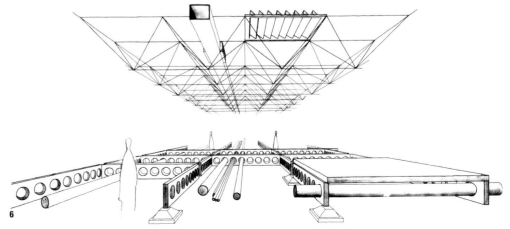

6

designs are neither exports from these countries nor an updated equivalent of a placeless International Style. Particularly since the design of the Menil Collection (Volume One p 141), the projects (besides importing new elements that might be used anywhere) are shaped not only as a response to immediate context, but also to the local materials and traditions and aspects of a broader culture. Yet, even earlier, the seminal UNESCO Neighbourhood Workshop experiment in Otranto (Volume One p 68) had fused and sought a balance between the input of the local culture, achieved through the participation of the community and its craftsmen, and the latest resources of contemporary technology, especially in the equipment used for surveying and documenting conditions.

Designed in the early 1970s, the Pompidou Centre epitomizes the ideals and optimism, particularly about technology, that were current in the 1960s in London and Paris, among other places. In retrospect, it also marks a climax of both the emancipatory project of the Enlightenment, in which culture would be enjoyed by all, and of the soon-to-be waning ideals of the machine age, in which technology was expected to ensure this democratic equality of access. Yet even the Pompidou can now be seen as having picked up on more local themes, connecting it with other phases in even longer cycles of history in which building technology was pushed to new limits. Thus (as already discussed in Volume One), it has striking affinities with

Notre Dame – both loom above their surroundings and have externalized their skeletal structures in the quest for transparency. It also seems to have resurrected developments in Paris (where Structural-Rationalism met Constructivism in the Maison du Peuple in Clichy by Beaudouin and Lods with Jean Prouvé, as well as the Maisons Suspendue and de Publicité by Paul Nelson and Oscar Nitschke respectively) that had been abandoned prematurely because of the Second World War. Although this might surprise many, it implies that the Pompidou is also the first of Piano's buildings to evoke some resonances with local history, even if these were not consciously intended.

Unlike Piano's early works, the Pompidou does not limit itself to being a delicately wrought, materially minimal enclosure. Instead, it is a flexible skeletal framework, serviced by exposed entrails, that takes a deliberately provocative stance against earlier notions of culture and the venerable city. Intended as an interactive mechanism (though one replete with organic overtones) for the living arts, rather than a pompous, elitist mausoleum for the art of the past, it is plonked like a newly arrived space-ship in its historic surroundings. Alternatively, it can be seen as a vast piece of gadgetry or furniture (a sort of 1960s 'room divider'/storage wall) in an urban room, its exposed structure and services acknowledging that it is the facades of the old buildings facing it that are the edges of the total work – of which the Place

10   UNESCO Neighbourhood Workshop by Piano Rice Associates, Otranto, Italy, 1979.
1 Plan of Neighbourhood Workshop opened up and in use.
2 Town meeting in piazza at night with main speakers under tent roof of Neighbourhood Workshop.

Pompidou Centre by Piano & Rogers, Paris, 1971–78.
3 Building in context, looming above the historic fabric of Paris.
4 Double-height gallery at northern end of fourth floor.
5 Cross section through Pompidou Centre and Place Beaubourg.
6 Typical floor laid out as gallery.
7 Old buildings facing Place Beaubourg are the outer walls of the complete work constituted by the new building and the square together.

1

2

3

4

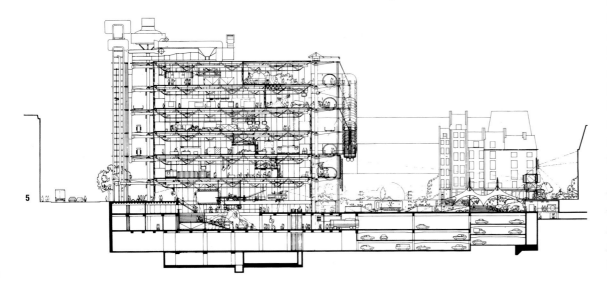

5

6

Beaubourg is as integral as the main building.

A mechanical contraption that makes space for, and services the unpredictable requirements of a multi-functional cultural centre, it is a framework of loosely coordinated and rearrangeable systems, always in process and incomplete. Although a mechanism at the service of humankind and culture, what it tends to show off best is itself, overwhelming artworks and people (even banishing human circulation to a dangling external tube, thrilling though this is to use). The Pompidou thus achieves the paradoxical status of monumentalizing the ideals, as much as realizing the actuality, of flexibility and function (previously thought of as anti-monumental ideals).

How utterly different is Kansai's passenger terminal. This is, of course, inevitable considering that it was designed for a very dissimilar location and function; but it was also designed in what is almost, just two decades later, a new epoch. It also exemplifies a very different attitude to people. Instead of being in the centre of a city, hemmed in by historic buildings, it is on an artificial island so recently constructed that part of it was still being filled in when the terminal's foundations were being laid. Rather than provoking and accommodating unpredictable demand, the terminal must function, day in day out, in the same smoothly preordained manner to reassure potentially nervous passengers. Also, far from being built at a time when the brute power of the machine was still widely

11

7

1

Pompidou Centre.
1 Central portion of west elevation
overlooking Place Beaubourg.
2 Pompidou Centre: east elevation facing
rue Renard is festooned with ducts.

admired, we are now in an age that demands technology (mechanical technology at least, though not yet such things as electronics or genetic engineering) be more deferential to nature and humankind, to which end the computer promises to provide the means.

Despite its vast size, and the fact that it is an interchange between various means of mechanical transport rather than a cultural centre, the Kansai terminal, unlike the Pompidou, is very much shaped around Man (though sceptics might say: only Man as scuttling passenger). In particular, it is given form by people's movement and the searching scan of their eyes. Although the shuttle trains run outside the outstretched boarding-wings, against which all the planes dock, circulation is not otherwise marginalized. It is not only central to the design, but every aspect of the building – space and views, even ceiling and structure – helps guide and urge along the circulation of passengers, while the flowing structure reassuringly keeps them company. Moreover, although the building is an interchange between sophisticated moving machines, and is itself machine-like in its clarity, efficiency and glider-like form, it is also highly organic. The finiteness of its form (the opposite of the mere extrusion that can be chopped into self-complete sub-parts) could be considered organic, and even more so could the tight integration between the building's various systems and components, several of which, such as the skeletal structural system, are

themselves biomorphic in form.

That architecture should approximate the mechanical or the organic, or better yet, conflate the two, is a dream that has run through modernism since its origins with Viollet-le-Duc and other nineteenth-century architect-theorists. Critics of this bio-mechanical strand, which first manifested itself in movements such as the Neo-Gothic and Art Nouveau, deemed this quest inappropriate as buildings do not move, unlike machines and organisms (they seemed to forget that plants tend to stay in one spot). So it is fitting that these organic ideals have at last been brought together in a building which (though it moves only relatively small amounts with seismic action and settlement) is so thoroughly dedicated to movement: that of people, baggage and air within it, and of various mechanical means of transport without.

It is movement of people, and the flow of the billowing and tapering spaces that pull them forward, as well as the continuities of the structure, that help unify the design into such an exceptional organic whole. But equally crucial in achieving the semblance of the organic, and the sense of utter inevitability and understatement that are other striking aspects of the design, is the extraordinary degree of integration between the systems and elements of the building (as if achieved, as in evolution, over generations of mutual accommodation) and the geometric discipline to which these are all subordinate.

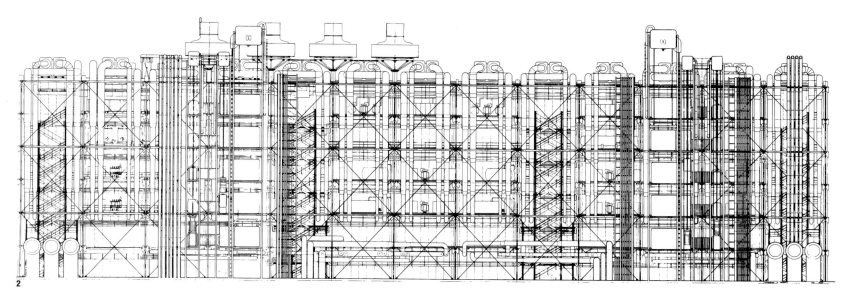

2

3

Kansai International Airport Terminal, Osaka,
1988–94: the tight integration between structure,
space, skin and services.

3 International departures hall.

4 Transit lounge between international departures
and boarding wing.

5 Section through boarding wing with main
terminal block in elevation behind.

4

These attributes, however, could only have been realized with the help of the computer.

The computer plays an increasing role in architecture. The new theoretical approaches in various branches of engineering, and the associated calculations on which many of the buildings in these volumes are dependent, are only possible using the computer. During the design process, the computer is used to simulate and predict not only the performance of structural systems and components under all sorts of stresses, but also such things as the changes in environmental conditions throughout the year, the acoustics of variable-volume halls and smoke accumulation and escape times in case of fire. Drawings are done on computer, some of which control the manufacture of components; also quantities are measured and specifications issued, flow charts prepared and progress monitored. Once a building is complete, a computerized building-management system controls environmental conditions throughout, perhaps moving excess heat from one part to another cooler part, even detecting which rooms are occupied and need light and ventilation and granting access to these according to a person's security status.

All of the above uses of the computer are increasingly familiar to most architects; but, as already argued in the introduction to Volume Two, the Building Workshop is one of the few architectural practices to have grasped its true potential in generating building form. This potential lies not in its ability to facilitate whimsy, including biomorphic forms, because it can draw quickly and then control the manufacture of one-off components. Instead the computer's potential lies in its capacity to generate new forms, particularly ones related to those it is now revealing as underlying nature, which can serve as an encompassing discipline – especially useful if they result in an exceptional degree of integration between the building's various systems, as well as new levels of economy and efficiency in both performance and manufacture. With industrially made components, it is high levels of repetition of identical pieces that constitute the equivalent of the organic order manifested in leaves or scales that, though controlled by the same genetic template, are different in size because they grow rather than are made.

Kansai's relation to organic order, however, goes beyond these dimensions. There are strong parallels between the way it was designed and the revolution that is taking place in the natural sciences. Until relatively recently, a science like biology was largely concerned with the classification of species and their parts. The computer has changed all this, making possible the study of dynamic processes, not just static products. In various ways it has made previously invisible or incomprehensible processes visible and available for study. It can slow down or speed up processes of transformation, growth and gestation, or it can create conceptual models with differing variables as exploratory and

13

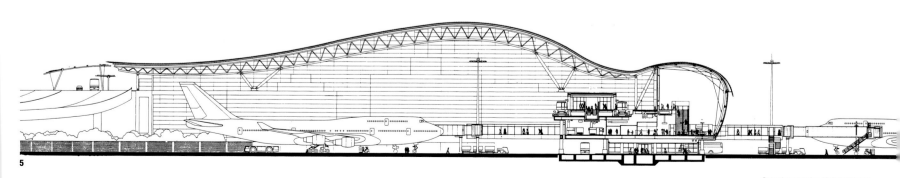

5

14   Kansai International Airport Terminal.

1 Diagram of geometric derivation of air-scoop in international departures hall.

2 Diagram shows close integration of structure and air-scoops; their shapes propel space as well as air forward.

3 Photomontage compares sizes of London's Hyde Park and terminal.

4 San Nicola Stadium, Bari, 1987–90.

5 IBM Travelling Pavilion, 1982–84.

6 National Centre for Science and Technology, Amsterdam, 1992–.

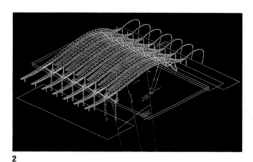

1

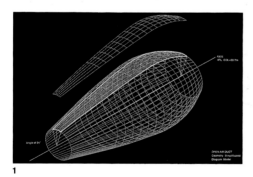

2

often very revealing analogues of natural phenomena. The consequence is that these sciences are moving away from an emphasis on taxonomy towards studying the processes of emergent form, exploring how those forms arise and how they transmute into other forms.

Kansai has been designed in a way that is analogous to a reversal of this process, hence the very tight meshing of elements that seem to have co-evolved together. Although some building components have been designed in a similar way, Kansai is the first building, and probably the first large-scale human artefact designed in this manner.

This is the most profound level at which Kansai could be said to be organic, thus realizing yet another dimension to Piano's quest for a natural architecture (a theme elaborated in the introductory essay to Volume One). It is also why Kansai seems so perfectly to symbolize the emergent era in which, for better or worse, the natural is increasingly engineered and technology increasingly models itself on nature (in its performance if not always in form). If the Pompidou belongs to a machine age of reductive analysis, resulting in independent systems that are disjointed and aloof from Man, the Kansai Terminal promises an electronic age when our dreams are of synthesis and reconciliation, of pulling the world together again and placing Man at its centre, though now in harmony with, and not elevated above, the natural world. Paradoxically, the Pompidou's fulfilment of the

dreams of its time also marks their passing, while Kansai, by realizing a far older dream, is the herald of the future.

There are other architects who claim to be using the computer to apply to architecture the new forms and topologies found to underlie nature, whether they are fractals, soliton curves, crystalline foldings or whatever. But there are profound differences between what they do and what has been achieved at Kansai. Instead of the form slowly emerging out of a thorough exploration and meshing together of all the building's systems, it is generated early on in the design process in an arbitrary and aleatoric manner. More often than not, only the outer envelope conforms to the computer-generated shape, and it has no logic in terms of the disciplines of construction or component manufacture. Inside, space is purely residual and amorphous, and structure and services follow their own disciplines without any synthesis with the skin or each other. Function accommodates itself as best it can. Except in their floor-to-ceiling heights, such buildings have very little relationship with Man, and are indeed proudly proclaimed as anti-Humanist. Such a position might be endorsed by some contemporary French philosophy (such as Deconstruction), but it is profoundly out of touch with much of what is happening at the leading edges of science and in the philosophy of science; in quantum mechanics, for instance, sub-atomic events are dependent on the presence and position of the per-

3

4

5

ceiver, or in the controversial Anthropic Principle, cosmologists argue that the evolution of mankind seems to have been predestined since the Big Bang. (Even those who consider the emergent era as post-Humanist do so not to belittle Man, but to recognize that what were once thought to be uniquely human attributes, such as consciousness, are shared in some degree by other creatures, and soon probably by machines too.)

To single out and contrast Pompidou and Kansai because of their size and seminal importance (not just for Piano, but for architecture generally), is a revealing exercise. It highlights how profoundly the world has changed in a very short time, and how little this is reflected in the work of most other architects. But this comparison also gives a distorting impression, not only because the work of Piano and the Building Workshop is far more varied than it suggests (and includes several other works of comparable quality), but also because the architects themselves have not pursued much further the approaches exemplified by either of these buildings.

In the case of the Pompidou Centre, this was no doubt because the building not only marks a climax, but also the end of an era. Early in its construction came the first oil crisis provoked by the Six Day War in the Middle East. By the time the building was complete, faith in energy-guzzling mechanical technology was wavering and there was widespread criticism of modern architecture,

particularly its urban failings. Conservationist attitudes were beginning to prevail, advocating the saving of existing buildings as well as energy, that wanted architects to be more sensitive and respectful of nature and historic settings.

After Pompidou, Piano formed a practice with Peter Rice and entered an intensely experimental phase, not just expanding the range of his concerns and expertise, but also reorientating himself. For instance, with the UNESCO Neighbourhood Workshop project (Volume One p 68), he sought a way to use a compatible mix of simple local and very sophisticated imported technologies to regenerate the social and physical fabric of relatively mundane historic towns. Following his founding of the Building Workshop, he went on to consolidate and expand much of this thinking. With Peter Rice, usually, as structural engineer, he explored how to introduce new technology harmoniously into various settings: old buildings at the Schlumberger Renovation (Volume One p 90); verdant nature with the IBM Travelling Pavilion (Volume One p 110); a low-key suburban setting with the Menil Collection (Volume One p 140); a pivotal urban site with the IRCAM Extension (Volume One p 202); an Arcadian landscape with the San Nicola Stadium (Volume One p 178). Apart from a tendency to colour-code the elements of a building, vestiges of the Pompidou (which unlike these later schemes does not temper its concern with technology

15

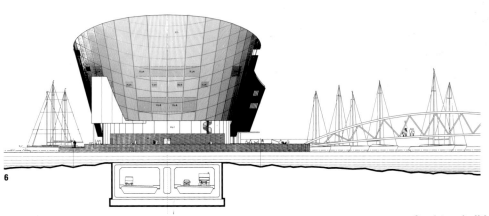

6

16

with an equal interest in context) resurface only occasionally, as with the external ducts and bright colours at the Thomson Optronics Factory (Volume Two p 34) and the exposed cylindrical air-conditioning ducts at Kansai.

Kansai's strong internal design rules and the pressures the design team worked under (which were a major reason for the adoption and submission to these design rules) helped to push the architects into all sorts of potentially fruitful new territories. However, Kansai's legacy has so far only manifested itself in a use of toroids for the roofs of the Mercedes-Benz Design Centre and the Rome Auditoria (p 102), and in the cladding of curves with repetitive metal panels, such as on the National Museum for Science and Technology, Amsterdam (Volume Two p 132). Perhaps too, the long vista and flowing sequence of spaces that will lead visitors through the latter design owes something to Piano's spatial discoveries at Kansai; but otherwise, the Building Workshop has again set off in other directions.

One reason the approach pursued at Kansai has not been taken further, for the time being at least, is that though it is probably particularly suited to such a vast and programmatically precise and predictable building on an open site, it is less relevant for more mundane structures on constrained sites. However, this approach is so in tune with what is happening in science and other fields that it seems certain in time to become widely applied. Until then, it is very likely that it will be taken up in product design: it is more usually in the design of cars and planes, than in buildings, that one can find increasingly tight integration between the various systems that constitute them.

Although none of the Building Workshop's current commissions would suit a similar approach to that pioneered at Kansai, they confront and deal with some of the most pervasive and pressing of contemporary problems in imaginatively innovative ways. These include repairing the fabric of the city core, and converting obsolete buildings, bringing these cherished monuments to life with new uses. Such projects restore a sense of wholeness to the city, and help it evolve to suit today's lifestyles, while retaining or re-establishing its roots in the past. As a corollary of this, most architects now strive to make their buildings 'contextual', but few display such diversity of ways of integrating their buildings into their settings as do Piano and the Building Workshop.

As well as repairing and fitting into the existing city, architects must also help cities develop in other ways to suit current and future conditions. As it evolves, the contemporary city is becoming increasingly poly-nucleated. The Building Workshop is currently building only one urban node that will eventually be contiguous with the urban fabric around it – the Potsdamer Platz project in Berlin (Volume Two p 210).

1

2

3

4

1 Columbus International Exposition, Genoa, 1984–92.

2 IRCAM Extension, Paris, 1988–89.

3 Schlumberger Renovation, Paris, 1981–84.

4 Bercy 2 Shopping Centre, Paris, 1987–90.

5 Rue de Meaux Housing, Paris, 1988–91.

6 Thomson Optronics Factory, Guyancourt, St Quentin-en-Yvelines, 1988–91.

But it is also working on other large projects which, despite forming isolated precincts because of contextual constraints, will add immensely to the resources and life of their respective cities. Some of these projects develop further a particular approach to making facades that are not only contextually sensitive and warmly urbane, but will weather to settle in even better with age. Yet now, too, to achieve greater energy efficiency, an outer enclosure of glass is being added to these terracotta-clad facades.

The range of strategies these projects employ to deal with a wide range of current urban, contextual and more general environmental and energy issues, make them all extremely topical. If the second half of this volume devoted to the Kansai terminal is a glimpse of the future, the first half is almost a manual about characteristic problems encountered in current practice. It is to emphasize this that the Kansai terminal, which chronologically should come first in the book, is placed as a climactic, forward-looking end-piece, and the rest of the projects are arranged not in strict chronology but as pairs, or a trio, that confront similar contemporary challenges. Most of the remainder of this essay highlights some of the comparisons this format of coupled projects affords, while also drawing some relevant parallels with projects in the first two volumes, so emphasizing the range and responsiveness of the Building Workshop's approaches to these challenges.

Among the most prevalent and pressing problems facing architects today is the legacy of 'functional' town planning and the Charter of Athens. These promoted simplistic notions of efficiency, sought in mono-functional zoning and unimpeded traffic flows, rather than the rich web of social relationships, in particular the urban life of the street. The once-continuous fabric of the city is now rent into fragments, or has been razed altogether to be replaced by freestanding buildings forlornly isolated from one another and the roads. In rediscovering the virtues of urbanity, architects face the challenge of reweaving into a new whole the fabric of the city and reinstating the opportunities it once offered for social interaction. Two large-scale projects by the Building Workshop that do precisely this are the Columbus International Exposition in Genoa (Volume Two p 94), which reconnects the historic city with the oldest part of the docks, now refurbished for public use, and the Potsdamer Platz scheme which, when complete, will be a bustling urban quarter that seamlessly reconnects what was once separated into West and East Berlin. At a somewhat less grand scale, so, too, do the Headquarters of the Banca Popolare di Lodi, in that city, and an unsuccessful competition entry outlining a design strategy for a large extension to the University Hospital in Strasbourg.

The Lodi bank headquarters are now nearing completion and so will be published at length in a future volume, and the Strasbourg scheme (as required in the competition condi-

17

5

6

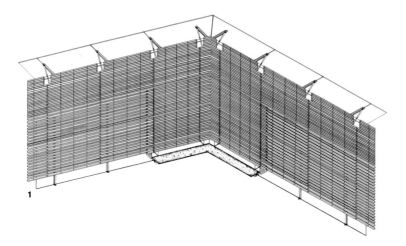

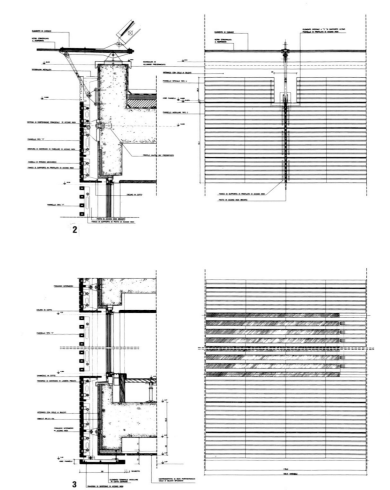

18 Banca Popolare di Lodi, Lodi, Italy.

1 Worm's eye isometric of terracotta-clad external corner capped by frosted glass cornice.

2 Section and elevation of head of external wall with cornice supported by metal brackets and terracotta cladding that extends in front of window as protective grille.

3 Section and elevation of external wall at first floor level.

4 Location and ground floor plan: **a** station **b** widened street with commuter parking **c** pedestrian precinct connecting station and town centre **d** auditorium used by bank and city **e** garden **f** ramps to underground parking.

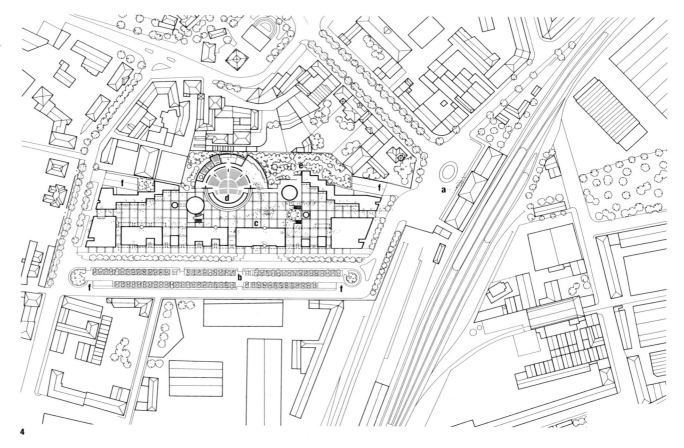

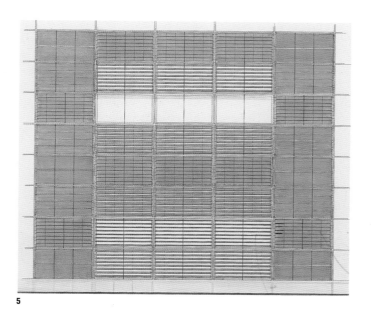

5

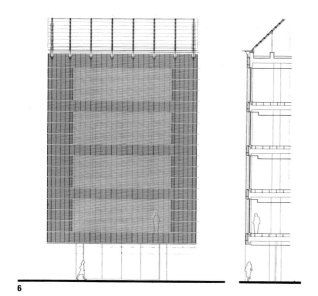

Banca Popolare di Lodi.

5 Part elevation of different cladding treatments. Windows are protected and shaded, partially or wholly, by different densities of terracotta grille.

6 Elevation and section of cladding bay (nearly two structural bays) of linear block.

7 Roof plan: **a** glass roof suspended from radial cables **b** auditorium **c** cylindrical towers housing strong rooms and plant **d** linear block **e** helipad.

8 West–east cross section through linear block along widened street, pedestrian precinct sheltered by suspended glass roof, auditorium and garden.

6

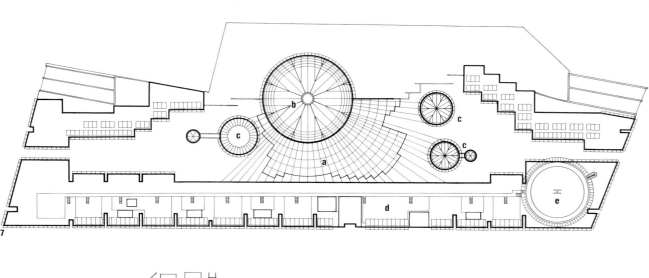

7

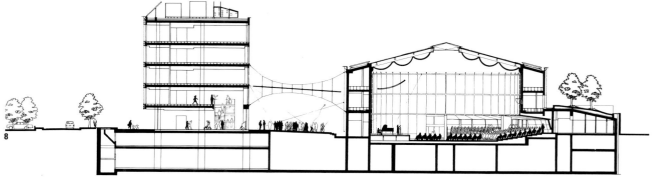

8

tions) is too schematic to show in detail. Both schemes are for sites that edge an urban core, and exploit similar strategies to reweave their surroundings. Both create a new piece of the public pedestrian realm that crosses the site to link the town or city centre with a major public facility: a paved and partially glass-roofed court leading to the station at Lodi; a glazed-in 'street' leading to a park at Strasbourg. In the transverse direction to these routes, both schemes present to one side relatively solid frontages, defining the space of the street and addressing the buildings across it; while towards the opposite side of the site their forms break down to interlock with gardens. At Lodi, specialized functions are housed in freestanding cylindrical elements that establish a relationship with the tower of a nearby castle and with the silos that are a prominent feature of the farms in the surrounding countryside. At Strasbourg, the hospital wards form fingers that interlock with rows of existing trees.

But to reweave and revivify the city, it is not enough merely to re-establish the street wall, recreate and reconnect pedestrian realms and reciprocate the forms of neighbouring buildings, or those associated with the surrounding area. It is also necessary to use materials that have a scale, texture and warmth, a visual vibration and vivacity that people might enjoy a prolonged proximity to – as well as weathering gracefully, so helping the buildings to settle into place. Hard, cold and overly smooth materials tend to result in buildings and outdoor spaces that are frigid and forbidding. Such buildings also lack the texture and detail that might catch the eye and so arrest the restless flow of space, thus creating a calm and comforting sense of place.

For such reasons, the Lodi building is yet another in a continuing series that uses terracotta units as a cladding. Here, though, instead of small units together making up a larger metal-framed panel (as at the IRCAM Extension and the Genoa Harbour Master's Office, Volume Two p 123), larger units span independently between recessed verticals, giving this big building an appropriately scaled and horizontally emphasized 'grain'. This cladding is an evolution of that used on the Cité Internationale de Lyon (p 74), though without the energy-saving, glass outer skin. At Lodi, there is also an elegant cornice of frosted glass to finish the building against the sky and to read as a sort of coving that helps define the adjacent public spaces as outdoor rooms.

As well as reintegrating the city, architects are increasingly engaged in restoring and converting old buildings which the public and the planners would rather see kept than replaced by contemporary architecture. Considering what so many current buildings are like, this is understandable. Yet it is ironic that some of those buildings now treasured as monuments were built only as functional industrial plant that would lose all raison d'être and be demolished when obsolete.

Terracotta claddings.
1 Cité Internationale, Lyons: beyond the terracotta cladding of office blocks on right is a second skin of large adjustable glass louvres that provides economies of energy consumption.
2, 3 Columbus International Exposition:
2 close-up of service spine and
3 Harbour Master's Office.

21

2

3

1

2

But then, when moving from one era to another, that which is left behind becomes properly visible for the first time. This, together with their loss of utility results in the characteristic environment and artefacts of that era being elevated to the status of art. So, as the Industrial Revolution overtook Britain, Constable's paintings celebrated the agricultural landscape. Now, as we leave the industrial era for that of electronics and services, or as robots replace people in automated factories, the old industrial landscape is cherished as an artwork. Its very lack of artistic pretension gives it a vital authenticity now treasured for its timeless aesthetic quality.

Hence obsolete industrial plants, like Turin's Lingotto Factory (p 40 and Volume Two p 150) and London's Bankside Power Station (p 54), are being converted into galleries, museums and other cultural complexes. The Pompidou Centre was prophetic: using an industrial vocabulary for a cultural institution, it was not only provoking a new view of culture but also recognizing the passing of the machine age that its architecture monumentalizes.

The Fiat factory in Lingotto, Turin, was designed by the engineer Giacomo Matté-Trucco. When completed in the 1920s its rigorous, stripped and repetitive forms were immediately recognized by Le Corbusier and other architects as those of a masterpiece. It was inevitable that when obsolete it would be renovated and reused. By contrast, the

Bankside Power Station, designed by the architect Giles Gilbert Scott, looked dressed up and dated when eventually completed in the 1960s, and what now seem rather powerful forms then appeared overly rhetorical. It is a minor work compared to the same architect's Battersea Power Station (which sadly has been dismembered, probably beyond repair, in another conversion that has been aborted).

Bankside is to be converted not because it is deemed a monument that must be saved; instead it is because of the widespread antipathy to modern and contemporary architecture, felt not only by a conservative British public but also by artists, even the most avant-garde of them. Significantly, the competition brief gave the impression of being less concerned with the viewing public than with flattering the aspirations of artists. In it, two of the most popular establishments in the world, New York's Museum of Modern Art and the Pompidou Centre, are dismissed because artists do not like them. Artists prefer the raw and provisional quality of converted industrial premises that resemble the studios they work in and the premises they probably first showed in. In such settings their work promises to retain a vitality and currency that might be tempered if it is entombed (perhaps prematurely in their eyes) in a purpose-built museum.

But the challenges in converting industrial premises into a museum for permanent or long-term display are quite different to those

3

4

5

Bankside Power Station, London.
1 Riverside elevation dominated by central chimney.
2 Turbine hall that extends full length and height of building.
3 Tate Gallery at Bankside competition entry, London, 1995: proposed axial route connects building to neighbourhood and, via a foot-bridge, St Paul's Cathedral and City of London.

Lingotto Factory Renovation, Turin, 1983–.
4 Aerial photograph of factory in early stages of renovation.
5 An insistent grid controls layout of park on west of site.
6 Landscaping plan: **a** park **b** piazza.
7 Southernmost court on roof of new gallery space.

of making good spaces for short-term display. Meeting all sorts of stringent standards for conserving both the displayed works and the building can be difficult to reconcile with keeping the gritty character that artists and others admire in old industrial buildings. To achieve this at Bankside, the Building Workshop proposed leaving the outer walls untouched and housing the galleries in a new structure standing free within this shell.

The Lingotto Factory renovation required a very different strategy. A vast building, even in comparison with Bankside, it now accommodates much more than just galleries and other exhibition facilities. There is a concert and congress hall that needs to be fully isolated acoustically and faced internally in materials of the right rigidity and acoustic reflectivity. And there are conference facilities, a hotel, and not-yet-completed large business centre and incubator units for fledgling businesses. All of these will be used primarily by business men, who might like old buildings yet not care for the raw and gritty qualities prized by artists, preferring their premises to be slick and sanitized. Besides, Lingotto lacked Bankside's large clear-span spaces so that any intervention is constrained by the ubiquitous close-spaced grid of columns. It is particularly unfortunate that Lingotto's exterior had deteriorated so much that the original windows have had to be replaced and the crumbling concrete surfaces protected by a special render.

All this has led to an inevitable compromise of the tough and frugal character that had constituted so much of the old factory's appeal. Sadly, this character can now only be glimpsed on the sides of the central service cores that close the internal courts and inside the central part of the trade fair hall. But otherwise it was largely impossible here to follow the strategy associated with Piano's early mentor, Franco Albini (which Piano had pursued himself when rehabilitating the Schlumberger Factory in Paris), of keeping old and new quite distinct, with the old as little changed as possible. (This same strategy later became somewhat caricatured by Carlo Scarpa, who often stripped back the old to make it more rough and ruinous than it had ever been, and has now become a pervasive and predictable cliché.)

Within their respective urban contexts, Lingotto and Bankside also presented similar challenges as to how to tie the aloof old buildings into their surroundings in an inviting manner suited to their new public roles. In both schemes, a major elevation now addresses the neighbourhood across a piazza, and on the building's opposite side an engineering solution (shuttles or footbridge) links it to a part of the city from which previously it had been isolated.

At Lingotto, steps climb through new openings in the eastern elevation to lead up from the piazza to the first floor. This is the main public circulation level and is conceived of as a piece of Turin, complete

23

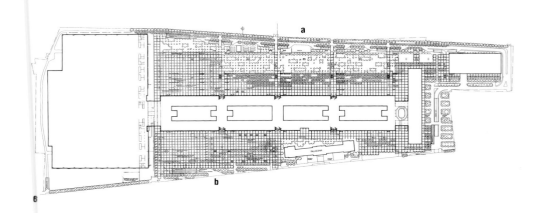

6

7

with shopping arcades and café-ringed court-yard-piazzas. On the west, a public transit shuttle on an elevated track will connect this public level to the city's central market. This lies across the railway lines that effectively divide Turin; these edge a new park, designed by the Building Workshop, which is being laid out alongside the old factory, on what had been railway marshalling yards. In the Bankside scheme, the so-called piazza on its southern side was a rather notional one, consisting of shopping pavilions below an oversailing roof. These marked a central axial route that passed through the building to emerge on the northern side and cross another notional piazza and then a proposed footbridge across the Thames. This landed at the base of the steps up to St Paul's Cathedral, thus connecting the new gallery with this major tourist attraction and to the City of London.

In both schemes, the intention behind this common design strategy was to encourage people to pass freely through the building without necessarily engaging in its activities. The idea was that the buildings and their activities would become familiar to people on a rather casual basis so that not only are members of the public encouraged to avail themselves of these resources, but they also become perceived as everyday parts of the city into which they are now integrated. As an important by-product of these new linkages, existing parts of the physical fabric of the city would also be better connected.

Today, however, it is not usually old buildings that need to be better integrated into context, though of course many of them (such as cathedrals and railway stations, as well as mills and factories) once towered over their surroundings. The more usual challenge is to integrate new buildings, especially huge ones housing modern functions. Though offices and shopping centres can be easily manipulated to fit their settings, other buildings such as sports stadia are much more problematic.

Two unsuccessful competition entries by the Building Workshop show, however, that stadia need not be isolated, out-of-town structures shaped without regard for setting or *civitas*. Instead, like their ancient prototype the Colosseum, they can be pivotal in an urban setting, not just gathering into them vast crowds of people, but also creating visual linkages with major features in the surrounding town and landscape. These designs show too that such structures can serve not only the crowd events of soccer matches and athletics meetings, but also have a more quotidian functional relationship with their immediate surroundings. Besides promising to achieve such rich relationships with their surroundings, the designs for the Grande Stade for Paris (designed in collaboration with Jourda & Perraudin) and the Saitama Arena, for the Japanese city from which it takes its name, are remarkable also for their elegant structural solutions and the unprecedented flexibility they provide.

24 **1** Grand Stade, Paris, 1994: perspective from south-west.

Most modern sports stadia, many of which are out of town or in suburban areas, are designed as if they were isolated objects, shaped by function and structural necessity alone and, just like the mooning hooligans they attract, turning ugly backsides to the world around. Piano's previous stadium, San Nicola, built near Bari in southern Italy (Volume One p 178) for the 1990 World Cup, might be an out-of-town, self-contained object that resembles a spaceship barely come to rest. But when there you are struck by how the inward focus on to the playing field is counterbalanced by an extraordinary sense of openness to the surrounding arcadian countryside, which is drawn into a close relationship with the stadium. The Grand Stade and Saitama Arena were designed for urban sites, yet ones that are cut off from their immediate surroundings by the adjacent transport infrastructure. But by crossing this with bridges and underpasses and using built form and vistas to make visual connections with elements in the distant surroundings, as well as by including small-scale functions to be used daily by the neighbourhood, these projects would have been thoroughly integrated into their surroundings while adding a powerful new dimension to them.

Like most Italian stadia, San Nicola is used for both soccer matches and athletic meetings, but the track around the soccer pitch distances spectators from the match. The competition brief for the Grand Stade required a stadium that would seat 80,000

spectators tightly packed around a soccer match, and yet, with fewer spectators, would also accommodate an athletics track. The Building Workshop solution harks back to when the Romans flooded the Colosseum to stage mock sea-battles. It was to put the sports field on a barge that could be raised and lowered by flooding the huge tank it floated in, and to retract or extend bleacher seating. The Saitama Arena exploited a similar system, though used jacks to raise and lower the floor, as well as other devices to achieve even greater flexibility to allow it to be used for very many other functions, both sporting and otherwise. However, the Saitama Arena was not only very much more flexible than San Nicola and the Grand Stade; it was smaller in capacity, seating up to 40,000 compared with their 65,000 and 80,000 respectively, and it was entirely roofed over.

A triumph of the San Nicola stadium is the design of its concrete superstructure. The raised upper tier of seats, with its soffit that seems to hang as lightly and softly as fabric, appears to hover over the landscaped mound that it crowns. The concrete structure of the Grand Stade promised to be every bit as impressive and beautiful. But with both this stadium and the Saitama Arena, the roofs were the most strikingly elegant structural features. The Grand Stade roof oversailed and floated at a jaunty angle over the upper tier, while that of the Saitama Arena used extraordinarily slender arched trusses.

2 Saitama Arena, Japan, 1994: parabolic roof truss.

3 Grand Stade: computer study of structural components of upper tier and roof.

4 Saitama Arena: north elevation.

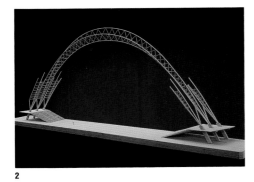

2

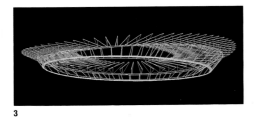

3

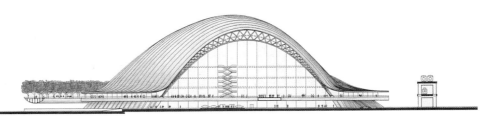

4

Both the Grand Stade and Saitama Arena projects were produced as entries for invited competitions, and were prepared in collaboration with major contractors. Though much the best entry in both cases (not least for being the only ones concerned with context, let alone the aptness and quality of that contextual response) neither was a winner. Though it is an immense pity that Piano and the Building Workshop have missed the opportunity to build two of their very best recent designs, the missed opportunities seem much more tragic for Paris and Saitama.

No matter what connections they make with their settings, structures as vast as the Grand Stade and Saitama Arena stand out from their context, which is inevitable and quite right considering their pivotal roles in those settings. Today though it is usually assumed that buildings, particularly smaller ones, should blend into their surroundings. Yet sometimes, and especially if they house some special function as do the Cy Twombly Gallery (p 56) and the Mercedes-Benz Design Centre, it can be more appropriate for relatively small buildings to contrast with adjacent existing buildings and draw due attention to themselves.

The pressure to be contextual was a much needed antidote to the dislocating impact of so much modern architecture, which ignored its setting, to be shaped only according to its internal arrangements. Too often, however, contextualism has led to simplistic dogma, timidity of design and confusion. Some build-

ings merely fit in unnoticeably, like the eponymous character in Woody Allen's film *Zelig* who blended into situations so well that nobody noticed him. And sometimes a single work presents several different faces to its surroundings, reflecting the contrasts and confusions in these as a more finely fragmented collage. In both cases the resulting buildings tend to lack a sufficiently independent identity, and thus fail to hold their own in, and enter into dialogue with, their surroundings.

Piano avoids constrictive dogma and approaches each context and how to respond to it afresh, as guided by his instinctual responses. Hence, the Building Workshop's designs have responded to context in various ways. Instead of different facades reflecting contrasting neighbours, characteristic elements taken from some of these might be interwoven in a new synthesis, which might be prominent or recessive as required. For instance, in the city (the historic centre of Paris) the IRCAM Extension forms a prominent pivot, its partially exposed steel frame stepping upwards and outwards to that of the Pompidou Centre, and its terracotta-cladding panels affirming a relationship with the old brick buildings that it links and extends. Outside of the city (on a hillside near Genoa) the UNESCO Laboratory-workshop (Volume Two p 76) nestles gently into nature, its stepping levels continuing the surrounding agricultural terraces, its retaining walls and stairs extending the pink-stucco vernacular of the old farmhouse it adjoins, and its glass roof

26 Menil Collection, Houston, Texas, 1981–86.
1, 2 Main museum building is clad in same grey clapboarding as surrounding bungalows.

1

2

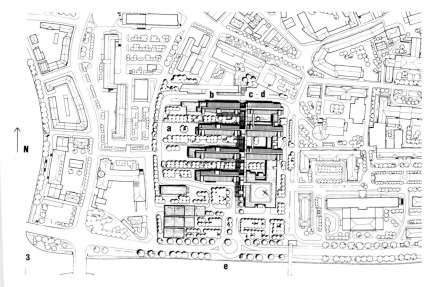

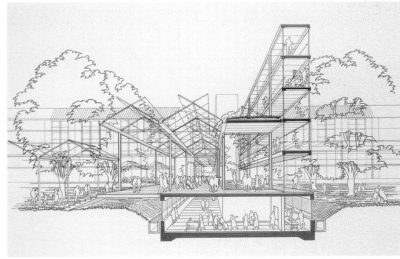

3

4

Extension to University Hospital,
Strasbourg, 1993.

Scheme, and its pedestrian spine, links city
centre to north with park across canal to south.
Existing trees extend park northwards up
west of site providing pleasant outlook for
wards while clinical block extends city centre
development southwards down east of site.

3 Location plan: **a** existing trees **b** ward
blocks **c** circulation spine **d** clinical block
e canal.

4 Sectional perspective of public pedestrian
promenade and adjacent cafés on ground level
with hospital circulation above and below.

5 Part west–east section through circulation
spine and clinical block.

6 West–east section through shady garden
between wards, pedestrian promenade and
courtyard of clinical block.

7 North–south section through ward blocks.

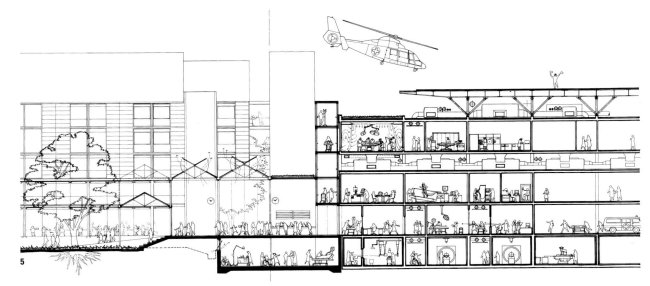

5

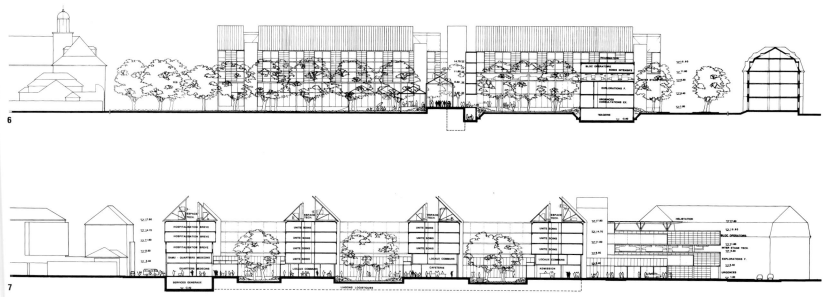

6

7

and walls recalling the agricultural greenhouses that cling to these mountain slopes.

Aspects of the approaches used in both of these projects were pioneered, and in some ways taken yet further, with the Menil Collection in the suburbs of Houston. The museum's exposed steel frame echoes those of the nearby Miesian buildings by Philip Johnson and its clapboard cladding is the same as that of the surrounding bungalows. However (as argued in Volume One), the Menil relates to more than its immediate setting. It also relates more broadly to American architectural culture, both in general (steel and balloon framing are its two quintessential construction methods), and to some of its high points. Thus the detailing of the steel frame and the shaping of the ferrocement and ductile iron elements of the roof canopy recall the work of Craig Ellwood and Charles Eames respectively, both of whom were leading exponents of the mid-century Californian modernism, which is now regarded as an apogee in American modern architecture. The covered walk around the building evokes distant resonances with the verandahs of southern plantation houses, as well as with stoas, and hence by association with the Greek Revival of American civic architecture. And the sense of space, extending freely through and outwards from the building, is again very American.

Current larger scale projects explore further contextual strategies. The Headquarters of the Banca Popolare di Lodi and the Strasbourg University Hospital extension do not echo closely the vocabulary of the buildings in their vicinity, but through responsive massing and by sheltering internal pedestrian routes they will both fit into and help reintegrate their surroundings. The Cité Internationale in Lyons, Île Seguin in Paris and Rome Auditoria are all strong formal statements, the first two of which might recall earlier buildings on their sites but otherwise mimic nothing in the immediate area. Yet these large and somewhat isolated complexes are all designed as calculated responses to their settings.

Both the Cy Twombly Gallery (p 56) and the Mercedes-Benz Design Centre are small in comparison with the buildings or complexes they extend, and are sited on the periphery of the grounds of the parent institution. If they were executed in the same vocabulary as the latter, they would appear to be mere outbuildings, too unimportant for their respective contents, and to not be terminating the expanded complex with sufficient formal force. Hence the independent stance both adopt.

The Cy Twombly Gallery, like the IRCAM Extension, confronted Piano with the challenge of responding to one of his earlier master works, in this case the Menil Collection. As at IRCAM, the new building is much smaller ·than the original and is set among others that frame the space in which the larger buildings sits; it is set among the bungalows that ring the grassy campus. Here,

28   **1** Cy Twombly Gallery, Houston, USA,
1992–95, and Menil Collection: east
elevation.

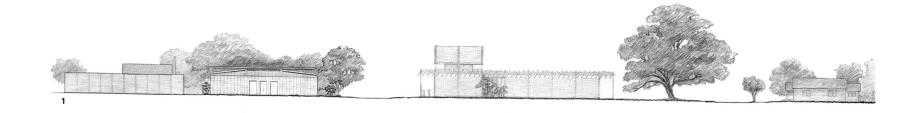

1

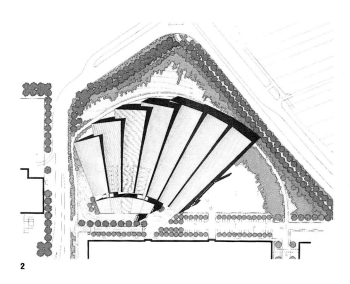

2 Mercedes-Benz Design Centre, Stuttgart, 1992–96: roof plan.

3, 4 Rome Auditoria: longitudinal and cross sections of large concert hall.

though, it is the earlier building which adopted the materials of those surrounding it (the clapboarding) so as to integrate itself among them, while the new building introduces a foreign material, reconstituted stone. While it might not have appeared too bungaloid if clad in the clapboard that gives the Menil its familiar and friendly demeanour, the new pavilion would have receded among its neighbours and not drawn due attention to the splendid collection it houses. Moreover, the large reconstituted stone blocks have a scale and solidity suited to its static squarish form, which in turn makes an emphatic punctuation on the periphery of the Menil Collection complex.

The Mercedes-Benz Design Centre occupies a prominent site on the edge of the huge factory outside Stuttgart. Here the fanning geometry contrasts with the prevalent rectilinearity of the surrounding buildings to give due emphasis to the important function it houses. It also creates a suitable terminating flourish to both the edge of the site and to a tree-lined axial walkway, which the Building Workshop has proposed to impart some urban order to the factory site. However, the toroidal curves that give grace to the fanning forms of the roof also place the design in another context, as one of a series by the Building Workshop that explores complex double-curved roofs in the sort of geometries that the computer now makes feasible. Yet here the radial geometry is somewhat at odds with a key instrument used to discipline a

major internal function, the parallel strip lights that reflect off the wet clay in which prototypes are modelled. At the urging of the client, Piano has let pursuit of propriety (dignifying the design department with a design of obvious flair) and response to context take primacy over a narrow adherence to functional dictate.

Challenges facing the contemporary city involve not only reintegrating its fabric, and new buildings into that fabric, and reusing existing building stock, but also helping it evolve into a new form better suited to current needs, technology and lifestyles. This often involves a better integration of the old core of the city and the newer mono-functional tracts that sprawl around it into an upgraded whole, updating the former with new uses and bringing the latter to life with a better mix of uses. To achieve this, cities are becoming, whether by planned intention or not, increasingly poly-nucleated. What were merely local centres are growing to acquire a mix and scale of uses that not only serve the immediate area around them better, but also draw on and serve the whole metropolis. Elsewhere entirely new nodes are being created, often focused around some specialized use. As each of these nuclei acquire their own distinctive character, the resources of the city are increased and its overall character and the experiences it can offer are enriched.

In the main such nuclei will continue to grow and change. Nevertheless, self-contained and complete nuclei built as single

29

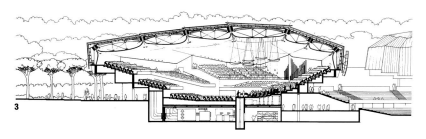

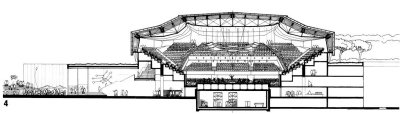

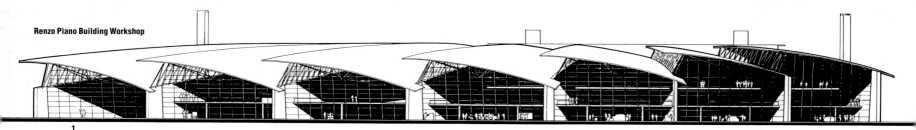

1

2

30   Mercedes-Benz Design Centre.
Radial walls support toroidally-curved shed
roofs whose clerestories admit north and
north-east light. The steel roof deck forms a
compressive element that is supported by
purlins and struts splaying out from the centre
line of a three-dimensional web of tension ties.

1 West elevation.

2 North–south section through full-size
mock-up workshops.

3 Reflected plan of roof structure.

4 Plan of radial walls supporting roof
structure.

5 Roof and site plan: **a** design studios and
workshops **b** translucent-roofed showroom
c administration.

6 West–east section: **a** workshop for
full-size mock-ups **b** design studio
c storerooms **d** model workshop
e administration.

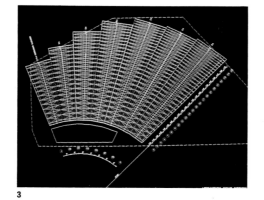

3

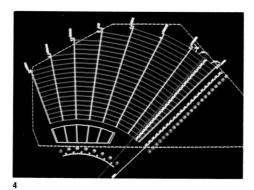

4

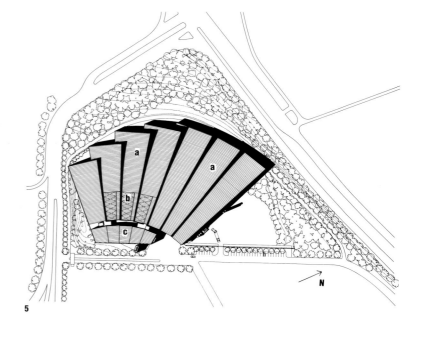

5

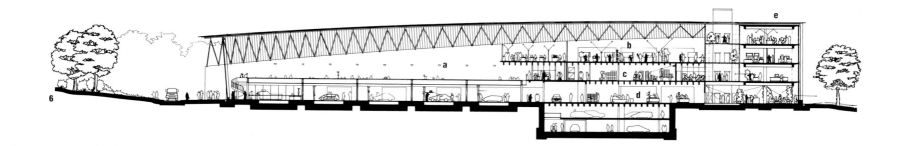

6

Mercedes-Benz Design Centre.
7–9 All reveal main structural and cladding components: **7** construction view from west **8** 'peeled-away' axonometric view of single bay **9** interior.
10, 11 Full-size models of connecting elements of roof structure.
12 Internal view of showroom roof that is clad in translucent sheet with large louvres below to control light.
13 Exploded isometric of framing and shading elements of glazing that closes west end of each bay.

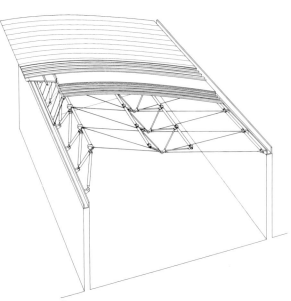

8

9

10

11

12

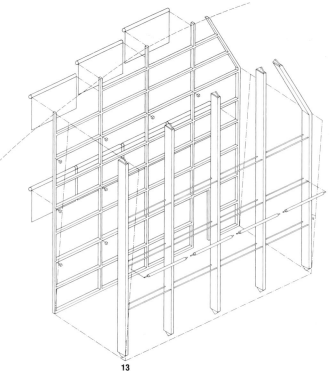

13

Terracotta cladding.

1 Rue de Meaux Housing: terracotta tiles hung on glass reinforced cement panels.

2 IRCAM Extension: terracotta units held away from structural frame in aluminium frames.

3 Cité Internationale de Lyon: a secondary skin of large adjustable glass louvres beyond provides economies of energy consumption.

4, 5 Researching the facades of Potsdamer Platz where a secondary external layer of glass louvres is used for energy efficiency.

6 Île Seguin and Bas Meudon: model view of north-western tip of the Île Seguin. A common external terracotta skin will unify the buildings by various architects.

(though maybe phased) developments can also have considerable impact on life in the cities in which they are built. The Building Workshop has designed a series of such large schemes on prominent sites that, though in peripheral areas of their respective cities, are constrained from further growth. These are the Cité Internationale de Lyon, the Rome Auditoria complex and the Île Seguin master plan for an island on the south-west edge of Paris, all of which started as competition entries.

The three projects are for visually prominent sites, isolated from the fabric of the city, that are prevented from growing because they are adjacent to major natural features, such as rivers, or semi-natural ones such as parks. Indeed both the Cité Internationale and Île Seguin are on conspicuous bends in two of France's major rivers, the Rhône and Seine respectively, and are also adjacent to or will include a park. All these projects form clearly defined precincts with their own individual identity, yet it will no doubt become part of the larger identity of their respective cities. In each case a greater civic role has been assured by focusing on a central pedestrian realm, which is planned with a sufficient mix of uses to bring it some life throughout most of the day and night.

The Cité Internationale de Lyon is yet another scheme in the expanding series of buildings clad in terracotta units that form a protective rainscreen to the main weatherproof and insulated wall. However, it is the first building in this series in which the terra-

cotta units are not grouped and supported in framed panels, but each spans independently between vertical rails to which they are clipped on site. The result is a visual grain of an altogether larger scale and more horizontal emphasis, better suited to the size and shape of these blocks and the distances they can be seen from over the park and river. The Cité Internationale is also the first in a series of schemes in which the Building Workshop has used yet another independent layer, a screen of frameless glass panes (some of which open as louvres) set some distance outside of the terracotta. This overlays the terracotta with its own larger-scaled grain that is also a dematerializing veil, constantly reflecting changes in the play of light. The result is what Piano refers to as 'pointillist', a shimmering liveliness that gives the facades an affinity with both the reflections on the river and the flickering leaves on the trees.

In terms of energy efficiency the outer glass screen with its adjustable louvres brings a number of advantages. It reduces wind force and intercepts rain so that the conventional windows behind it may be open at any time, no matter what the weather or how high up the building (where wind speeds and pressure normally make openable windows impractical). This allows all the offices to be naturally ventilated for much of the year and thus, just as importantly for Piano, for the occupants to feel a connection with the outdoors. In winter, if the outer louvres and inner windows are closed, air is trapped in the gap between

1

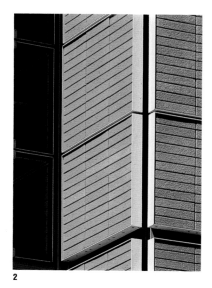

2

3

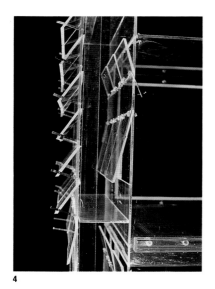

4

5

them to be warmed by the sun and the heat escaping from the interior, thus forming an effective insulating jacket of intermediate temperature. In summer, the louvres are opened so that the gap forms a thermal chimney with the warmed air rising and escaping from the top, pulling behind it cooler air that also enters the open office windows. And because rain and strong wind does not reach the inner windows, these can be left open at night to admit cool air to chill the internal fabric of the building so that it might absorb heat built up during the next day. The double facade at the Cité Internationale has not eliminated the need for heating and air-conditioning, but it extends considerably the period during which neither of these is needed and natural ventilation will suffice.

This system of terracotta cladding and an external glass skin has been further refined, with the addition of light shelves to reflect light deep into the offices, for the office blocks that the Building Workshop is now constructing as part of the Potsdamer Platz project. For this, extensive research was undertaken in conjunction with the services engineers of Ove Arup & Partners and Drees & Sommer and funded by the EU as part of the Joule II research programme. The research involved the use of two purpose-made pieces of equipment, the solar box and the climate box, as well as full-size mock-ups (in both Vesima and Berlin) and various forms of computer simulation. All of this will be reported on in detail when the completed

scheme is published in a future volume. Suffice it to report for now that the research predicts that the double facade will allow offices at the top of a tower to be naturally ventilated for nearly forty per cent of the year and those towards the bottom to be naturally ventilated for fifty-five per cent of the year, thus reducing by forty per cent the energy needed to heat and cool the building.

These facades and this research illustrate further dimensions of Piano's concern with what has been characterized in the introductory essays to the first two volumes as a natural and participative architecture. Using what in energy terms are known as passive means, the facades exploit the ambient natural conditions, drawing heat and light from them and using them to draw away excess heat. Yet at the same time they allow occupants to experience, and so sense some participation in these processes and the conditions outside. Furthermore, the facades have other qualities that might be thought of as natural. The terracotta units not only have an earthy warmth, but will look better as they mellow with weathering. The proportions of the individual terracotta units, and the panels they form between the vertical supporting rails and horizontal floor demarcations, as well as the different spacings of the joints between all these, induces a slight jittery flicker in the eye, or vibration as Piano calls it, that invests these facades with an inherent liveliness. Thus they become a fitting backdrop, and themselves an analogue for the

33

6

1

34   Lingotto Factory Renovation.

1 Concert–congress hall.

2 Courtyard on roof of concert–congress hall overlooked by cantilevered, glass-domed conference room.

3 Ground floor corridor of conference centre.

Brancusi Studio, Paris, 1994–.

4 Constantin Brancusi in his original studio.

5 Roof of model viewed from above.

6 Model viewed from south against sloping edge of Place Beaubourg.

2

liveliness nature manifests in rustling leaves and the light dancing on the ripples in water.

Besides the ongoing refurbishment of Lingotto and the unsuccessful entry for the conversion of the Bankside Power Station, the Building Workshop is currently refurbishing a building once reviled by many as resembling some such industrial plant as an oil refinery. This building, the Pompidou Centre, has now almost achieved the status of a revered and sacrosanct historic monument. Open for nearly twenty years, it has suffered the ravages of not just time, but also of very much more intense use than was ever anticipated. The Building Workshop is currently refurbishing the exterior, and, in consultation with Richard Rogers, will supervise the refurbishment of the interior. In accord with EU rules for public commissions, this will be the subject of a series of competitions.

Outside, the fireproofing that was becoming unsightly on the external beams and the stainless-steel sleeves that clad it are being removed, and the beams cleaned and treated with intumescent coatings. In terms of a modernist ethos, the simplicity of the naked beams represents a conceptually more honest and elegant solution. Some, however, might miss the metallic sheen of the sleeves, that seemed so much part of the futuristic imagery. Along the rue Renard, the brightly coloured ducts that swarm down the facade are being reorganized – to achieve a revised pattern of air distribution – and repainted. Revisions to the ground floor and its external

3

paving will make this street edge more approachable and hospitable. Here, on this and the other sides, once under the perimeter of the building above, the rough cobbles will give way to smooth paving slabs that are easier to walk upon. Similarly, parts of the sloping Place Beaubourg in front of the Pompidou will be paved as shallow steps so as to be more comfortable to sit on, thus also tending to restrict sitting to those areas while leaving others free for movement.

A small project, with which Piano nevertheless strongly identifies, that is going ahead as part of the refurbishment of the Pompidou Centre, is the construction of a new version of the sculptor Constantin Brancusi's original shack-like studio. As Piano has explained (Volume Two p 71), Brancusi's interest lay not only in the individual sculptures. For him, the most significant work was the totality of all the sculptures together within the setting of his studio, along with the sculptures he was working on and even those blocks of wood and stone that lay around as only potential sculptures. It was being able to ponder the relationships between all these that brought him insight and inspiration. To keep altering gradually these relationships, so that he might always see them afresh, some of the sculptures were placed on slowly rotating turntables.

When Brancusi bequeathed his works to the nation, it was with the stipulation that they be displayed in his studio which was to be preserved intact. But the studio was demolished, to eventually be replaced by a rough replica that stood in front of the north-west corner of the Pompidou, above and adjacent to the retaining wall that forms the northern edge of the Place Beaubourg. This was never a satisfactory solution; the shack merely looked scruffy in its prominent location, and this did nothing to dignify the works. It was also impossible to arrange access and security so that the public could view the works as Brancusi intended.

The new studio is being built in the same place as the replica, but set somewhat lower and enfolded by an ambulatory, the windowless wall of which will define this as a separate precinct. The studio itself will be more or less identical to the original in shape and dimensions, but will be rebuilt in a more robust and contemporary fashion to meet modern curatorial standards. The public will not enter the studio, which, like the original, will be brightly lit through the clerestories of shed roofs. Instead they will look in from the ambulatory through openings where the original windows and door were. One corner of the ambulatory will widen into another exhibition space outside the studio, and adjacent to the stairs down to the new building's entrance will be an external court for further sculpture.

To protect the glass of the shed-clerestories and of the rooflights over the ambulatory, as well as to present a neat view to those looking down from the Pompidou, the whole

35

4

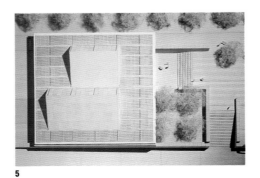

5

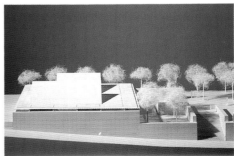

6

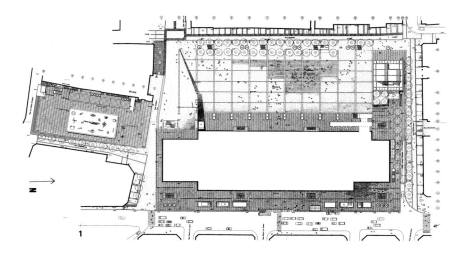

1

36 Pompidou Centre Renovation and
Brancusi Studio, 1994 –.
1 Site plan: Brancusi Studio is west of
northern end of Pompidou Centre and paving
replaces the cobbles under the latter's
overhanging upper floors.
2 Tree-shaded court of Brancusi Studio
model seen from south.
3 Plan view of Brancusi Studio model with
roof removed.
4 North elevation.

Brancusi Studio.
5, 6 Model without and with roof.
7 North–south section.
8 Plan: **a** entrance **b** ambulatory **c** exhibition
space **d** reconstructed studio **e** tree-planted
court **f** stair up from Place Beaubourg
g escape stair of Pompidou Centre.
9 East elevation of studio in context.

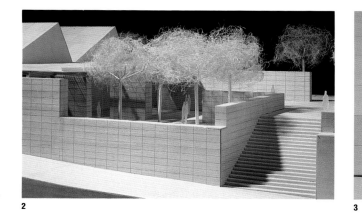

2

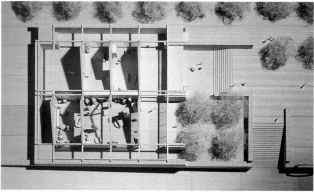

3

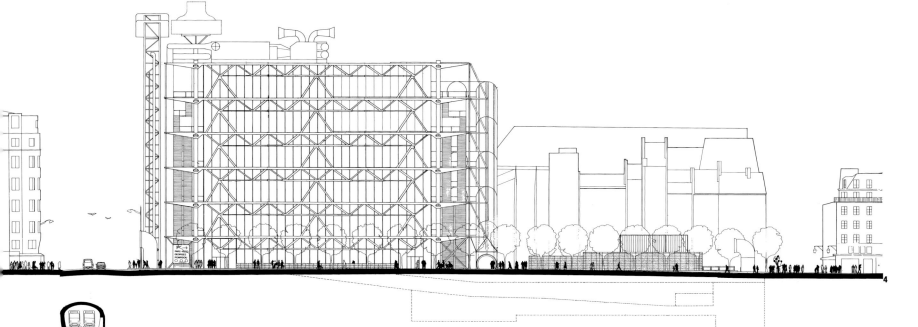

4

5

6

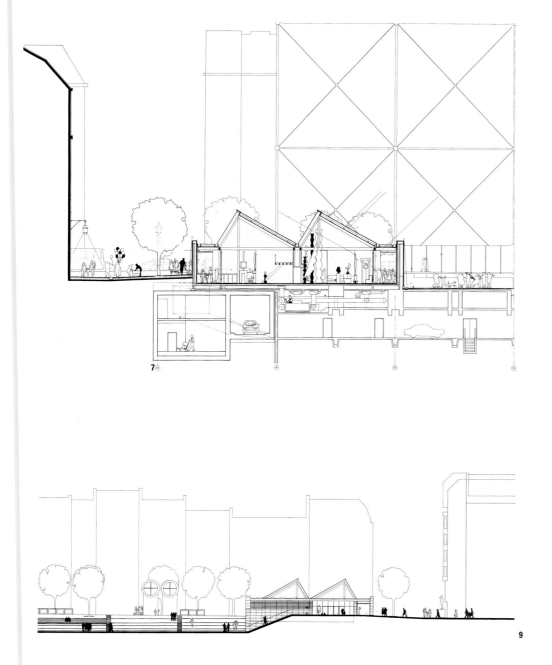

7

9

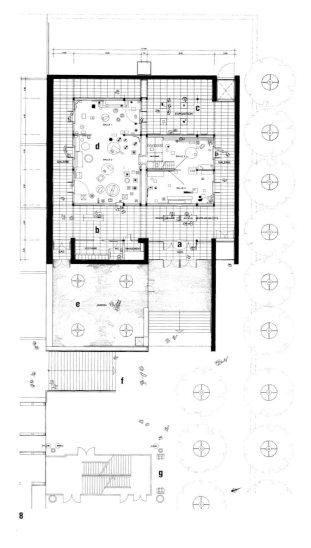

8

roof is to have an outer cladding of stainless-steel panels, perforated where light and ventilation are required, a solution first explored at the Bercy 2 Shopping Centre (Volume Two p 16). The steel-panelled roof and stone-clad ambulatory walls will present a very different character to that of the original flimsy timber shack. But inside this defensive, crisp carapace, the white-painted exposed wood frame (with plastered walls) of the new studio will also be more robust and neat in character than the original. Nevertheless, it should assert a similar quiet dignity of its own.

When designing the Brancusi studio and finding out more about the sculptor and his attitudes to his work, Piano recognized that he felt something similar about his own projects and their relationship to the Building Workshop's premises, particularly the laboratory-workshop at Vesima (Volume Two p 76). When moving between its stepping levels, the different projects and the teams at work on them all belong, in his mind, to a single unfolding adventure in which each project both explores new approaches and reinterprets those that have already been applied, or elaborated on, nearby drawing boards.

With many architects it is possible to grasp all there is to be learnt from them by studying a single work, and even with most of the greater architects, a select few works will suffice as they tend to rework familiar themes. With Piano, however, it is the total *œuvre* that is important, and whatever the successes and failures of individual works, each has its lessons. This is because he keeps moving on, not in search of trivial novelty, but as his ideas expand and evolve, in response to the promptings of his finely tuned instincts and the contributions of his collaborators, as well as to the clues and constraints offered by each project, and to the potentials of the times.

This exceptional fluidity comes about because Piano's architecture is not so much *imposed* as it *evolves* in a spirit of participation with every pertinent factor. An example of this participatory attitude that has already been discussed in this essay, is Piano's selective combination of, and balance between, the constructional traditions of the local culture and the leading-edge technology available to our global civilization. Another such example is the energy-saving exploitation of ambient conditions without forfeiting a sense of contact with the natural environment. So the architecture of Piano and the Building Workshop is one of acting *with* rather than *on* the world. In participating with the world it seeks a desperately needed reconciliation between technology, the evolving city and its history and traditions, as well as between technology, mankind and nature. This is most clearly seen in the way the Renzo Piano Building Workshop tackles topical and pervasive problems, but is also evident in such epoch-defining works as the Pompidou Centre and Kansai Airport.

38

1 UNESCO Laboratory-workshop, Vesima, 1989–91.
2 Pompidou Centre: revisions to ground floor of north-east corner ease pedestrian access.
3 Kansai International Airport Terminal: portion of air-side elevation.

1

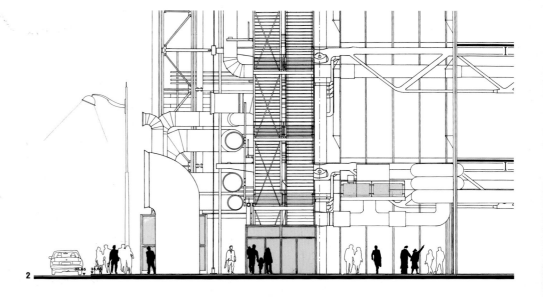

2

40 **Concert and conference facilities**
Concert–congress hall completed 1994,
'Bubble' conference room completed 1995.

Lingotto Factory Renovation Turin, Italy **1983–**

The conversion of the famous Fiat Lingotto factory into a cultural/educational/ business resource for Turin and its region is such a large and complex undertaking that it is taking several years of continuous work to complete. The overall design strategy, whereby a machine-age monument becomes a multi-functional, megastructural microcosm of the post-industrial city, is explained and illustrated in Volume Two, as are the conversion of the main exhibition spaces and some exhibition installations within these, which were carried out by the Building Workshop.

Since the publication of Volume Two, various facilities for conferences and concerts have been completed. The largest of these are two subterranean halls: a concert and congress hall seating up to 2,000, which is below one of the original courtyards, and a 480-seat conference hall that extends below the piazza in front of the old building. There are also a range of smaller auditoria on the ground floor that can seat between fifty and just over two hundred. Crowning the building, cantilevered above and to the side of one of the old building's stair and service towers, and counterbalanced by the circular pad of a heliport, is a glass 'bubble' containing a conference room. Together the heliport and the bubble are a conspicuous futuristic addition to the local skyline and loom dramatically over the courtyards below them, signalling the transformation of the old factory into a space-age complex.

Ironically perhaps, these elements also acknowledge that, no matter how much the new Lingotto is conceived of as a place for the people of Turin, culture (whether high or pop) and business still have their elites. Here, however, stretch limos will not have to negotiate throngs of fans and other plebs. Instead each star, like a *deus ex machina*, will drop in and be whisked away by helicopter. And although Lingotto is no longer a factory with prototype cars whizzing around the roof-top test track, captains of industry will still pay flying visits. They will meet those who have come up from the business centre or incubator units below to wait for them in the conference bubble, or descend to address larger groups in the conference halls.

Each of the conference and concert facilities has its own appropriate mode of access. The conference bubble in the sky is reached by the mechanical

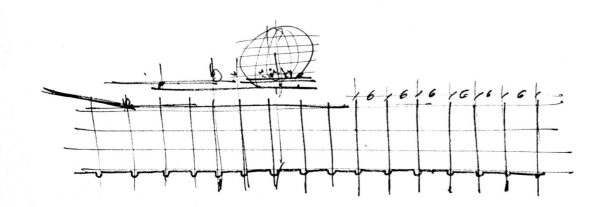

42

Lingotto Factory Renovation

Previous page Portion of interior of conference dome with inner layer of frameless panes of glass to dissipate acoustic focus.

1 Glass-domed conference 'bubble' and helipad are visible from a distance, updating the futuristic aspect of the old building (the helicopters adding the dynamism once given by the cars on the roof-top track).

2 Arcade-flanked courtyard on roof of concert–congress hall with moving sculpture-fountain by Susumu Shingu.

3, 4 Landscaped garden on floor of courtyard at centre of hotel.

5 Close-up of Shingu sculpture-fountain.

1

2

4

3

5

means of either a helicopter or a pair of elevators. The medium-sized conference rooms, together with their ancillary facilities, are reached directly from the piazza in front of the building and are part of the business-orientated ground floor. Broad corridors connect some of these auditoria to the exhibition facilities (some conferences might be organized in conjunction with an exhibition), the foyer of the four-star hotel (where delegates may stay) and, overlooking the hotel's garden-courtyard, a reception room (that can be annexed for both conference and hotel functions). Though semi-subterranean, the large concert hall is entered from the first floor, which is the main public level and is conceived as an internalized fragment of Turin, complete with shopping arcades and courtyard-piazzas.

Not only do the heliport and conference bubble suggest an elitism, somewhat at odds with the spirit of the rest of the Lingotto project, but the bravura cantilevers and blatantly futuristic forms seem to look backwards, rather than forward, to an earlier phase of Piano's career: to the London-influenced high-tech of the Pompidou that he has otherwise outgrown. Compared with the massive rectilinear cantilever beams that support them, the radial structures of the bases of the heliport and bubble are dainty; indeed the bubble looks like a dinky bauble in relation to the structural effort with which it is supported. The original design for the supporting structure had included slanting props and was more refined in form. But Piano feels that the rough and rudimentary built solution is more in keeping with the old factory.

The bubble is shaped as an onion dome for structural and visual reasons, with a sectional geometry generated as tangential arcs of circles of differing radii. It is framed in curved vertical and horizontal tubes: vertical members are only 38 millimetres in diameter, achieved by using a tube with an 8-millimetre wall thickness, and horizontal members are 60 millimetres in diameter with

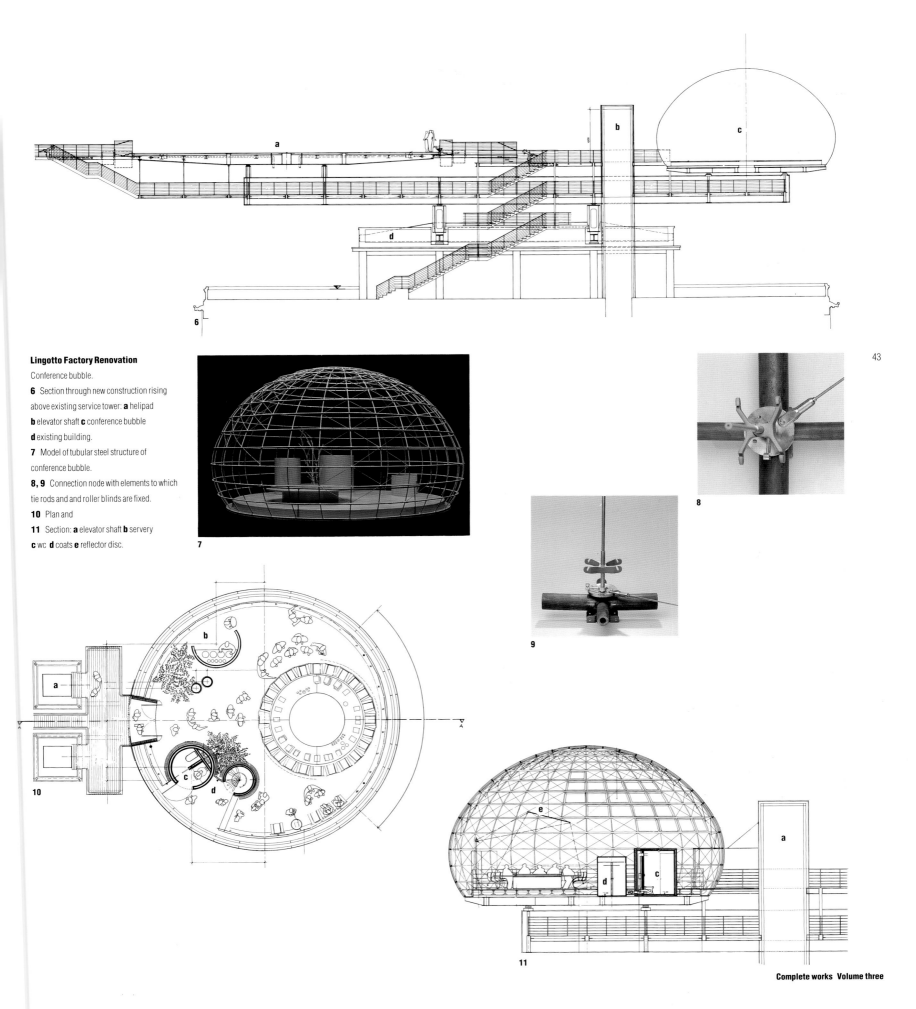

Lingotto Factory Renovation

Conference bubble.

6 Section through new construction rising above existing service tower: **a** helipad **b** elevator shaft **c** conference bubble **d** existing building.

7 Model of tubular steel structure of conference bubble.

8, 9 Connection node with elements to which tie rods and and roller blinds are fixed.

10 Plan and

11 Section: **a** elevator shaft **b** servery **c** wc **d** coats **e** reflector disc.

43

1

a 5-millimetre wall thickness. Outside of this cage are double-curved units of bluish, reflective-coated double glazing that differ in size and shape with each row: the outer pane is tempered 6-millimetre glass, the void is 12 millimetres and the inner pane is made of two 4-millimetre sheets glued together. On the inside of the dark grey-painted tubular cage are stainless-steel cross-bracing rods (6 millimetres in diameter). Inside of these, on those parts which will receive most of the direct sunlight, are motorized blinds set between the outer glazing and another set of panes that are supported independently, without frames. This inner glazing is an acoustic reflector, the panes angled to scatter sound and eliminate any acoustic focus. For all the complexities and difficulties that must have been encountered in detailed design, the dome achieves the impression of being both very light and effortlessly resolved. It was built as a specialist subcontract by Bodino, a firm that usually makes exhibition stands and mobile displays.

Inside the dome is a circular table that can seat twenty-four people, and curved screens that enclose a kitchenette-servery, lavatory and coat cupboard. Inlets in the floor admit conditioned air; in winter, this is also extracted through the floor and recycled, and in summer, a circular glass pane at the apex of the dome is lowered to vent the stale air.

44 **Lingotto Factory Renovation**

Conference bubble.

1 As seen from helipad.

2 Beyond conference table is panoramic view of Turin; above it is tilted disc that reflects light from uplighter. Blinds shield sunlight where it falls directly on dome.

3 View down into court over concert—congress hall.

4 Sectional detail of side of dome: **a** 6 mm reflective-coated tempered glass **b** 12 mm void **c** 2 x 4 mm sheets of glass bonded together **d** 38 mm diameter steel tube **e** 60 mm diameter steel tube **f** 6 mm stainless steel tie rod **g** fixing element for roller blinds **h** frameless glass panes.

5 Sectional apex of dome. Central circular glazed unit rises to exhaust air in hot weather.

6, 7 Details with **7** showing close-up view of connection node supporting roller blinds and frameless glass.

8 View into dome with sun blinds closed.

9 Sectional detail of junction of dome to floor.

2

3

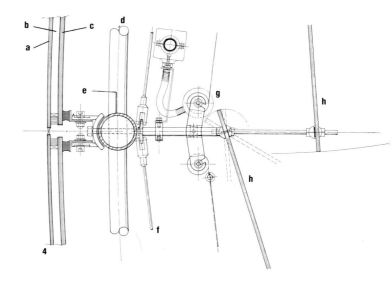

4

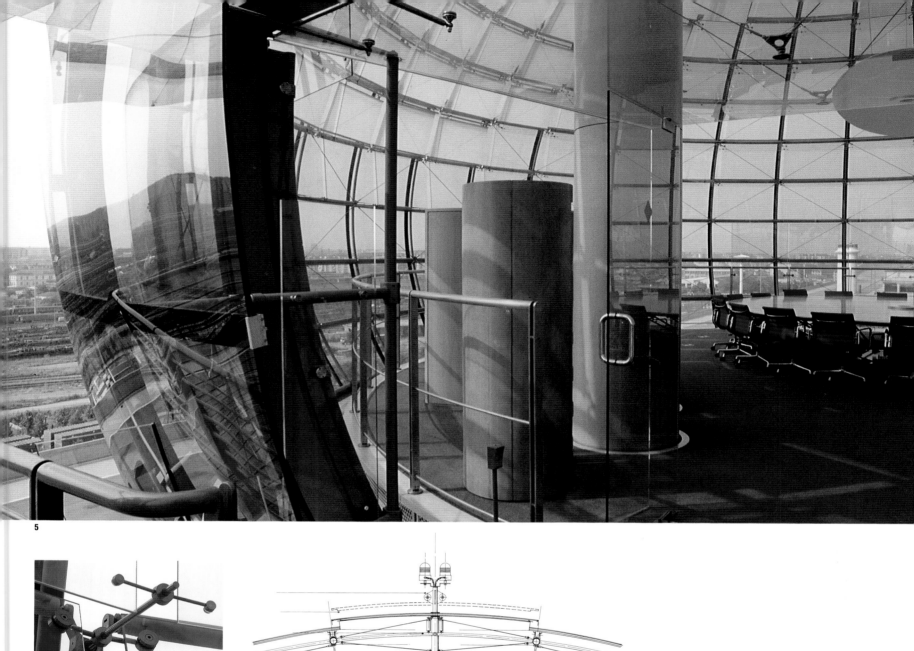

5

7

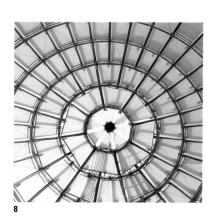

8

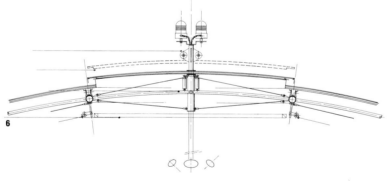

6

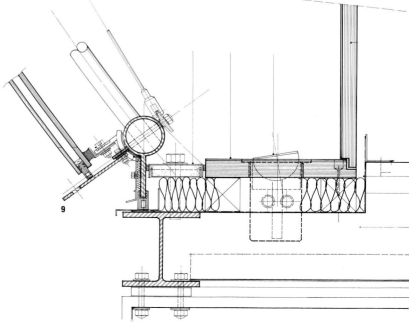

9

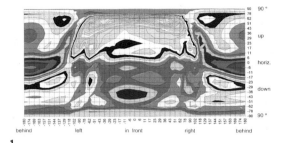

1

Lingotto Factory Renovation

Concert–congress hall.

Previous pages Hall as seen from choir seats behind stage.

1 Computer prediction of spatial distribution of sound energy.

2 Seat, designed by Building Workshop, with stowable table out for conference use.

3 Ground-floor plan of balcony level of concert–congress hall and surrounding conference centre (scale 1: 1000): **a** stairs up to public concourse **b** escalators to and from public concourse **c** concert–congress hall lobby **d** stairs down to hall **e** balcony **f** escape stairs **g** conference centre corridor **h** conference room **i** stairs down to 480-seat auditorium **j** reception room.

There are nine conference auditoria on the ground floor: four of 50 seats, two of 75, one of 120 and two of 210. All are flat-floored, comfortable and relatively conventional, although some have windows, either looking out on to the front piazza or on to a broad internal corridor from which passers-by can look in when the blinds are open. More striking is the larger 480-seat auditorium beneath the piazza; a very handsome room entirely panelled in wood, it is detailed as an obvious relative of the large concert–congress hall. But

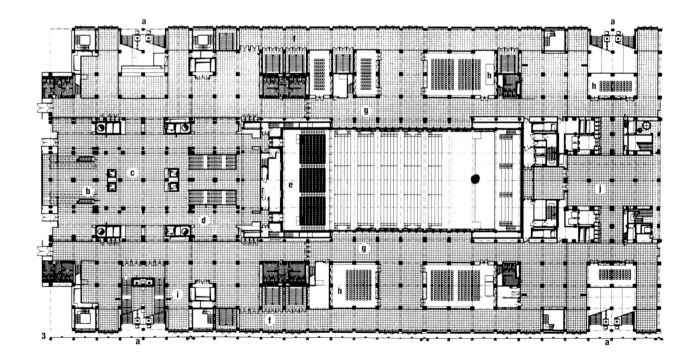

2

while in the latter the structure is exposed on the long sides so as to modulate the scale of the room, here everything is sheathed in the same size rectangular panels (some with slots for acoustic absorption) with recessed joints to give the emphatic, horizontally dominant gridding that is a Piano hallmark.

The large concert–congress hall has been constructed below one of the old building's four central courts, the floor of which is now raised to first floor level. Here it forms a piazza between the arcades that extends the length of the main public and shopping level. Under this, the bottom of the court has been excavated 14 metres down, well below the level of the old building's foundations, to achieve the hall's requisite volume and raked floor. To do this, the edge of the excavation had to be

retained with mini-piles, clusters of which underpin each of the old column footings. For acoustic isolation, the new structure of the hall is completely independent of the old structure. The concrete frame expressed on the hall's long sides supports steel beams and concrete decking which are independent of the steel beams that support the 350-millimetre-deep concrete slab of the courtyard floor. For further sound dampening, both sets of beams are mounted on rubber pads.

Apart from the sloping floor, what has been created is a shoe box-shaped volume (lined on its long sides by two galleries and a row of translation booths above these), into which has been inserted a balcony at one end and a fully adjustable stage at the other. If measured from the front of the balcony, this is almost exactly the 48-metre-long by 24-metre-wide by 20-metre-high volume that Arup Acoustics had recommended when originally consulted. Also adjustable is the suspended ceiling of convex curved segments made of very dense chipboard (weighing 50 kg per square metre) and veneered in wood. Each segment of the ceiling, and of the lighting grids between them, can be independently lowered and raised.

The hall is used at its maximum volume, 21,500 cubic metres, for symphony concerts when it seats 1,800 and has a reverberation time of 1.9 seconds. With some electronic amplification for speakers, it can be used at this volume for conferences, with the front of the stage

3

4

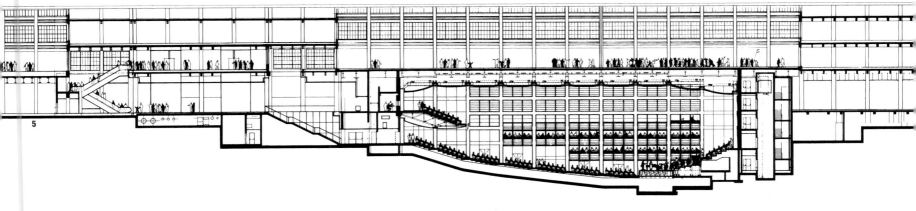

5

4 Hall in use for public rehearsal of
symphony concert as seen from choir seats
behind stage.
5 Longitudinal section showing access from
public concourse level and ground-floor lobby
as well as hall.

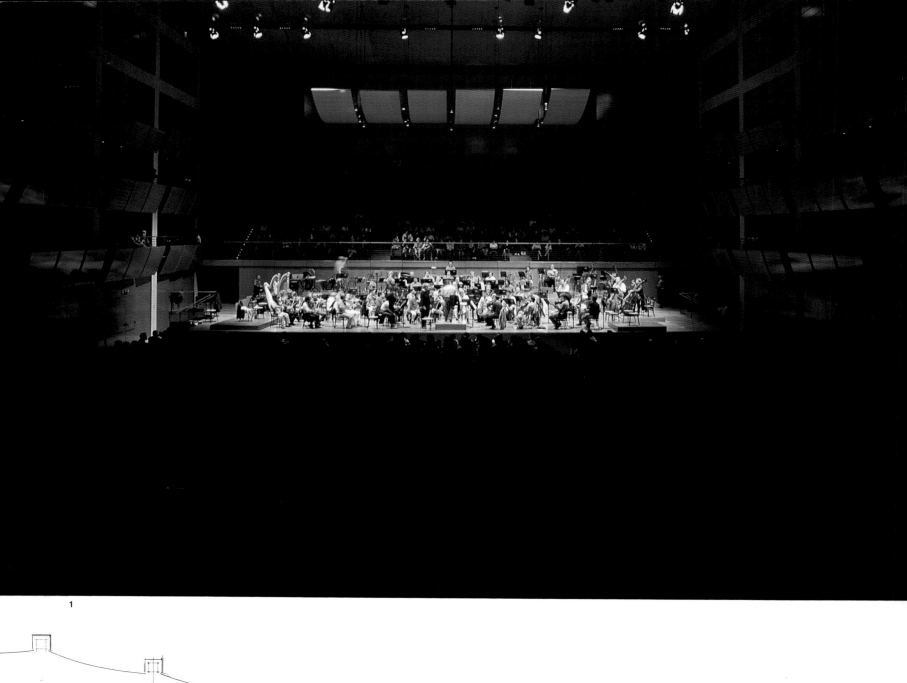

1

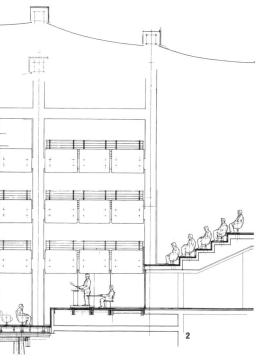

2

3

4

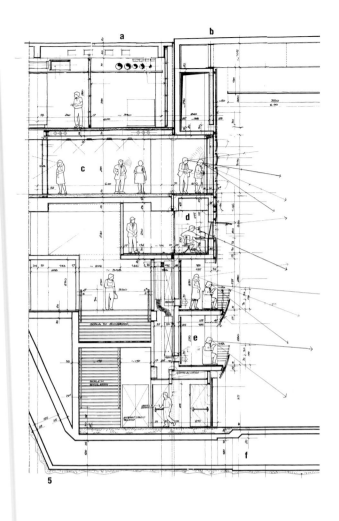

5

6

7

8

9

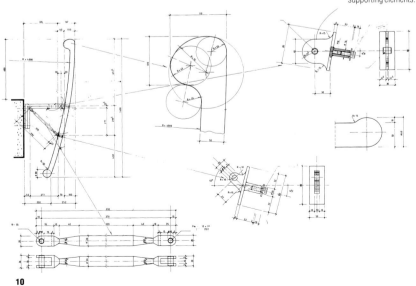

10

Lingotto Factory Renovation

51

Concert–congress hall.

1 View from balcony.

2 Section through front of hall with stage arranged for congress.

3 Curved and angled acoustic reflectors to front side galleries.

4 Front of hall seen from side gallery with stepped tier of choir on left.

5 Section through side of hall showing separation of old and new construction: **a** first floor (public concourse level) of existing building **b** raised new courtyard floor **c** broad corridor on ground floor with glimpses into hall **d** translator's booth **e** side galleries **f** plenum.

6 Side gallery overlooking the hall.

7 Circular grilles admit conditioned air beneath the seats.

8 Close-up view of stairs in side aisles.

9 Oblique view along side of hall.

10 Details of acoustic reflectors and supporting elements.

lowered for more seating to accommodate 2,000. For chamber concerts and smaller conferences, the ceiling can be lowered by as much as 6 metres decreasing the volume of the hall and adjusting the acoustics. At its lowest, the ceiling aligns with the front of the balcony, shutting it off so that the hall only seats 1,080. It then has a volume of 9,400 cubic metres and a reverberation time of less than 1.5 seconds. When lowering the ceiling height and volume of the hall, the acoustics can be further dampened and fine-tuned by opening or closing banks of louvres along the walls that thereby increase or decrease sound absorption.

The conceptual engineering work of the heliport, bubble and concert–congress hall was originally done by Ove Arup & Partners: Philip Dilley was responsible for the structure, Alistair Guthrie the services and Richard Cowell the acoustics of the main hall. But the structural and services work was finally executed by Fiat Engineering, and the detailing of the acoustic concept by Müller BBM. Arups had already built and tested a 1:50 scale working model of the hall, and Müller's execution has remained loyal to the original concept, though the ceiling has been considerably simplified. The result is a triumph. Although the moving ceiling is not fully commissioned as yet, the acoustics for symphonic concerts have been hailed by musicians and other *cognoscenti* as magnificent. The room is also exceedingly handsome, with a warm and festive atmosphere, the rich and lively grain of the cherry wood veneer animating the almost entirely wood-panelled walls and ceiling.

52

1

2

3

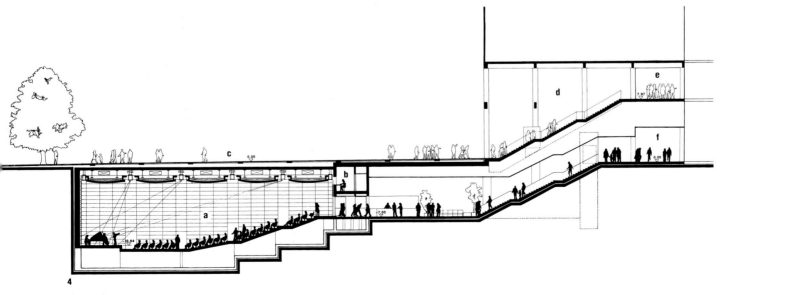

4

5

Lingotto Factory Renovation

1, 2 Ground floor lobby of concert–congress hall that is reached by escalators from public concourse level above.

3 Ground level entrance from piazza to conference room corridor.

4 Section through 480-seat auditorium and access to it: **a** auditorium **b** translator's booth **c** piazza **d** entrance to public concourse level **e** public concourse level **f** ground floor lobby.

5 480-seat subterranean auditorium seen from back of hall.

6 Plan of concert–congress hall and 480-seat auditorium.

7 480-seat auditorium viewed from stage.

8 Ground floor conference room with flat floor.

Lingotto Factory Renovation
Client Lingotto Srl
For credits to earlier phases see Volume two

Heliport and Bubble conference room 1992–95
Design team R Piano, S Ishida (associate in charge), M Carroll (architect in charge), M Cattaneo, S Scarabicchi
Assisted by S Arecco, L Lin, M Nouvion, M Piano, D Simonetti
Model maker D Cavagna
Structural and services engineers Ove Arup & Partners (concept design)
Acoustics Ove Arup & Partners
Lighting Piero Castiglioni
Contractor Associazione temporanea d'impresse: Del Favero, Maltauro, Aster
Subcontractors Primary steel structure and heliport: De Valle, Maeg; structure, glazing system and fittings of bubble: Gruppo Bodino; insulated glass units: Hardglass; lighting: i Guzzini

Concert–congress hall 1992–94
Design team R Piano, S Ishida (associate in charge), M Varratta (architect in charge), M Cattaneo, D Magnano, S Scarabicchi
Assisted by D Guerrisi (CAD), M Nouvion, D Simonetti
Model maker D Cavagna, Biskitalia, Milan
Structural and services engineers Ove Arup & Partners (concept design), Fiat Engineering
Foundation engineers Studio Vittone
Acoustics Müller Bbm
Lighting Piero Castiglioni
Graphics P L Cerri
Contractor Associazione temporanea d'impresse: Del Favero, Maltauro, Aster
Subcontractors Stage and movable ceiling: SAM; parquet flooring: Frigo Srl; acoustic timbers: Gabella Pascal; handrail, parapets and fittings: Gruppo Bodino; seats: B & B Italia; audio facilities: Euphon; lighting: i Guzzini

53

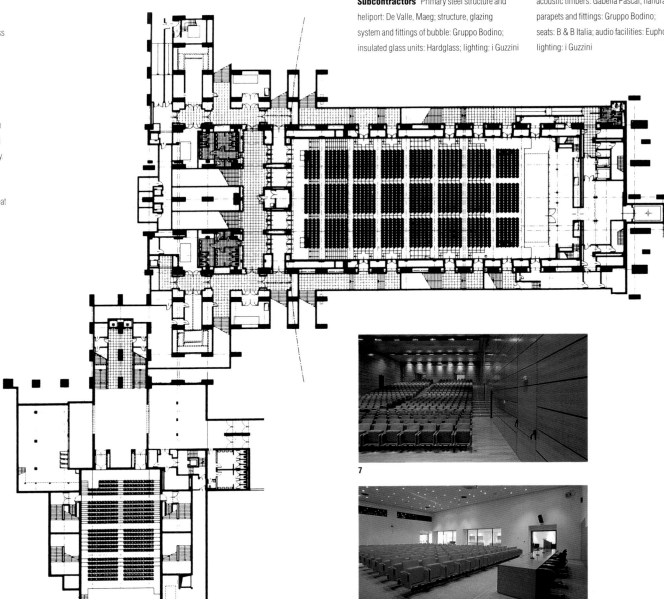

6

7

8

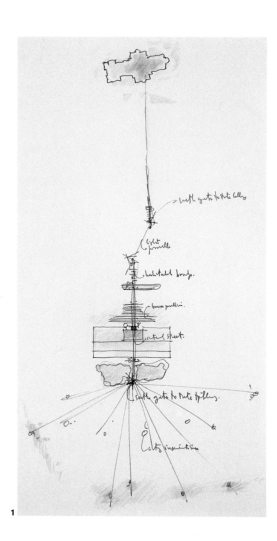

1

Tate Gallery at Bankside London, UK **1995**

The Building Workshop were finalists in an international architectural competition to convert the Bankside Power Station in Southwark, London, to house the Tate Gallery's modern art collection. Its scheme was eminently pragmatic and functional. But because it reflected Piano's reluctance to impose unduly, some misunderstood it as obvious and dull.

The power station had been divided into three east–west strips: the boiler house along the river; the turbine hall extending the length and height of the building's middle; and the switch house to the south.

Piano's characteristic respect for the old building led to following its strict symmetry with only low-key external additions. To tie the aloof old structure into its surroundings, Piano skewered it, and the notional 'piazzas' proposed to north and south, on a central pedestrian axis that was to be a twenty-four-hour-a-day public route. This passed through the old building at its existing ground level.

But all floor levels inside were adjusted so that the internal bridge connecting the axial entrances did so 3 metres above the new floor of the turbine hall. This became a semi-public 'urban room' shared by the museum, which displayed large-scale works there, and the city, whose citizens could pass through the building without entering the museum proper. Yet they would notice the throngs and the museum's attractions, and so be enticed down into the turbine hall and then, perhaps, into the museum itself.

Although the roof was now glazed, the building's shell was otherwise left untouched. Inserted into the boiler house, without touching existing walls or columns, was a multi-level, self-supporting structure containing flexible galleries insulated and serviced to the highest standards. All galleries were given natural light: the top floor through the roof; the lower floors through windows into the brightly-lit turbine hall or top-lit wells against the windows onto the Thames. This solution allowed exceptionally energy-efficient environmental controls: most parts needed only passive systems of ventilation and shading. Temperatures would have fluctuated greatly at the tops of the tall volumes, but always would have been comfortable around people and art works. These parts also formed a buffer surrounding the air-conditioned galleries, reducing considerably the heating and cooling loads.

2

3

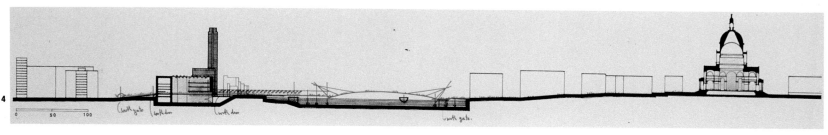

4

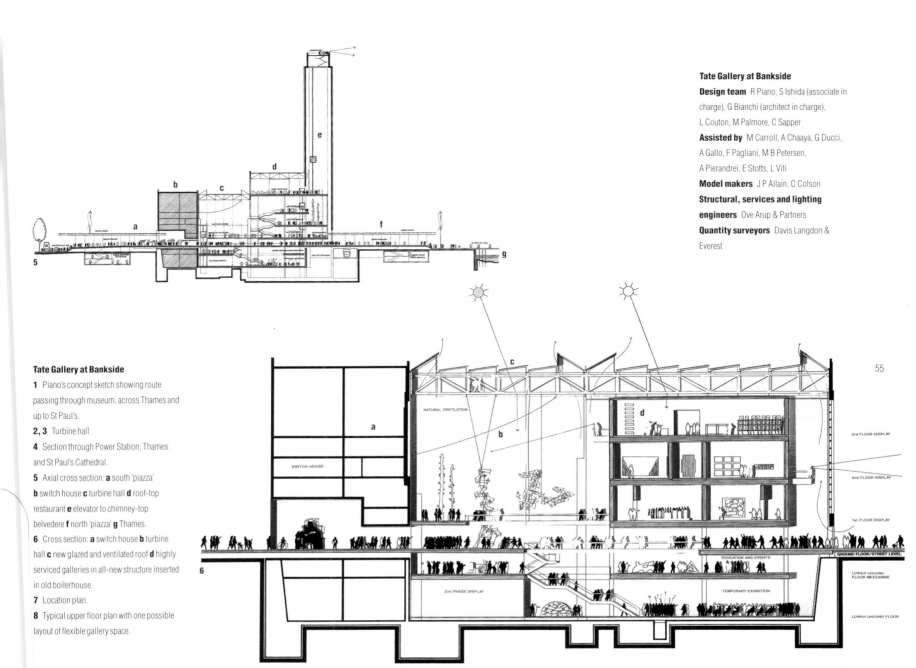

Tate Gallery at Bankside
Design team R Piano, S Ishida (associate in charge), G Bianchi (architect in charge), L Couton, M Palmore, C Sapper
Assisted by M Carroll, A Chaaya, G Ducci, A Gallo, F Pagliani, M B Petersen, A Pierandrei, E Stotts, L Viti
Model makers J P Allain, C Colson
Structural, services and lighting engineers Ove Arup & Partners
Quantity surveyors Davis Langdon & Everest

55

Tate Gallery at Bankside

1 Piano's concept sketch showing route passing through museum, across Thames and up to St Paul's.

2, 3 Turbine hall.

4 Section through Power Station, Thames and St Paul's Cathedral.

5 Axial cross section: **a** south 'piazza' **b** switch house **c** turbine hall **d** roof-top restaurant **e** elevator to chimney-top belvedere **f** north 'piazza' **g** Thames.

6 Cross section: **a** switch house **b** turbine hall **c** new glazed and ventilated roof **d** highly serviced galleries in all-new structure inserted in old boilerhouse.

7 Location plan.

8 Typical upper floor plan with one possible layout of flexible gallery space.

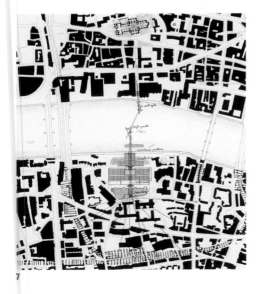

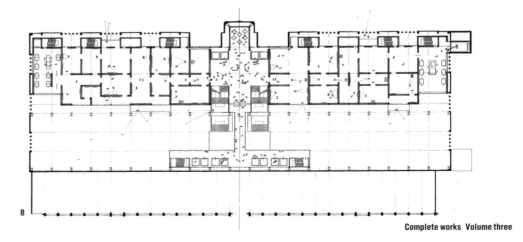

Cy Twombly Gallery Houston, USA 1992–95

Built for the Menil Collection's holdings of works by the artist Cy Twombly, the gallery is the latest in a group of buildings in the suburbs of Houston, Texas, that together make up the Menil Foundation. The largest of these buildings is the museum for the Menil Collection by Piano & Fitzgerald (Volume One p 140). This occupies most of a block which, together with that to its east, forms a grassy campus ringed by bungalows that are also owned by the Menil Foundation. Designed as an unpompous 'village museum', Piano's earlier building is clad in the same clapboard siding as the surrounding bungalows which house some of its ancillary functions; and it is ringed by a welcoming colonnade that establishes a reciprocal relationship with the porches of the bungalows.

The new gallery stands among the bungalows that frame the campus, but it lacks a porch or colonnade and is not clad in clapboard. If it had been, it might have receded inconspicuously among the bungalows and have seemed to be a mere outbuilding of the Menil, lacking the dignity and emphasis due to its contents. Instead its solid, mostly windowless walls are faced in big reconstituted stone slabs.

These give it a scale comparable to that of the museum, while also making it more mute and monumental.

Besides size, siting and the desire to make the gallery quietly conspicuous, there are other reasons for the differences between the buildings. Unlike the museum, which houses several functions, the new building contains only galleries. The original museum's galleries take the form of a large flexible space subdividable by moveable partitions, whereas the new galleries are fixed rooms. These are tailored around specific works by a single artist who was closely involved with the design, having strong opinions about such matters as materials and colours. In this sense, the Cy Twombly Gallery has affinities with the Rothko Chapel, designed by Philip Johnson and executed by Eugene Aubry and Howard Barnstone, on the block adjacent to the one which the museum came to occupy. But while the latter is, as Rothko intended, very dimly lit, the new building, though very much brighter, has lower light levels than the main museum. This is because unlike the museum, where the works are rotated for short-term show from the collection stored in the elevated

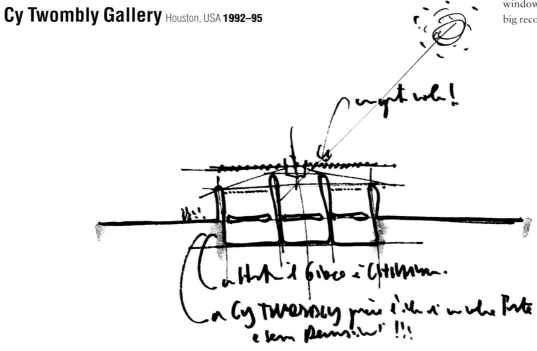

1

Cy Twombly Gallery

Previous page Sunshading canopy floats above walls of reconstituted stone slabs. In background is clapboarded Menil Collection.

Views of model.
1 Pondering roofless model in Vesima laboratory-workshop.
2–4 Elements that shade and diffuse the light: **2** sunshading louvres **3** structural grid that supports louvres **4** light-diffusing fabric ceilings.
5 Fully assembled model.

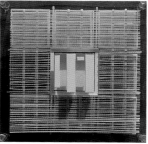

2

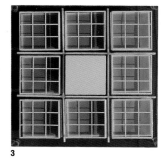

3

4

treasure house, the gallery has a permanent display that is thus much more susceptible to light damage. Also, reflecting the changed conditions and concerns that have arisen since the museum was built, the gallery is very much more energy-efficient.

The gallery sits across the street from the museum's south-east corner. To assert its autonomy from the latter, it is not only clad in reconstituted stone (whose huge blocks and ochre colour contrast with the grey clapboarding of the

museum and bungalows), but it turns its entrance sideways away from the larger building so that it is approached along its eastern side. Moreover, its square form contrasts with the elongated rectangle of the museum. Although both buildings are lit through a glass roof with a conspicuous shading canopy, these emphasize the differences in plan form. The roof of the museum consists of linear elements that oversail the external walls to reach dynamically outwards. The square form of the gallery is made yet more static by the central emphasis given to the sloping glass roof, which is hipped around its flat opaque central portion.

All this is reflected in the plan of the rooms below, which are laid out on a planning grid of 0.9 metres (3 feet). The exhibition rooms occupy a square made up of nine smaller squares with sides of 4.9 metres (27 feet) and separated by walls of 0.9 metres. Except where one room fills two squares, each square is an independent room.

All of these, except the central one, which is entirely artificially lit, are naturally lit through the roof. A strip extending from the eastern edge of this square of rooms houses a central entrance, an archive, lavatories and a service stair to the basement, all below a flat opaque roof. Matching the glass entrance doors and its flanking windows are another set of windows and glass doors on the opposite side facing west. All of these are framed in massive concrete architraves. This is one of the very few buildings in which the most apt responses to propriety and context have led Piano to deliberately seek heaviness in a design – though he has also emphasized the weight of the walls to ensure that the roof and its shading canopy look very light by contrast.

Despite their thickness and perceived mass, neither the external nor internal walls are structural. Both conceal air-conditioning ducts: the internal walls are hollow between their plastered skins of 18-millimetre plywood; the external walls are hollow between the plastered plywood inner linings and the core of insulating block. (Between the latter and the facing blocks there is another smaller cavity.) Also concealed in the internal walls, in the corners of the innermost square,

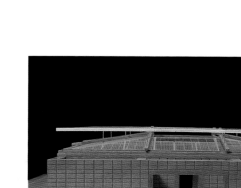

5

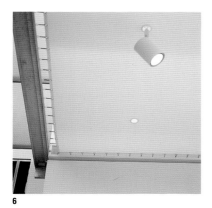

6

Cy Twombly Gallery

6 Corner of cotton ceiling with turnbuckle fixings.

7 Full-size plywood mock-up of external corner to check scale of outer blocks.

8 Erecting mock-up in final materials on site.

9 Inspecting completed on-site mock-up.

7

8

9

are four I-sectioned steel posts; and concealed in the multi-layered external walls are concrete posts at 2.7 metre and 0.9 metre centres.

Together these posts support the roof with its sloping external beams. Propped up from these is a flat steel grid supporting above it a canopy of fixed steel louvres that shade the glass and admit only north light. Suspended from the sloping beams is the double-glazed roof (with clear ultraviolet-excluding glass) and below that another steel grid filled with horizontal adjustable louvres.

Because the upper canopy of fixed louvres does not oversail beyond the external walls, direct sun falls on the lower and outer edges of the glass. In these places it is fritted (at between 20 and 80 per cent coverage depending on location) to limit the amount of direct sun admitted. Stretched below the louvres are translucent ceilings that are each a single sheet of white cotton. These diffuse the light further, giving a softness to both it and the ambience of the room. The adjustable spotlights that provide artificial illumination are supported on arms that pass through holes in these fabric ceilings to the tracks above them.

The resulting exhibition spaces are very different to those of the museum. Instead of the conspicuous and curvaceous 'leaves', which float in the light that floods down between them, and offer glimpses of the bone-like cast structural elements with which they are integral, there is the quiet, flat plane of the velaria that hides all other light control elements and

structure. (These elements are now only vaguely detectable shadowy presences although they were all very neatly ordered in case a more translucent fabric was chosen.)

The light levels in the gallery are lower and more constant than in the museum. The motorized blinds above the fabric ceilings are designed to maintain the modern conservation standards of 200–300 lux, with sensors automatically adjusting the louvres above each room independently. But the blinds can open to admit a maximum of 700 lux. Yet even this is well below the museum's range of 1,000–2,000 lux. The light is also considerably more diffused, though still somewhat directional, thus allowing any relief in the works to read clearly. There is also even less fall-off in the intensity of light from the top to the bottom of the pictures than in the museum, in part because more 'spill' light is reflected off the floor.

In the entrance areas the floor is stone; but as in the museum the gallery floors are wood. Instead of being painted black, however, the 200-millimetre-wide boards are of pale American oak, a palette preferred by Twombly and readily agreed upon by the architects, the client and Ove Arup & Partners, who were the

59

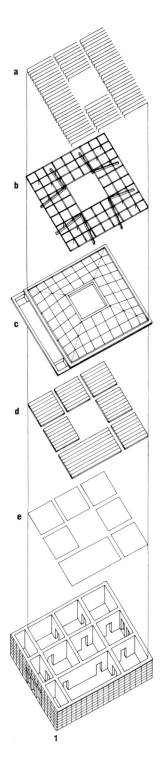

a

b

c

d

e

1

Cy Twombly Gallery

60

1 Exploded axonometric of roof and shading elements: **a** fixed sunshading louvres **b** structure that supports louvres **c** glazed roof **d** adjustable louvres to control light intensity **e** light-diffusing fabric ceilings.

2 Overhead view of model without sunshading louvres.

3 Model of corner of roof and sunshading canopy.

4 Concrete framed entrance doors in east elevation with Menil Collection to right.

5 Location plan: **a** Menil Collection **b** Cy Twombly Gallery **c** Rothko Chapel.

6 Oblique view of entrance elevation when approaching from the street.

services engineers. However, air-conditioning inlet grilles, such as those used in the museum, would have been conspicuous in this floor. Instead, the inlets in each gallery are at the heads of two opposing walls where they are connected to ducts within the wall that rise from the plant in the basement. Channels set in the other two walls allow air to pass around the edge of and rise above the fabric ceiling, where it is extracted from under the glass roof.

As at the museum, this is a low-velocity system and totally silent – the latter is achieved by careful design. All bends are perfectly radiused and all ducts are perfectly sized to achieve a balanced distribution without other controls. Unlike the museum, no direct sun is admitted through the glass roof, and also because of these lower light levels, air-conditioning loads are much reduced. Though consuming twice as much energy per square metre as the Beyeler Foundation Museum (Volume Two p 170) that is now under construction (in temperate Basle, rather than hot and humid Houston), this is a very energy-efficient system, using only a quarter as much energy per square metre as the museum.

As always with a Building Workshop design done in collaboration with Arups, development involved much model-making and testing. The natural lighting, for instance, was first tested on a 1:50 scale model at the University of Michigan; and to be sure of the scale of the big facing blocks, a corner of the building was mocked-up in place and at full size. The result is a low-key but commanding building, the blankness of its walls alleviated by the flourish of the crowning canopy. However, the roof, with its structure supporting what could almost be independent sun-excluding and light-diffusing layers, rather lacks the conceptual economy of the original museum in which sun excluding, light-reflecting and structural elements are all fused into an integral unit.

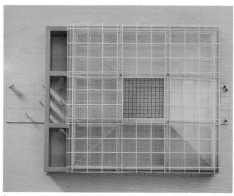

2

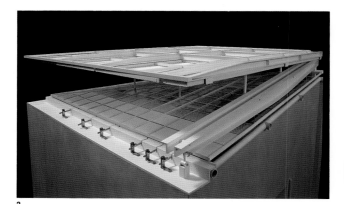

3

4

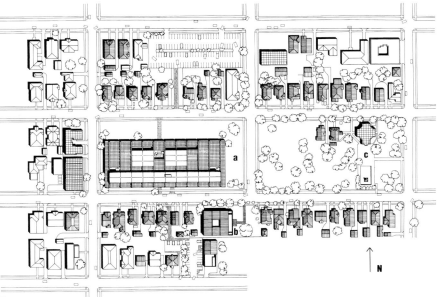

5

6

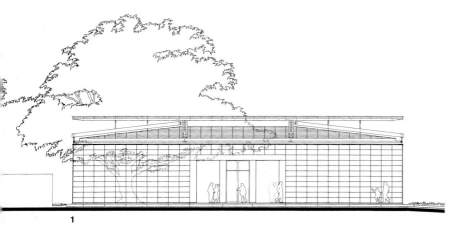

1

Cy Twombly Gallery

1 East (entrance) elevation.

2 Plan.

3 Entrance at dusk.

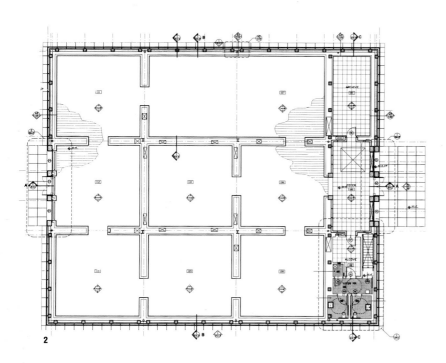

2

3

1

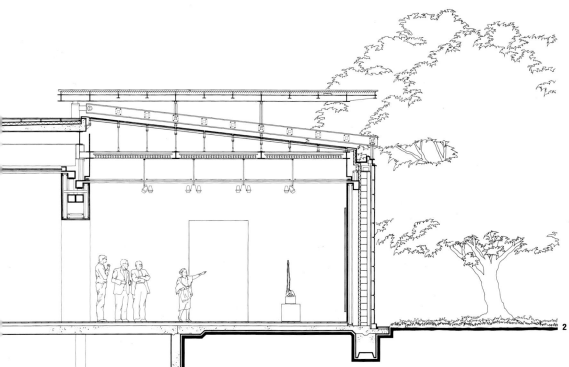

2

Cy Twombly Gallery

1 Central gallery on east side with entrance lobby visible through glass doors.

2 Section of single gallery.

3 North–south section.

4 West–east section.

5 Entrance lobby.

6 Central gallery on west.

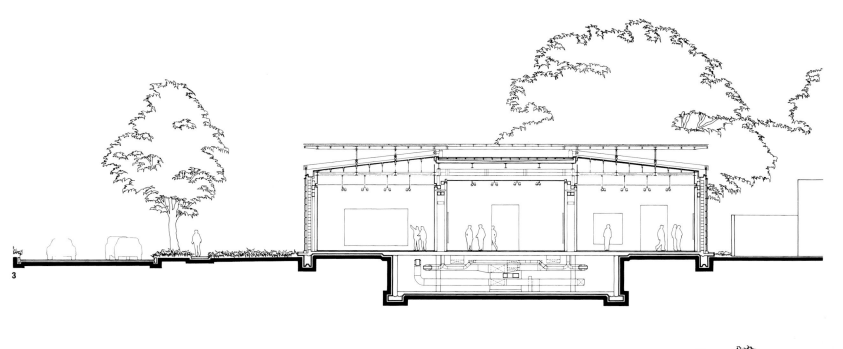

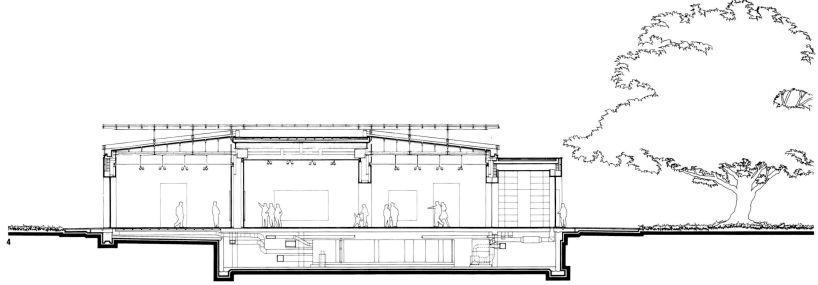

1

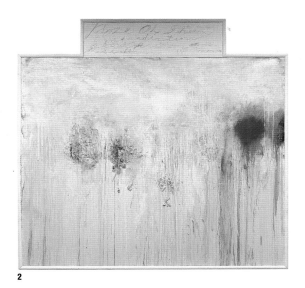

2

Cy Twombly Gallery

Works from the collection.

1 'Untitled (Archilocos Line)', 1989.

2 'Analysis of the Rose as Sentimental Despair', 1989 (central panel).

3 'Untitled', 1978, 1990.

4 'Thermopylae', 1991.

5 'Untitled', 1971.

6 'Untitled', 1977.

7 'Untitled', 1970.

8 'Winter's Passage LUXOR', 1985, 1990.

9 'Untitled (On Wings of Idleness)', 1994.

10 'Untitled' 1983.

11 'Rotalla', 1986, 1990.

12 'Analysis of the Rose as Sentimental Despair', 1985 (left panel).

3

4

5

6

7

8

9

10

11

12

1

Cy Twombly Gallery

1 View into central, artificially-lit exhibition space.

2 Gallery in north-west corner.

3 Large northern room with opening into exhibition space in north-western corner.

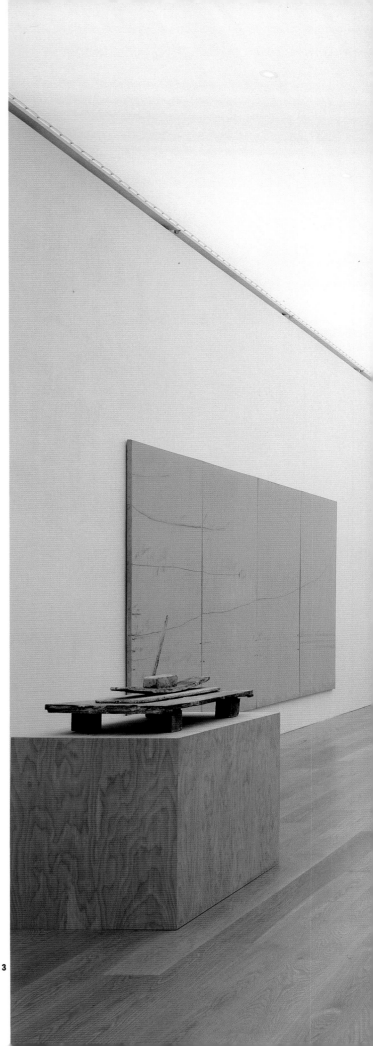

2

3

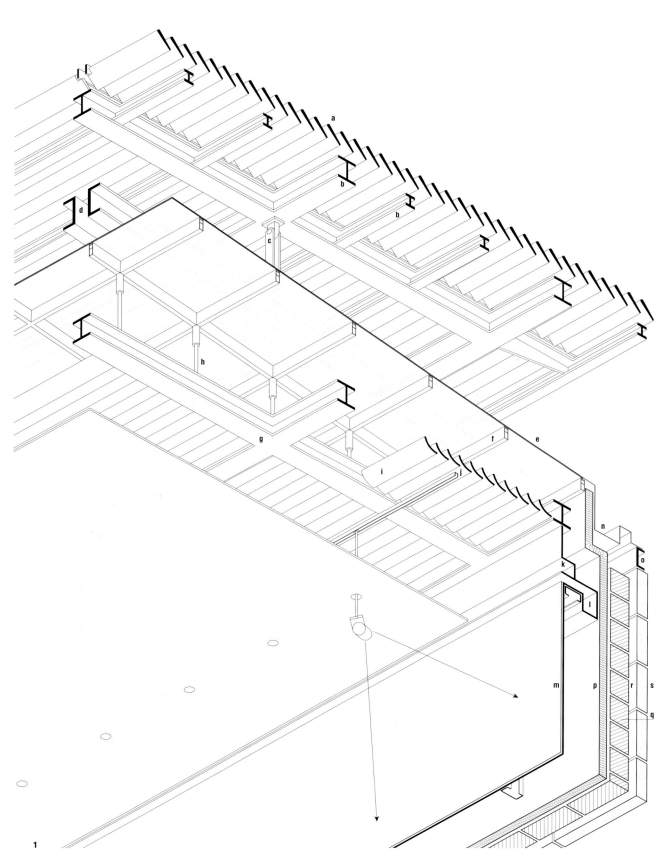

Cy Twombly Gallery
Client Menil Foundation
Design team R Piano, S Ishida & M Carroll
(associates in charge), M Palmore
Assisted by S Comer, A Ewing, S Lopez
Modelmaker M Bassignani
Local architect Richard Fitzgerald &
Associates (R Fitzgerald, G Krezinski)
Structural and services engineers Ove
Arup & Partners (T Barker, J Hewitt, K Holden,
S Meldrum, M Parker, J Peel Cross, A
Sedgwick)
Local structural engineers Haynes
Whaley Associates Inc, Houston, Texas
Local civil engineers Lockwood Andrews
& Newnam, Houston, Texas

1 Worm's eye isometric showing
constructional detail of head of external wall,
roof and shading canopy: **a** fixed extruded
aluminium louvres **b** steel canopy: 100 x
100mm universal section checkerboard within
200 x 200mm universal section grid **c** canopy
support strut from **d** double 300 x 150mm
steel channels **e** ultra-violet filtering clear
glass double-glazed units **f** supporting
framework for aluminium framed double-
glazed units **g** 200 x 200mm steel universal
section grid **h** props for glazed roof
i mechanically adjustable aluminium louvres
j lighting track **k** return air reveal **l** supply air
duct **m** plaster on 18mm plywood **n** pressed
steel gutter **o** 150mm steel channel fascia
beam **p** 75mm fibreglass insulation **q** 200mm
concrete blockwork **r** 75mm cavity
s reconstituted stone slabs.
2 Oblique view of west elevation shows
contrast between floating filigree of shade
canopy and serene solidity of walls of
reconstituted stone slabs and stark heavy
concrete frames around openings.

1

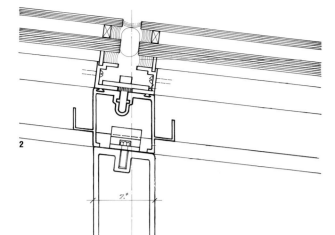

3

4

Cy Twombly Gallery

1 Close-up view of shade canopy and head of external wall.

2 Detail of junction of double-glazed units of roof and supporting sub-structure and drip collectors.

3, 4 Views between shading canopy and glazed roof.

5 Detailed section of single gallery: **a** fixed louvres **b** structural grid **c** prop for shade canopy **d** double-glazed roof **e** prop for glass roof **f** mechanically adjusted louvres **g** channel allowing return air around edge of fabric ceiling **h** inlet for conditioned air **i** 18 mm plastered plywood **j** cavity.

6 Detail of internal mechanically adjusted louvres that can be hinged down for maintenance: **a** prop supporting glazed roof **b** sprinkler head **c** electrical conduit for spot lights **d** location of electric motor and gear box **e** 87mm wide aluminium slats.

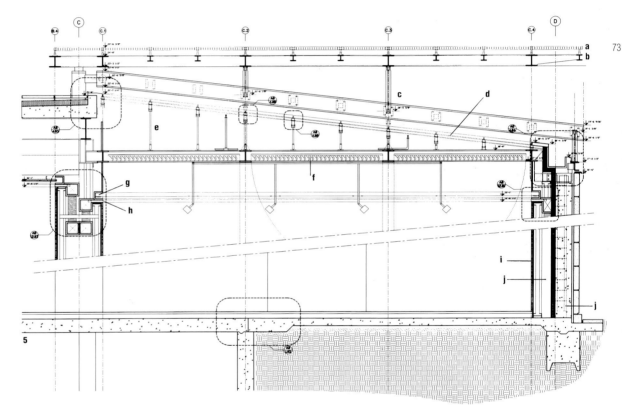

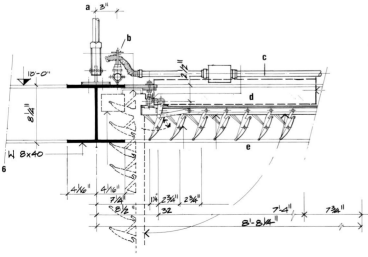

74 **Competition** 1985
Final scheme 1989–
First phase completed 1995

Cité Internationale de Lyon Lyons, France **1985–95**

Close to the city centre, yet somewhat isolated from it, the Cité Internationale de Lyon will be neither city nor suburb as we know them, but a dense multi-use precinct in which people live, work, meet and play. Although it brings new conference, cultural and leisure facilities to the citizens of Lyons, it is being built primarily to attract and serve the larger international community to which Lyons is well connected. This urban microcosm is a dense linear development, with chains of buildings of different uses on either side of a central pedestrian spine, on a prominent site between the River Rhône and the Parc de la Tête d'Or. Like most of Piano's works, it is also designed to make connections with whatever nature is nearby, in this case cementing new links between park and river, in pursuit of his ideal of bringing contemporary life into harmonious relationship with the natural. The buildings are also part of the series by the Building Workshop that is clad in terracotta, as well as the first in a series using a secondary, external glass skin to achieve savings in energy consumption.

Lyons started as a settlement on a sandbank between the Rhône and Saône rivers. It is France's third largest city after Paris and Marseilles, to both of which it is now well connected by the TGV line (*Train à Grande Vitesse*, the French high-speed rail system), as well as to Geneva. To capitalize on these connections, an architectural competition was held in 1985 to rehabilitate the premises for the Foire Internationale de Lyon (an international fair) and to add to them a new conference centre so that, individually and together, these might be used for international events. This competition was won by the Renzo Piano Building Workshop in collaboration with the landscape-architect Michel Corajoud, thus initiating their involvement with the project.

The buildings for the Foire had been built in 1918 as a series of slab blocks that fanned in an arc between the nineteenth-century park and the bank of the Rhône. The Building Workshop scheme proposed linking the old blocks with a curving pedestrian mall and improving their connection with the park by moving most of the traffic from the road between them and the park to a major new road along the river bank. It also proposed a direct connection between the park and the river bank with a pedestrian bridge between the congress halls.

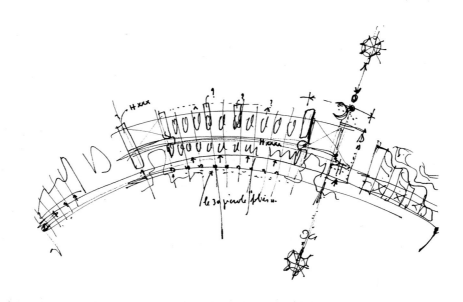

Having won the competition, further investigation revealed that, even if modernized, the old blocks would not attract tenants because they faced each other, rather than the park or the river. So in 1989 it was decided to demolish all the blocks, except the old entrance pavilion known as the Atrium, and to rebuild following the broad precepts of the competition scheme. The new blocks, though, were to be aligned as pairs on either side of the pedestrian spine (and so overlooking the river or park) rather than straddling it. The

Building Workshop and Corajoud, in collaboration with the city's road engineers, have master-planned an area that stretches from beyond the Churchill Bridge, to the west, to beyond the Poincaré Bridge, more than a kilometre to the east. The new urban boulevard between these bridges is now open, its edges and the river bank landscaped and half the first phase of buildings along the pedestrian spine completed. The busy old road along the park is now a quiet access way with street-edge parking.

Where the new road passes the Cité Internationale, traffic is slowed down by traffic lights, which also allow pedestrians to cross it; the road is also pushed against the river to leave as much space between it and the buildings as possible. This area is being densely planted to screen the traffic from view and muffle its noise, and includes a drop-off road immediately in front of the new buildings. This little road in turn gives access to the ramps that descend to the three-level parking garage extending under the basements of the new buildings.

Along the boulevard's river edge is a stone-faced, sloping concrete retaining wall with broad steps and ramps, all neatly detailed by the Building

Workshop, which descend obliquely to a gravel path close to the water's edge. West of an exhibition hall built in the 1960s (which will form the western end of the Cité Internationale), the boulevard swings gently away from the water's edge. Corajoud has landscaped this area between the boulevard and the river, and the entire length of the immediate water's edge, to look as natural as possible. Instead of a concrete or stone embankment, fibreglass matting stabilizes the soil and is hidden by the plants that grow up through it. Towards the Churchill Bridge, stands of willows screen the river and march right to its edge.

The first phase of construction consists of five pairs of buildings, including and stretching east from the Atrium. This is being converted and extended into a museum of

76 **Cité Internationale de Lyon**

Previous page The layer of adjustable glass louvres outside the terracotta facade and conventional windows brings economies of energy consumption and 'pointillist' reflections of leaves, sky and water.

1 Opening banquet for the Foire Internationale de Lyon in 1918.

2 Photomontage of 1985 competition-winning proposal for rehabilitating the premises of the Foire Internationale. These stretch between a curve in the Rhône and the Parc de la Tête d'Or.

1

2

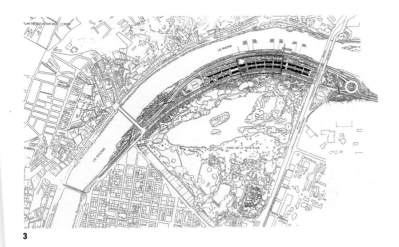

Cité Internationale de Lyon
The design now being executed.
3 Location plan, with Phase One shown in red.
4 Model of all phases.
5 Site plan.

4

contemporary art, and the new building across the pedestrian route from this will be a fourteen-screen cinema complex. Such cultural/leisure facilities not only add to the resources of Lyons, but are an important factor in attracting international businesses to visit or locate there. The pair of blocks to the east of this will be a four-star hotel. However, no backer has yet been found to fund or operate it, despite the nearby conference centre, its splendid site and the importance of its presence in a credible international centre. Next are a pair of office blocks and beyond these the conference centre, all of which are now complete. Eventually, another pair of office blocks will conclude the first phase. More offices and housing will be built, both to the east and west of this first phase, following a similar layout.

To unify the whole, all the blocks with their different heights, functions and fenestration will be clad in the same components. Here, the innovations are both in the size and fixing of terracotta units, and in the use of another layer of glass units outside of them. Unlike the IRCAM Extension (Volume One p 202) and the Harbour Master's Office in the Genoa docks (Volume Two

p 223), the terracotta units are not framed into larger panels. Instead, on these much larger buildings, the units are also larger, and span independently up to 1.4 metres between the vertical elements that support them. As on the earlier buildings, the terracotta units are extrusions, except for the pressings used on external corners. With further refinements, a similar system is being used on the Headquarters and Safety Deposits of the Banca Popolare di Lodi (now nearing completion) and the Potsdamer Platz buildings (begun on site, Volume Two p 210).

As with those works in the series that come before and after the Cité Internationale, the terracotta cladding provides a protective finish that is warm to look at and weathers well. It also gives an enlivening delicacy of 'grain' to the buildings, with the horizontal emphasis of these

77

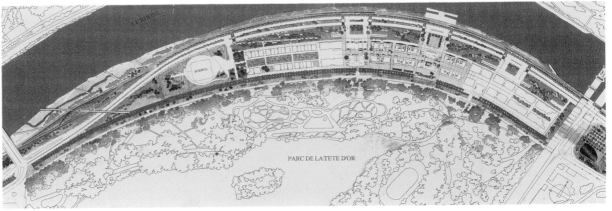

5

large units being matched to the chains of big buildings that are seen also from a distance across the river and park. Adding to the grain, and giving a shimmering dematerializing effect which Piano refers to as 'pointillist', are stretches of unframed glass panes, some of which pivot as louvres, projecting forward from the terracotta facade.

These buildings are the first in a series of projects to use such a device to achieve energy efficiency, while still allowing occupants a feeling of contact with the outdoors. Piano is adamant that he will not sacrifice the latter of these goals (that are often assumed to be incompatible) which are achieved by increasing the air supply during the portion of the year when even tall and exposed buildings can be naturally ventilated. (This solution is also being used at Potsdamer Platz.) The outer glass panes break the force of the wind and intercept the rain so that the conventional windows behind them can always be open. In summer, the night air cools the buildings, while during the day the gap behind the outer glass layer acts as a thermal chimney, with warm air rising to escape through open louvres at the top while drawing in cool fresh air behind it through louvres lower down the facade. In winter the louvres are closed to trap air, warmed by the sun and heat escaping from inside to a temperature that is immediate between indoors and out, which forms an effective insulating layer, thus cutting down heating loads.

These outer, ventilated glass skins are not used on the sheltered facades along the pedestrian spine, and only face the park and the river. On the typical nine-storey blocks, they curve back above the seventh floor. Where they continue over an eighth-floor double-height space, they give way to weather-tight double glazing that curves to form flat glazed roofs. Where they wrap over roof terraces, they maintain the same profile, but in the single glass panes. This gives the blocks a very distinctive profile, which complements the double facade with its diaphanous, crystalline skin projecting forward from and extending past the warmly coloured terracotta walls punctuated by conventional windows.

These facades pursue Piano's concern with the natural in their passive systems, in the use of a warm, earthy material that will weather gracefully, and in the flickering vivacity of its pointillist optical effects. Yet the use of terracotta and passive energy systems, together with the shapely cast elements that

78

1

2

3

4

Cité Internationale de Lyon

1 Site plan of first phase.

2, 3, 5 Views of the bank of the Rhône.

4 Perspective of pedestrian mall flanked
by office blocks.

6 Close-up of glass houses in the Parc de la
Tête d'Or. The curves and diaphanous skin of
these buildings is reflected in the Cité
Internationale's outer layer of glass.

6

5

both support the louvres and
serve as curved racks to the
electrically-driven pinions that
open them, are all updated
versions of nineteenth-century
equivalents. But this, as argued
in the introduction to Volume
One (p 8), is a characteristic of
much of Piano's work that is,
nevertheless, more topical than
dated: it harks back to a time
when engineering (whether
cast-iron structure or ingenious
ventilation controls) often gave
a building a distinctive character
that afforded people a sensual
relationship with the elements
of both architecture and nature.

Also distinctive is the
rhythmic system that disciplines
the layout of the blocks along
the central spine. Between the
blocks, open cross routes link
the river and park, while the
mid-block lobbies (between the
two wings which make up each
block) also form cross routes
between these. Both the open

routes and the lobbies taper
in plan so that the rectangular
wings between them align
with the curving spine.

Of the buildings so far
completed, the offices are more
typical than the conference
centre. This is because they
make more extensive use of
the double, ventilated facade
system, and also because they
form a pair of full-height blocks
on opposite sides of the glass-
roofed pedestrian spine. (The
conference centre, like the
planned four-star hotel, is a
single building straddling the
central route, which passes
through its fully enclosed
ground-floor lobby.) Both office
blocks consist of two wings with
eight floors of offices above a
ground level of shops and
separate entrance halls for each
wing. The six typical floors are
20 metres wide with a central
core of vertical circulation and
services flanked on both sides
by corridors and offices. Linking
the wings is an area for meeting
rooms or more offices. The top
two floors of offices are set back
on both long sides, behind
terraces overlooking the
pedestrian spine roof, or under
the curving outer glass skin that
roofs double-height office suites.

Part of the conference centre
extends into the basement of the
office blocks. The two largest
halls are underground. They are
reached by escalators and stairs

79

that descend from the ground-floor lobby, and also by external stairs that descend to a pair of courts sunk at first and second basement levels between the building and the park-side road. Entered from a lobby that stretches along and opens into the lowest of these courts is a large, elongated multi-purpose hall. It has a flat floor, walls lined with the same terracotta units that are used externally and a ceiling of exposed air-conditioning ducts and regularly spaced white panels. These reflect the same uplighters as

were designed for and used in the Lingotto Factory Renovation in Turin (Volume Two p 150). Intended for exhibitions and large meetings, this hall can also be subdivided into two or three smaller rooms for a mix of functions such as receptions and lectures.

Opening into the upper court is the lobby for the handsome 900-seat auditorium with a raked floor. Much of the detailing is the same as, or a refinement of that of the concert–congress hall at Lingotto (p 40). The same seats, designed by the Building Workshop, are used, but here each is self-supporting rather than sharing a supporting rail, so that conference attenders are not disturbed by fidgeting neighbours. At the client's insistence, the rows are curved so that the audience can see participants sitting in the same rows as them (when asking questions for instance). The walls are again wood-panelled, though here the long sides are not relieved by galleries but by concrete columns that line the inside edge of the side aisles. Flexibility in the use of the stage is simply achieved by moving panels suspended from a track to create such options as a proscenium and wings and differing depths of stage.

On the park side of the central route are the only two large spaces above ground level, and these can be used together or separately. One is the Salle Panoramique, a reception room overlooking the park through a stretch of the double facade. The second is another handsome auditorium with a raked floor that is quite different in character to the larger auditorium. Walls and ceilings of the 400-seat hall are formed as a single faceted shell constituted of large overlapping rectangular plywood panels supported on a concealed steel frame – a simple device that gives an enveloping intimacy to the room. On the river side of the central route, the building is a bit taller. Here there are two floors of meeting–reception rooms, and a third floor of VIP accommodation with adjoining terraces.

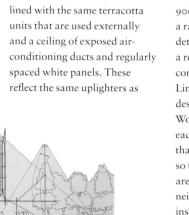

80

1

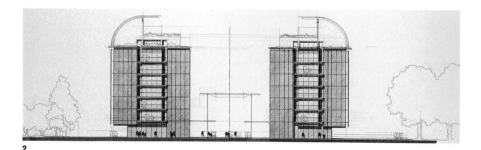

2

3

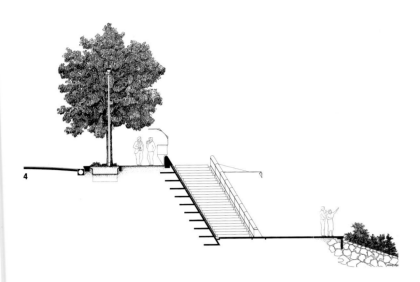

4

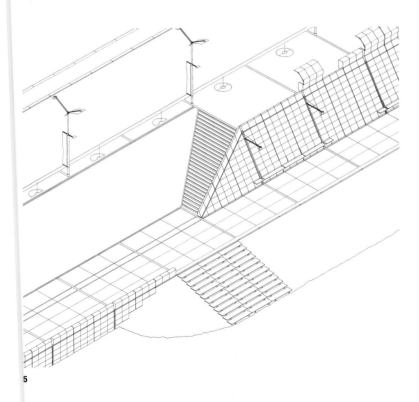

5

Cité Internationale de Lyon

1 End (east) elevation of conference centre.

2 End elevation of office blocks.

3 Aerial view of office blocks and conference centre (on left) overlooking Rhône with park behind.

Treatment of river bank.

4 Section through boulevard sidewalk, sloping retaining wall, riverside walk and planted river edge.

5 Isometric view of area from boulevard to water's edge.

6 Close-up of head of retaining wall that edges riverside walk.

Tall glass walls enclose part of the pedestrian spine, the roof of which continues uninterrupted, to form the lobby of the conference centre. The detailing of the roof and its supporting trusses, and of the frameless glass walls and their supporting structure, is deliberately downbeat. Piano was determined to avoid both the over-worked virtuosity of high-tech and the slickness associated with shopping malls, preferring something that should feel part of the everyday public realm. This attitude prevails everywhere along the central spine. Between the low (and low-key) glass canopies that extend from the shops, the central glass roof is raised high on slender steel posts, between which there is only cross-bracing. (Though roofed, the pedestrian route is naturally ventilated and provides an animated outlook for the windows of the adjacent blocks. To give some privacy to the lower floor offices, the lower part of the windows are fritted with horizontal stripes.) The floor of the central route is simply rough concrete, and the slightly stark hardness of the whole is tempered only by the warmth of the terracotta walls and by trees and other planting.

Although the design was largely dictated by the site and the precedent of the previous buildings on it, a chain of buildings along a pedestrian spine that goes nowhere might seem a rather problematic and dated solution, reminiscent of such schemes as the Coin Street project by Piano's erstwhile partner, Richard Rogers. But the megastructural bravado of these has been tempered by the liberal use of terracotta, the passive energy systems, the understated detail and earthy finishes of terracotta and rough concrete. Moreover, this is both an important transitional project for the Building Workshop, a stepping stone towards many aspects of the Potsdamer Platz scheme, and also one exemplifying many themes dear to Piano, such as the connections made across the spine to the two major natural elements of river and park.

81

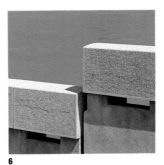

6

Renzo Piano Building Workshop

82   **Cité Internationale de Lyon**

South elevation of office block overlooking the
Parc de la Tête d'Or. The outer layer of glass
louvres serves several purposes. It breaks the
force of wind and rain so that the windows
behind may be left open at all times. The air in
the gap between louvres and building is
warmed by the sun: in summer it rises and
escapes drawing cool fresh air up and into the
windows; in winter the air is trapped to form a
thermal jacket. In material and form, the outer
layer suggests affinities with the glass houses
in the park, while the dancing, broken
reflections on the glass, together with the
gridding of the louvres and their supports and
that of the terracotta cladding behind give the
lively visual effect Piano calls 'pointillist'.

1

Cité Internationale de Lyon

1 Congress centre, on left, and offices seen from across the Rhône.

2 Cross section through riverside boulevard, ramps down to parking, large underground auditorium and ground floor lobby, parkside road and park.

3 Ground floor plan of first phase: **a** Atrium museum of contemporary art **b** multiplex cinema **c** public rooms of hotel **d** shops below office blocks **e** foyer of conference centre **f** ramp down to parking **g** riverside boulevard **h** riverside walk.

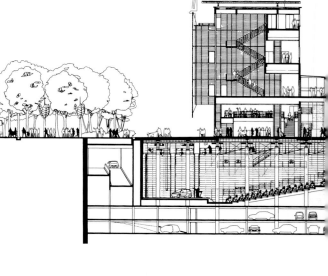

2

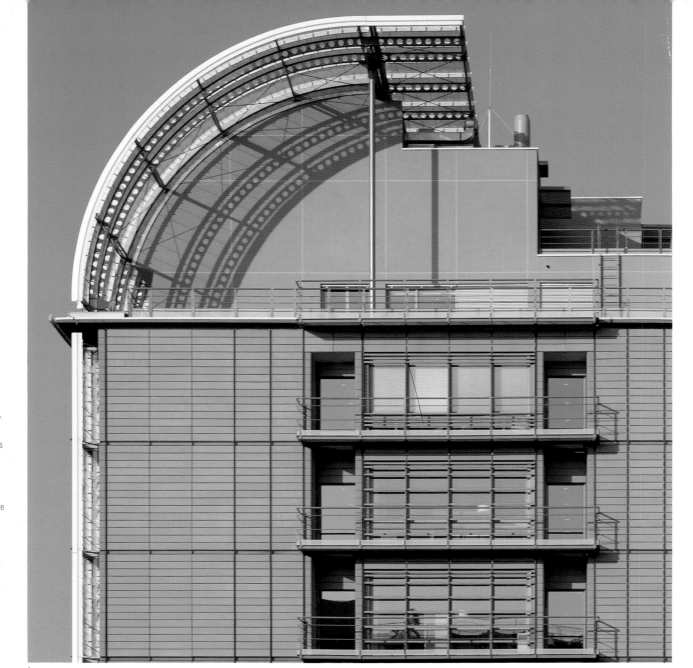

86 **Cité Internationale de Lyon**
1 Upper corner of office block.
2 Section along central mall looking north. From left to right are multiplex cinema, hotel, offices, conference centre and offices.
3 Glass-roofed mall flanked by office blocks leading to lobby of conference centre. Detailing and finishes are kept low-key so that mall should not resemble a slick shopping centre but seem a normal part of the public realm.

2

3

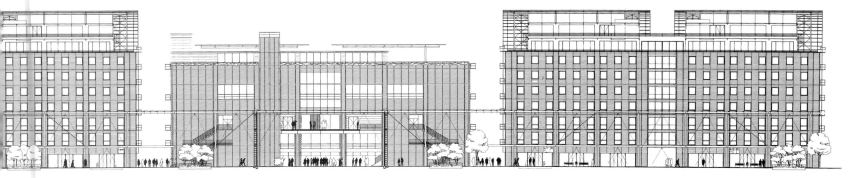

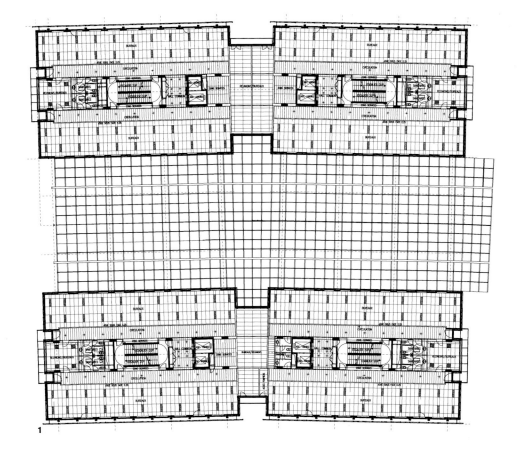

1

88   **Cité Internationale de Lyon**

The office blocks.

1 Typical floor plan.

2 Ground floor plan with office entrances
and shops.

3 Looking east along the park-facing facades
of the office blocks and, beyond them, the
conference centre. The basement of the latter
extends under the office blocks and can be
reached via the sunken court onto which opens
a large lobby.

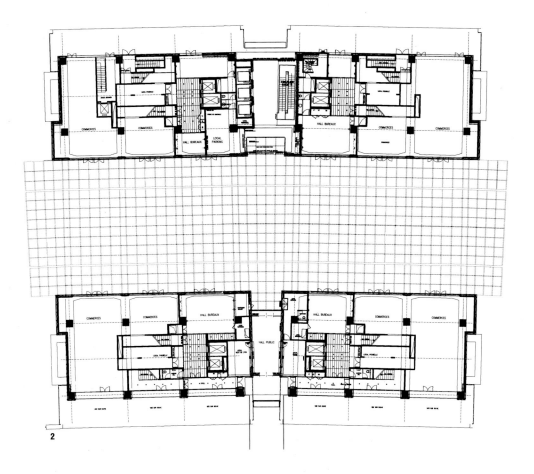

2

1

90 **Cité Internationale de Lyon**

Secondary skin of glass louvres.

1 External view of louvres, some of them wide open, with shading venetian blinds in cavity behind.

2 Close-up view from inside of louvres and their supporting and opening mechanism.

3 Elevational detail of supporting and opening mechanism.

4 Office facade with all the louvres closed.

2

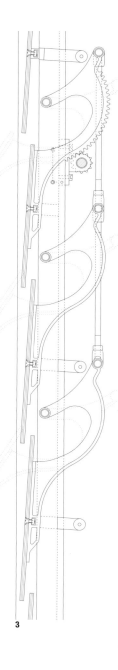

3

Cité Internationale de Lyon
Client SEM; City of Lyon; Grand Lyon;
SPAICIL (site developer)
Design team R Piano, P Vincent
(associate in charge), A Chaaya, A
Gallissian, M Howard, A El Jerari, M Henry,
C Jackman, J B Mothes, E Novel,
M Pimmel, A H Téménidès, B Tonfoni
Assisted by C Calafell, J A Polette,
M Salerno, W Vassal
Model makers J P Allain, O Doizy
Project management Syllabus
(A Vincent)
Site supervision Curtelin-Ricard-
Bergeret (associate architects) with
C Valentinuzzi
Engineering and quantity surveyor
GEC
Structural engineer ESB, Agibat
Electrical services engineer Merlin,
Jeol, HGM, Fusée
Mechanical services engineer
CSTB, Barbanel, Courtois, Inex
**Associate architect for electricity
sub-station** Archigroup
Road engineers DDE
Landscape architect M Corajoud
Landscape engineers Vegetude
Associate architect for cinemas
Alberto Cattani Associates
Stage equipment consultant
Labeyrie
Acoustics Peutz & Associés
Signage designer Ruedi Baur
& Associates

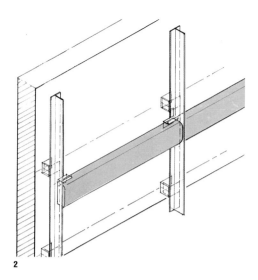

2

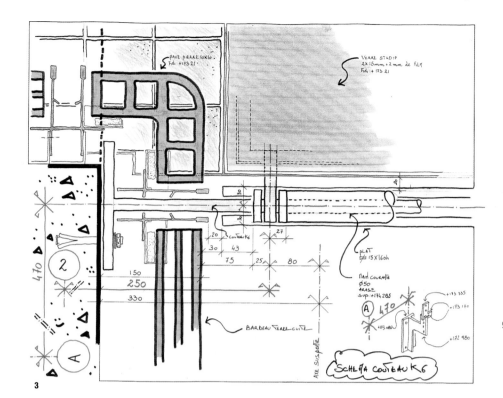

Cité Internationale de Lyon

Terracotta cladding.

1 Close-up view of projecting first-floor corner of office block shows how outer layer of glass louvres sails past main facade. Clearly visible too are the elements of the terracotta cladding system: the typical extruded units and pressed corner units, the vertical fixing rails and recessed channel string course.

2 Sketch detail showing how each terracotta unit spans between vertical supporting rails.

3 Sketch plan detail of fixing of balcony between extruded terracotta unit and pressed terracotta corner unit.

4 Sketch sectional detail of fixing of balcony to concrete structure. Channel between extruded terracotta units serves as string course marking floor level inside.

5, 6 Close-up views of cladding interrupted by supporting rails and recessed channel string course.

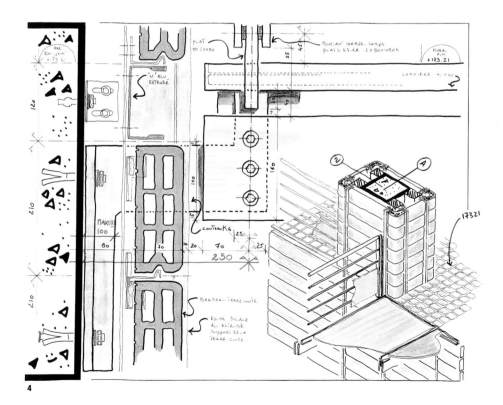

4

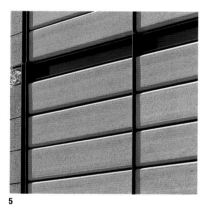

5

6

93

1

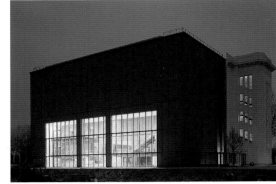

2

94 **Cité Internationale de Lyon**

Atrium museum of contemporary art and cinema complex.

1 Retained facade of the Atrium, which was the main entrance into the Foire now fronts the museum of contemporary art.

2 North elevation of museum. Forward of the old stair shaft on the right is entirely new construction. Glass roof of mall and cinema complex on its opposite side have yet to be built.

3 Basement plan of storage and service areas of museum and and smaller cinemas of multiplex cinema.

4 Entrance lobby of Atrium museum.

5 North–south cross section of multiplex cinema, mall and museum of contemporary art. Part of the museum occupies the shell of the old Atrium building.

6 Gallery overlooking park on top floor of Atrium building.

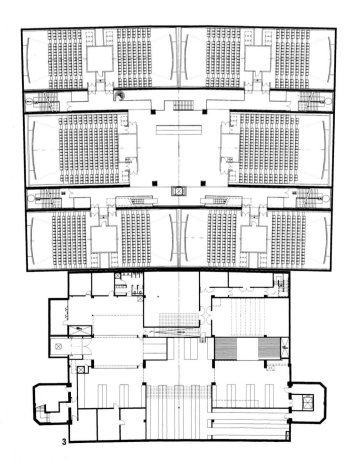

3

4

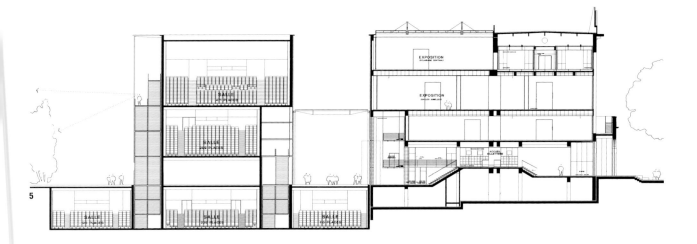

5

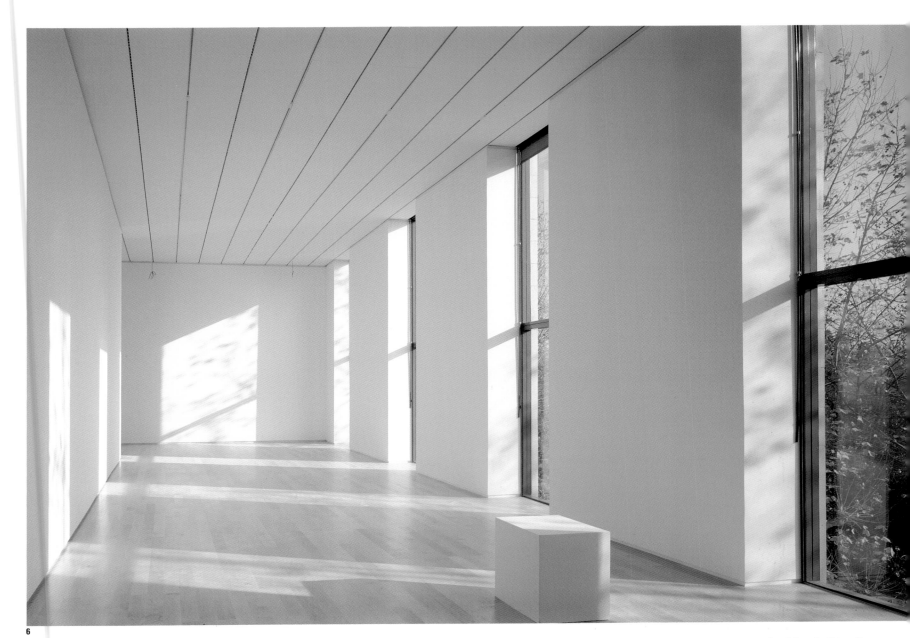

6

1

Cité Internationale de Lyon
Conference centre.

1 Elongated lobby in the basement that extends under the office blocks. Through glass doors on left is large subdividable multi-purpose hall used for exhibitions, receptions, banquets and conferences. Glass doors on right open onto sunken external court.

2 900-seat subterranean auditorium.

3 400-seat auditorium on first floor.

4 First floor plan: **a** 400-seat hall **b** Salle Panoramique **c** Meeting–reception room.

5 Ground floor plan.

6 Central part of the entrance lobby is a glassed-in portion of the glass-roofed mall that passes through it.

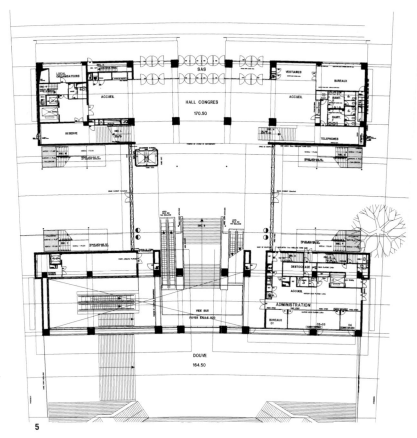

2

3

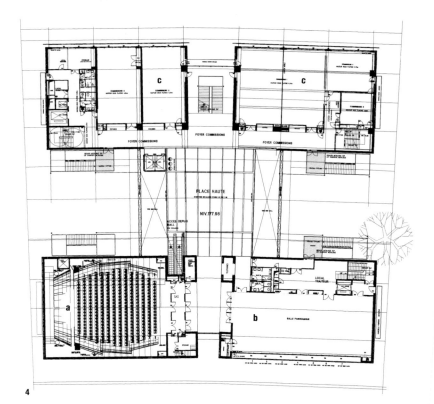

4

5

The huge Renault factory on Paris's ship-like Île Seguin, together with those on the Seine's banks to either side, are now defunct. No winner has been announced yet of the invited competition to master-plan the redevelopment of the island and a pocket of sloping land, the Bas Meudon, on the river's left bank.

Attending to what Piano calls 'memory', a place's history and memorable features, the Building Workshop scheme treats the sites differently. The Île Seguin is entirely rebuilt with a mix of uses around a central park that recalls the meadows and orchards that the factory displaced. The Bas Meudon's factories are demolished too; but other buildings are retained and joined by housing blocks organized around a web of planted courts and pathways that preserve or recall those already there.

Towards either end of the island is a piazza: that towards the south-east end is connected by existing road bridges to both river banks; the other is connected, north-eastwards and southwards by a new road bridge and a new footbridge respectively. An emergency and service vehicle road rings the island.

Building volume is deployed with equal clarity; yet results in an urban quarter of richly varied experiences. The island's perimeter is again edged by continuous building that now steps up towards each end. The largest buildings flank the piazzas and from these, rise taller, axially-aligned elements that enhance the island's ship-like silhouette.

Where it edges the park, the riverside building is housing raised above ground-floor promenades on the roofs of underground car parks. Along the promenades are bars, cafes and shops. To let winter sun into the park, the housing along the park's south-west edge is a storey lower in height than that across the park. The promenade below it is oriented primarily to the river: the intention is that large craft be confined to the river's right stream, and that the stretch between the bridges on this side be reserved for sporting uses.

The most intensive development is around and beyond the piazzas. Above ground are offices and hotels, below ground are auditoria, exhibition halls and parking garages. The hotels (and

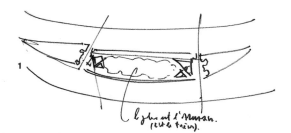

1

Île Seguin and Bas Meudon Paris, France 1995

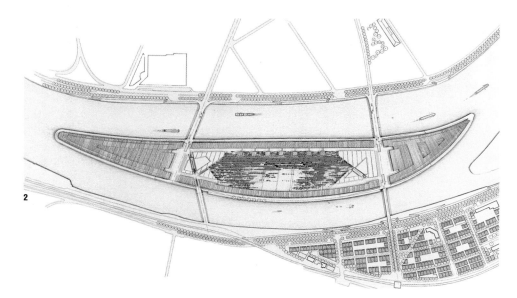

2

98

3

Île Seguin and Bas Meudon

1 Piano's concept sketch of Île Seguin.

2 Site plan of Île Seguin (the island) and Bas
Meudon (on southern bank of Seine).

3 Aerial photograph of existing situation.

4 Plan view of model.

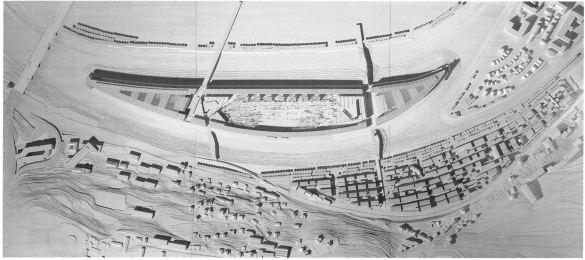

4

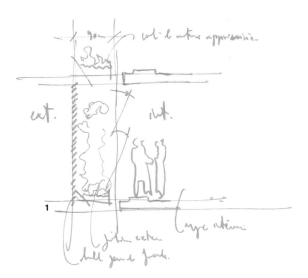

serviced apartment blocks) are between the piazzas and the park, the offices extend around internal gardens towards the island's ends.

Design guidelines will be most stringent for the perimeter buildings, dictating roof and soffit lines, and double-skin facades with an outer layer of repetitive terracotta units. The roof landscaping, visible from slopes above the Seine, will be unified by a grid to which rooflights, paving slabs and rows of planting all conform.

100 **Île Seguin and Bas Meudon**

1 Piano's sketch of proposed double facade allowing freedom of internal planning and winter gardens behind a standardized facade.

2 Aerial view of island as it is with Bas Meudon in the foreground.

3 Section through centre of island.

4 South-west elevation of island.

5 Model viewed from south-east with housing blocks of Le Bas Meudon on left and Île Seguin with both tips built up as corporate headquarters and hotels, and middle of housing flanking a central park.

6 Closer view of island from east.

7 Section through Bas Meudon showing housing blocks around planted courts.

8 Silhouette of ship compared with that of island, and island with proposed open ground floor promenade under perimeter buildings. Below is an elevation of the island.

2

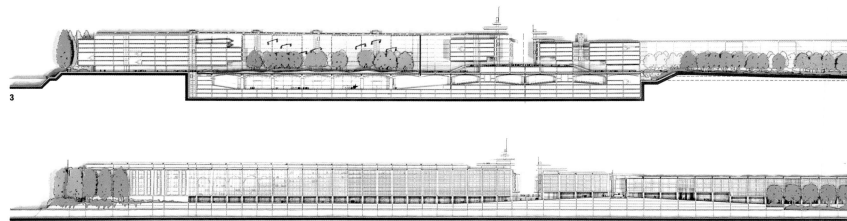

3

4

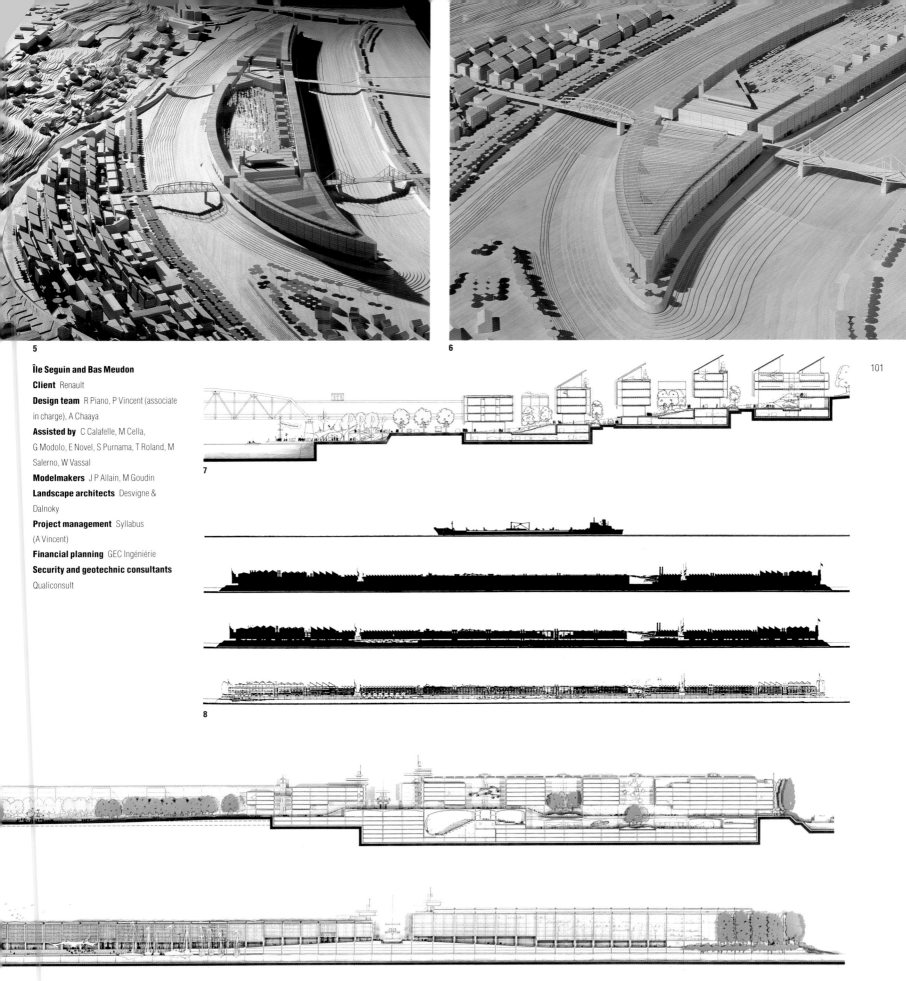

5
6

Île Seguin and Bas Meudon

Client Renault

Design team R Piano, P Vincent (associate in charge), A Chaaya

Assisted by C Calafelle, M Cella, G Modolo, E Novel, S Purnama, T Roland, M Salerno, W Vassal

Modelmakers J P Allain, M Goudin

Landscape architects Desvigne & Dalnoky

Project management Syllabus (A Vincent)

Financial planning GEC Ingéniérie

Security and geotechnic consultants Qualiconsult

7

8

Rome Auditoria Rome, Italy **1994–**

Rome has long lacked an adequate venue for classical music, let alone one commensurate with the city's importance as a major European capital. This will soon be rectified with the construction of one of the most lavishly complete centres for musical performance in the world. It will be perhaps the best appointed musical centre to be built anywhere, including as it does, four auditoria of differing size and configuration with ample rehearsal and changing facilities, a comprehensive music library, a museum of musical instruments, shops for CDs and sheet music, and cafés, bars and restaurants.

The design, for which the working drawings are out to tender at the time of writing, is an evolution and expansion of that with which the Building Workshop won an invited international competition in 1994. To give insight into the architect's design approach, the competition and the design that went to tender and its revisions are illustrated here. The changes between these schemes are the result of revisions in the programme made by the client, and those that are inevitable when a complex of this sort is studied more fully with a range of experts in all its exacting technical aspects. They have also been provoked at a later stage by the discovery on site of important archaeological remains. Excavations have revealed the remains of a large Roman villa. Preserving these as an integral part of the complex has led to further revisions, also shown here.

Such a large complex could not easily be accommodated on a central city site. So it is to be built in the north of Rome, near the facilities for the 1960 Olympics. The Olympic Village extends northwards from the site, and Pier Luigi Nervi's Palazzetto della Sport is to the west. To the south-west and even closer, just across the elevated motorway ramps that edge this part of the site, is the Flaminio soccer stadium. Rising steeply to the east is the park that was the grounds of the Villa Glori, and on land that rises more gently to the south are the housing blocks of Parioli.

As always with Piano today, the design responds to its context, extending key features of the surroundings on to and across the site. Like the freestanding sports stadia, the three auditoria asked for in the competition brief are independent, sculpted elements, each enclosed in its own beetle-like shell. These dominant

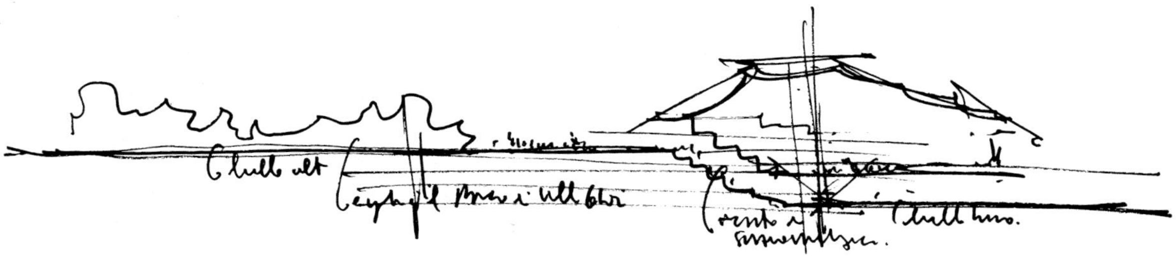

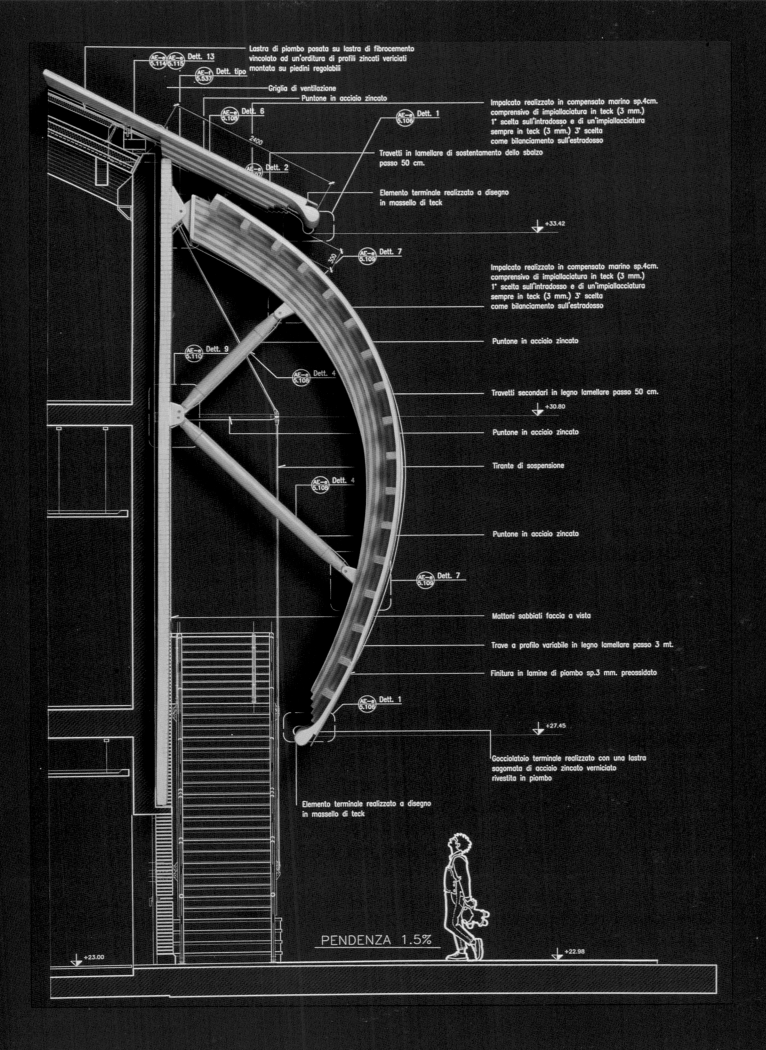

Lastra di piombo posata su lastra di fibrocemento
vincolato ad un'orditura di profili zincati vericiati
montata su piedini regolabili

Dett. 13
AE-e 5.114 AE-e 5.115

AE-e 5.537 Dett. tipo

Griglia di ventilazione

Puntone in acciaio zincato

Dett. 6
AE-e 5.108

Dett. 1
AE-e 5.106

2400

Impalcato realizzato in compensato marino sp.4cm.
comprensivo di impiallacciatura in teck (3 mm.)
1° scelta sull'intradosso e di un'impiallacciatura
sempre in teck (3 mm.) 3° scelta
come bilanciamento sull'estradosso

Dett. 2
AE-e 5.107

Travetti in lamellare di sostentamento dello sbalzo
passo 50 cm.

Elemento terminale realizzato a disegno
in massello di teck

+33.42

300

Dett. 7
AE-e 5.109

Impalcato realizzato in compensato marino sp.4cm.
comprensivo di impiallacciatura in teck (3 mm.)
1° scelta sull'intradosso e di un'impiallacciatura
sempre in teck (3 mm.) 3° scelta
come bilanciamento sull'estradosso

Puntone in acciaio zincato

Dett. 9
AE-e 5.110

Dett. 4
AE-e 5.108

Travetti secondari in legno lamellare passo 50 cm.

+30.80

Puntone in acciaio zincato

Tirante di sospensione

Dett. 4
AE-e 5.108

Puntone in acciaio zincato

Dett. 7
AE-e 5.109

Mattoni sabbiati faccia a vista

Trave a profilo variabile in legno lamellare passo 3 mt.

Finitura in lamine di piombo sp.3 mm. preossidato

Dett. 1
AE-e 5.106

+27.45

Gocciolatoio terminale realizzato con una lastra
sagomata di acciaio zincato verniciato
rivestita in piombo

Elemento terminale realizzato a disegno
in massello di teck

PENDENZA 1.5%

+23.00

+22.98

1

Rome Auditoria

Previous page Relief study of section of external shell of auditorium. Projecting beyond lead waterproofing are shapely hardwood lips giving an appearance of tactility and warmth and suggesting a resemblance to a gigantic musical instrument.

2

elements are arranged in an arc and between them will flow lush landscaping and trees. It is proposed that these trees should continue across the flanking roads so that the site will seem to be an extension of the park of the Villa Glori. The competition design also proposed that the trees continue on to the islands in the motorway junction and beyond to envelop the soccer stadium.

The composition is unified by the configuration created by the three beetles eating from the same bowl – an outdoor amphitheatre, the fourth auditorium. Below the stepped seating of the upper tier of the amphitheatre is a subterranean foyer that links and gives access to the auditoria. The foyer also wraps around the back of, and overlooks the lower steps and stage of the amphitheatre. This stage, which is the central focus of the whole scheme, is also the termination of a piazza which slopes down, as a contained and urban space with adjacent cafés,

into the site from the street to the north.

Raising the auditoria, which need no natural light, and exposing them to the noise from the elevated roads and aircraft overhead, while burying the foyer, which could benefit from abundant natural light, is perverse as an abstract concept. But as a response to the context, it seems an appropriate solution, especially as it produces a fourth auditorium, also a lively piazza, as the heart of the scheme. Moreover, Piano asserts that when built, the independent auditoria will evoke no insect analogies, but rather the image of gigantic musical instruments, thus perfectly expressing the function of the complex.

In all phases of the design, the auditoria are arranged by size, with the largest to the east, the smallest to the west and the medium-sized hall in between and aligned exactly north–south. In the competition design, the auditoria were in the

same sequence, but somewhat differently aligned, with the largest hall orientated due east–west. This 2,700-seat auditorium followed a similar concept to Hans Scharoun's Berlin Philharmonie, with the orchestra stage set to one end of the hall but entirely surrounded by seating arranged in sloping banks, referred to by Scharoun as vineyards. This solution was hailed by musicians and critics for bringing about an entirely new, more unified relationship between orchestra and audience. The smallest, 500-seat chamber music hall followed a conventional layout, with a stage at one end and a sloping tier of seats. The 1,200-seat medium auditorium was an amalgam of the other two, with a stage at one end and a lower tier very much like that in the smallest auditorium, but with another raised tier of seating along both the sides and the back of the lower tier.

In this first design, the outer surfaces of the auditoria roofs

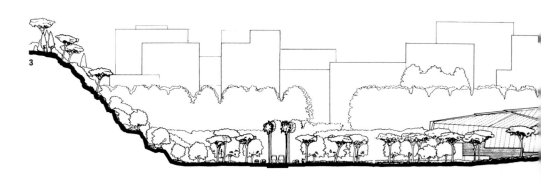

3

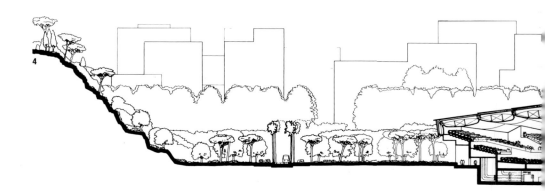

4

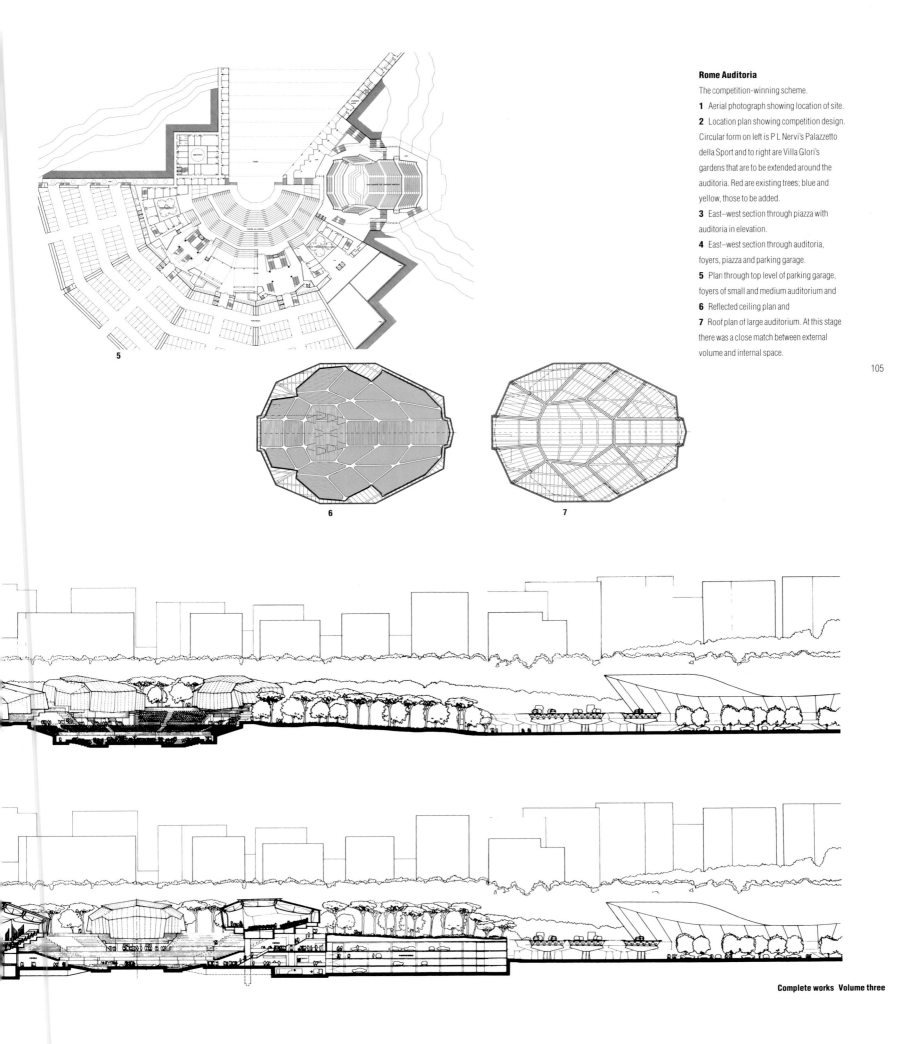

Rome Auditoria

The competition-winning scheme.

1   Aerial photograph showing location of site.

2   Location plan showing competition design. Circular form on left is P L Nervi's Palazzetto della Sport and to right are Villa Glori's gardens that are to be extended around the auditoria. Red are existing trees; blue and yellow, those to be added.

3   East–west section through piazza with auditoria in elevation.

4   East–west section through auditoria, foyers, piazza and parking garage.

5   Plan through top level of parking garage, foyers of small and medium auditorium and

6   Reflected ceiling plan and

7   Roof plan of large auditorium. At this stage there was a close match between external volume and internal space.

105

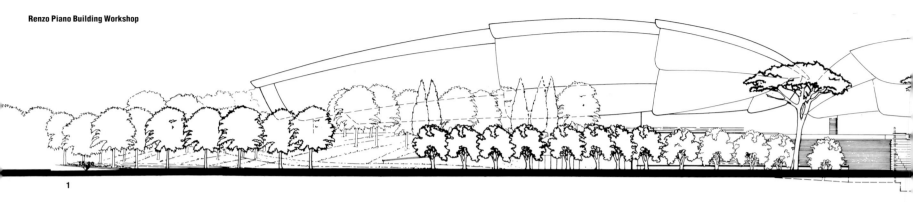

1

Rome Auditoria

Intermediate scheme.

1 North elevation from street with largest auditorium on left and library and shops on right.

2 Section of small flexible auditorium, foyer and parking garage.

3 Plan of small flexible auditorium.

4 Plan view of model.

5 Plan of medium-sized auditorium.

6 Section of parking garage, medium-sized auditorium, foyer and outdoor auditorium–piazza.

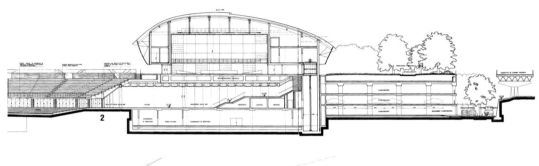

2

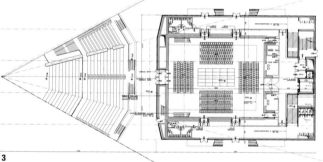

3

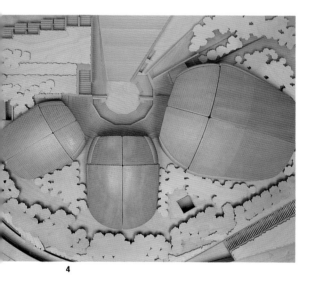

4

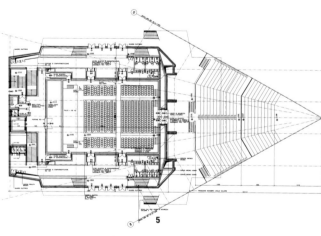

5

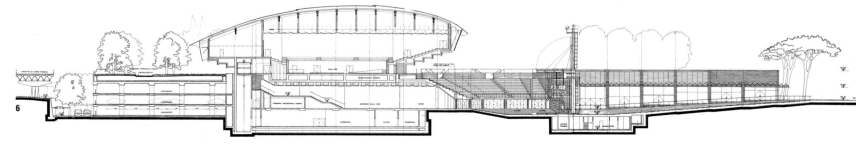

6

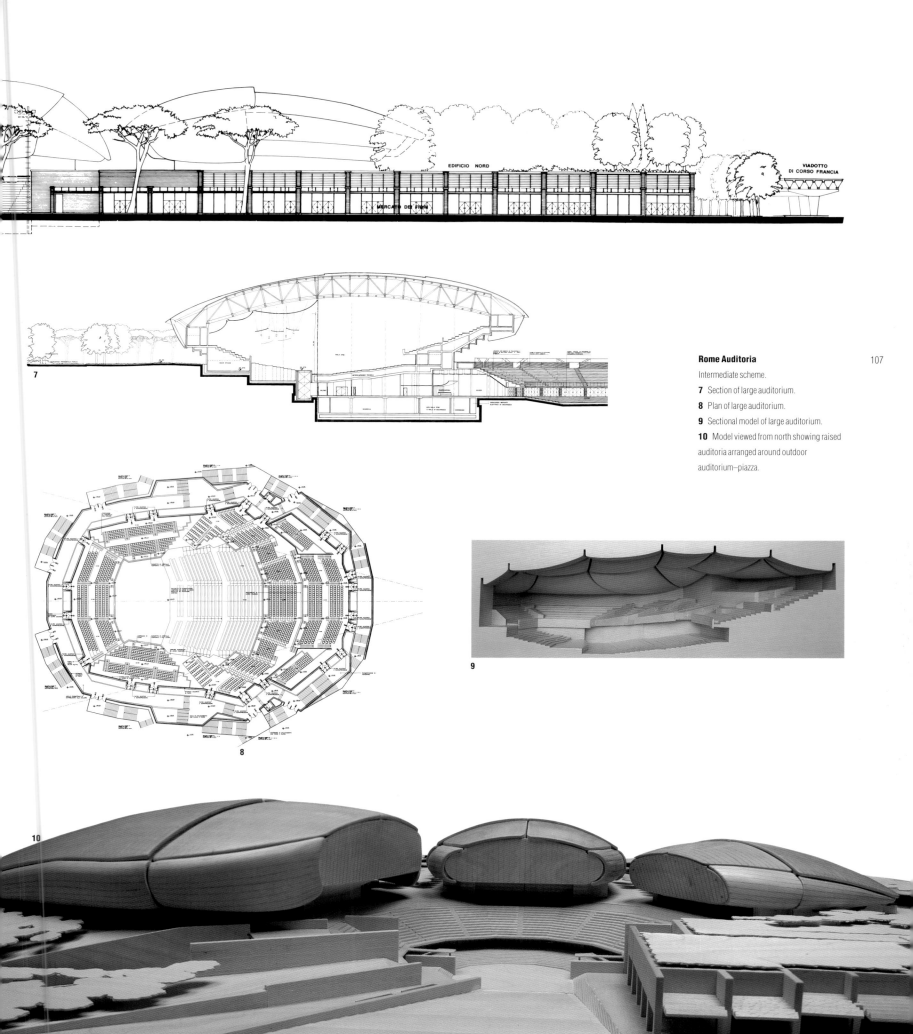

Rome Auditoria

Intermediate scheme.

7 Section of large auditorium.

8 Plan of large auditorium.

9 Sectional model of large auditorium.

10 Model viewed from north showing raised auditoria arranged around outdoor auditorium–piazza.

1

Rome Auditoria

Final scheme.

1 Study model of interior of large auditorium.

2–4 Diagrams showing derivation of toroidal geometries of auditoria roofs. Each roof is made up of segments cut conceptually from top of torus.

5 Model of large auditorium ceiling painted silver to reflect laser beams when studying patterns of acoustic reflection.

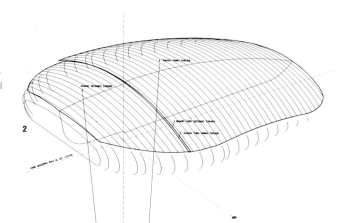

2

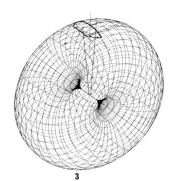

3

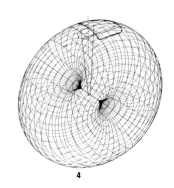

4

followed fairly closely the shapes of the halls' ceilings, though the roofs and ceilings were separated by a space accommodating the roof structure and service catwalks. Although there was a certain honesty in the way outer volume reflected the space inside, this was achieved at some conceptual cost to the structure, the laminated timber frames of which were shaped in a way that was neither structurally efficient nor expressive of their structural purpose.

Yet the way the faceted exterior echoed the interior achieved a further conceptual goal that Piano and Kenny Fraser, who worked on the competition with Shunji Ishida, were then keen on: that the bigger the hall, the greater the number of facets that formed the ceilings and roofs. This reflected their interest in fractals, whereby forms are built up from self-similar sub-parts, as well as their wider interest in nature's geometric order.

By the tender design such ideas had been abandoned and the halls have become, in their internal organization, less of a family as they were modified in line with further input from the client and consultants. The biggest hall, to be used for symphonic concerts, remains much the same in concept, though greatly revised after detailed acoustic study. But,

the smallest hall has become a completely flexible space, modelled on the auditorium of IRCAM in Paris (Volume One p 202), with an adjustable floor and ceiling, and walls that can be adjusted in their acoustic properties. The 1,200-seat hall for chamber and contemporary concerts has also acquired a degree of flexibility. The stage and lower tier of seating are on a flat floor and so can be rearranged in several ways, with the stage varying in size and position, from being at one end to being in the middle of the hall. And the volume of the hall and its acoustics can be changed by raising and lowering the segments of the adjustable ceiling, a solution very similar to that used in the concert–congress hall at Lingotto, which though originally designed with Arup Acoustics, was eventually realized with the same acousticians used here, Müller Bbm.

Design development of these auditoria was a drawn-out process involving discussion with Rome's National Academy of Santa Cecilia, composers like Luciano Berio and Pierre Boulez, conductors like Claudio Abbado and Ricardo Muti, as well as, of course, the input of the consultants with whom several different methods of simulating and testing performance were undertaken. Large-scale models were built (that for the biggest hall

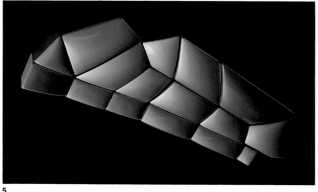

5

measuring some 6 metres by 4 metres) and their surfaces made reflective so that patterns of acoustic reflection could be charted with lasers. From these, mathematical models were created on the computer and the form of the hall further refined. After revising the models in accordance with these, actual sound tests were made, the results of which were then adjusted to predict the performance of the full-size hall.

Although the interiors of the halls now differ more than they did in the competition scheme, their roofs are more similar than they were and no longer reflect the volume inside. They do, however, allow for structural elements to be less contorted and more efficiently shaped than those of the competition scheme. They also express more clearly the notion that the auditoria are musical instruments, resonating chambers with the familial resemblances of violin, viola and cello. Instead of being angularly faceted as they were, they are smoothly formed, being made up of overlapping double-curved shells.

Once again these roofs, like those of Kansai (p 128) and the Mercedes-Benz Design Centre, exploit toroidal geometries. Each consists of a number of segments cut from toroids of differing shape and size, the double-curved segments resulting in the beetle-like carapaces. Because the curvatures of the segments differ, apart from those that are mirror images and meet along the centre line, they are overlapped where they meet. The segments have an outer lining of zinc (a material which resembles the lead on the domes of Rome), but where a segment overlaps that below, the zinc is omitted to reveal externally a broad rim of iroko hardwood edged with a delicately rounded moulding. This sensual touch reinforces the idea of the auditoria being huge musical instruments.

Behind the foyer, and similarly subterranean, are rooms for rehearsal and teaching. There are 7,000 square metres of rehearsal space, including rooms the same size as the stages of the two larger halls, so that up to 400 musicians can rehearse simultaneously down here. At the same levels and around a sunken court set between the two largest halls are the changing rooms. Forming an outer ring around all this accommodation is a three-level subterranean parking garage. In the daytime, this will be used as part of a park-and-ride system by commuters who leave their cars here and proceed into the city by tram. The stop for this new line is at the top of the sloping piazza on the road along the site's northern edge. The mechanical plant is also underground and aligned along an access trench beyond the parking garage and in the south-east corner of the site.

In the competition scheme, the administration offices and music library were also underground, to the north of the smallest auditorium. This component has grown to become a large building that fills the north-west corner of the site, stretching along the broad pavement on its northern edge as far as the sloping piazza. The landscaping between the

109

Rome Auditoria

Final scheme.

6, 7 Studying acoustic reflectors on large-scale model of large auditorium.

8 Model of large auditorium showing terraces of seating surrounding stage.

6

7

8

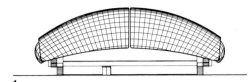

1

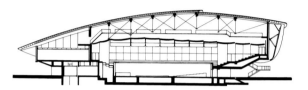

110 **Rome Auditoria**

Final scheme: elevations and sections of
auditoria

1 Flexible medium-sized auditorium.

2 Fully adjustable small auditorium.

3 Large auditorium.

4 Plan at auditoria level: **a** roof of block
containing library, administration, shops etc
b 500-seat auditorium **c** 1,200-seat
auditorium **d** 2,700-seat auditorium
e piazza/stage of outdoor auditorium
f remains of Roman villa.

5 Plan view of model.

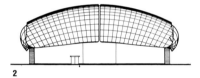
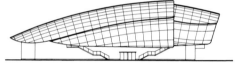

2

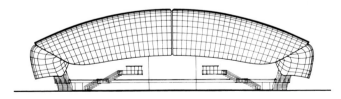
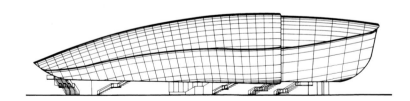

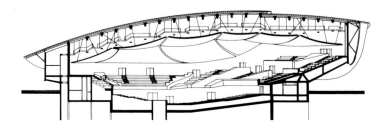

3

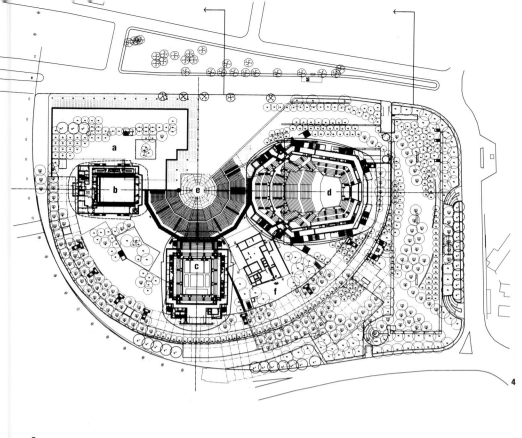

Rome Auditorium

Competition design 1994

Client City of Rome

Design team R Piano, S Ishida (associate in charge), K Fraser (architect in charge), C Hussey, J Fujita

Assisted by G Bianchi, S Canta, G Cohen, S Comer, G Langasco, L Lin, M Palmore, E Piazze, A Recagno, R Sala, C Sapper, R V Truffelli, L Viti

Model makers M Bassignani, E Doria

Team coordinator A Giordano

Acoustics Müller Bbm (H Müller, G Müller, J Reihnold)

Services engineers Ove Arup & Partners (T Barker, S Hancock, H Marsden, D Johnston)

Structural engineers Ove Arup & Partners (J Wernick, C Jackson)

Urban design and landscaping F Zagari

Quantity surveyors Davis Langdon & Everest (C Malby, T Gatehouse, R Hopper)

Landscape engineers E Trabella

Fire engineers Ing Bertolino

Rome Auditorium

Construction documents 1994

Client City of Rome (Ufficio Speciale Auditorium)

Design team R Piano, S Ishida & M Carroll (associate architects), D Hart, S Scarabicchi & M Varratta (architects in charge)

Assisted by M Alvisi, W Boley, S D'Atri, M Ottonello

Model makers D Cavagna, S Rossi

Structural engineers Studio Vitone e Associati

Services engineers Manens Intertecnica

Acoustics Müller Bbm

Quantity surveyors Austin

Landscape architects F Zagari, E Trabella

Security consultants Tecnocamere

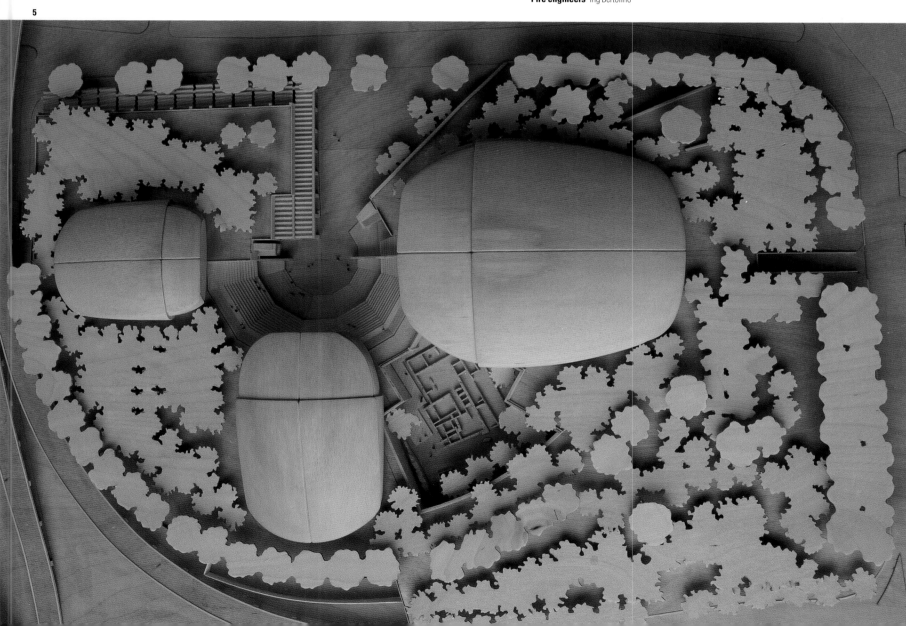

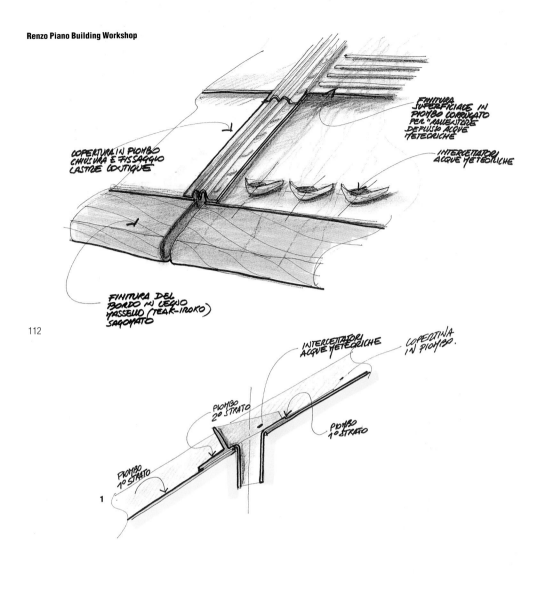

112

auditoria still extends over the roof of this building, which now accommodates no less than eleven different uses. Some of these are related to music and the auditoria, while others are orientated to the surrounding city.

Top-lit and filling much of the first floor is the library for books on music, scores and recordings. These will include tapes of all the concerts held in the complex, and of earlier concerts recorded in Rome. Also on this level and top-lit, though they have windows as well, are the administrative offices. There is also a museum of musical instruments, an educational department, an ethno-musicology centre and a laboratory for the scientific study of sound and its generation. On the ground floor, around the foyer that opens off the bottom end of the sloping piazza, are the box-office, shops for CDs and scores, bars and restaurants. In the basement, there are five cinemas seating 300 people each.

Along the northern edge of the ground floor, and spilling out onto the broad pavement, are florists and a flower market.

Across the sloping piazza from these is a glasshouse for public displays and advice on gardening and landscaping. This broad mix of uses in the northern part of the complex is intended to keep the street along this edge and the sloping piazza busy by day when the auditoria are not in use.

The project that went to tender is now being revised to preserve and display, as an integral part of the centre, the remains of a large Roman villa from the second century BC. The spacing of the radially-aligned auditoria is being adjusted, leading to a looser configuration. But any compromise to the diagrammatic clarity of the overall layout is compensated for by the clearer pattern of the circulation areas, in which some of the artefacts discovered on site will be displayed. Moreover, not only will the artefacts and views of the villa add interest to the subterranean foyer, but the introduction of an outlook and light from another direction will considerably enhance the space, while also affording vistas through it and thus some of the transparency Piano so often seeks.

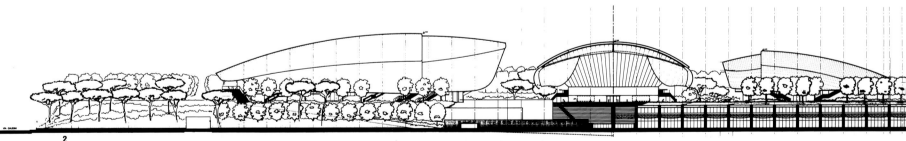

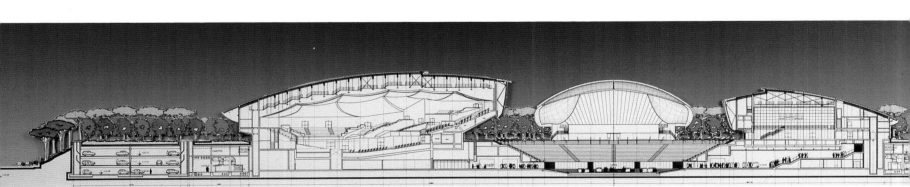

4

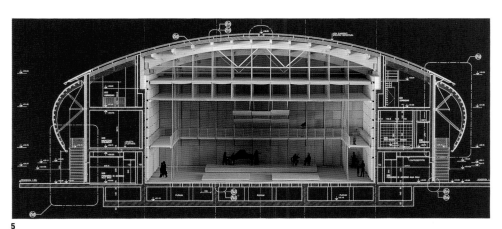

5

Rome Auditoria

Final scheme.

1 Perspective and sectional detail sketch of outer shell. Corrugations in lead finish slow flow of water that is collected in down-pipes before lead gives way to exposed hardwood lip that edges each segment of outer shell.

2 North elevation.

3 East–west section through parking garage, large auditorium, outdoor auditorium-piazza and small auditorium.

Exhibition models of auditoria interiors set into drawings of sections.

4 Large auditorium.

5 Small fully adjustable auditorium.

6 Medium-sized auditorium.

6

114   in collaboration with Jourda & Perraudin

Grand Stade Saint Denis (Paris), France **1994**

Piano's proposed design for Paris's Grand Stade could, with considerable justification, be considered a contemporary Colosseum. This unsuccessful competition entry would also have been a very urban monument, playing a pivotal role in the surrounding townscape and presenting a perimeter that is properly considered as a public face. Although it would not have hosted sea battles, nor would Christians be fed to lions there, it could have accommodated a variety of events, with its centre flooded to achieve this flexibility. It would also have sheltered the spectators on its sloping tiers with a translucent roof, a contemporary equivalent of the Colosseum's velarium.

Like the San Nicola stadium in Bari (Volume One p 178), the Grand Stade was to be built for World Cup soccer matches, yet also to accommodate athletics meetings. Although bigger than Bari (80,000 seats as compared with 65,000) and for an urban rather than rural site, there are similarities between the two designs. The lower tiers of seating were concealed in a mound-like base and ringed at the top of this by a broad ambulatory. Raised on slender columns above this was the upper tier with its translucent roof.

However, the urban location and larger size made this a much more complex design than Bari. Especially problematic was the brief's conflicting requirements that the seating encircle the soccer pitch as closely as possible, and yet that this same field should include a perimeter athletics track. For Piano a further challenge, typical of those he sets himself, was to resolve the potentially contradictory demands that the stadium be an immensely efficient machine (not only in offering this flexibility, but in terms of such things as sightlines and speed of evacuation), yet also be thoroughly embedded in its context, visually and functionally. To achieve the latter, it had to serve not only the large matches, but also more day-to-day activities.

The competition was not just to design the stadium, but also to locate it on, and master-plan the large 27-hectare site in Saint Denis in the north of Paris. This site is in a run-down industrial area and isolated from its surroundings by the elevated A1 motorway along its western edge, the A86 motorway to the south and the curving Canal de Saint Denis to the north and east. The existing master plan for the whole district proposes that from the south a boulevard,

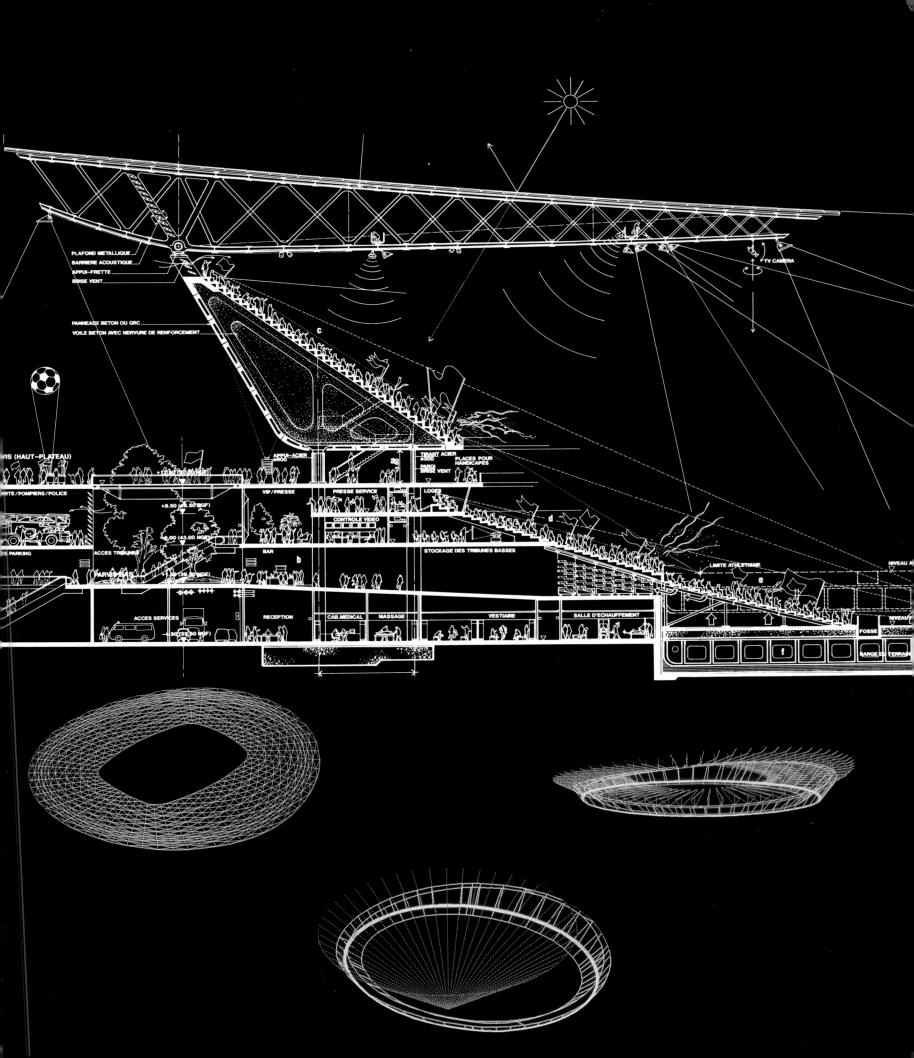

PLAFOND MÉTALLIQUE
BARRIÈRE ACOUSTIQUE
APPUI-FRETTE
BRISE VENT

PANNEAUX BÉTON OU GRC
VOILE BÉTON AVEC NERVURE DE RENFORCEMENT

TV CAMERA

c

VIS (HAUT-PLATEAU)

APPUI-ACIER

TIRANT ACIER

PLACES POUR HANDICAPÉS

d

RITE/POMPIERS/POLICE

VIP/PRESSE

PRESSE SERVICE

LOGES

+8.50 (46.50 NGF)

CONTROLE VIDEO

ES PARKING

ACCÈS TRIBUNES

6.00 (43.00 NGF)

STOCKAGE DES TRIBUNES BASSES

BAR

b

PARVIS

(39.50 NGF)

LIMITE ATHLÉTISME

e

NIVEAU

ACCÈS SERVICES

RECEPTION

CAB. MÉDICAL

MASSAGE

VESTIAIRE

SALLE D'ÉCHAUFFEMENT

NIVEAU

50 (36.50 NGF)

FOSSE

ARGE D TERRAI

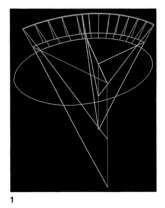

1

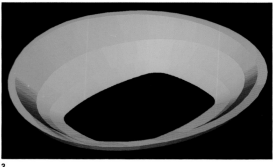

2

3

116   **Grand Stade**

Previous page Section through one side of
stadium with barge and playing field lowered
and bleacher seats extended for soccer match.
Below are computer studies of upper tier and
roof. **a** plinth-top ambulatory **b** lower
ambulatory **c** upper tier **d** intermediate tier
e bleachers **f** barge.

1 Setting out diagram for geometry of
upper tier.

2 Computer perspective of upper tier.

3 Computer perspective of all tiers.

4 South–north section.

5 Plan at same level as top of extended
bleachers with barge and playing field
lowered: **a** lower ambulatory **b** ramp up to
parvis at head of intermediate tier **c** ramp
down to seating **d** players' entrance **e** lowest
level of administration offices **f** snack bar
g emergency vehicles **h** car parking below
sloping parvis **i** storage for bleachers
j access to players' facilities

with a broad tree-planted
central island, would run due
north and under the A86 to
connect with the site. The
Building Workshop and
collaborators Jourda &
Perraudin, proposed that, once
under the A86, this boulevard
bifurcate into two avenues.

The Avenue Ouest veered
slightly west towards the front
of some existing buildings that
were to be retained along the
western edge of the site. Here
it returned to due north to then
terminate by the canal where
new footbridges crossed to
another north–south boulevard
with a broad central island.
This boulevard gives pedestrian
access to a metro station which
many spectators would use. The
Avenue Est veered east to cross
the canal and connect with yet
another tree-lined street.

Placed between these avenues,
and closer to the western one, the
stadium was placed with its long
axis oriented at 15 degrees west
of north–south. This is
considered to be the ideal align-
ment at this latitude to cope with
sun angles and wind direction,
especially if the upper tier is
raised higher on the west than
elsewhere so as to shield low
afternoon sun (as was done
here). East of the stadium an area
was allocated for a future field to
practise soccer and athletics. On
the opposite sides of both
avenues, sites were allocated for
other forms of development.
Trees along the avenues and
around these development sites
were extended and connected to
the bands of trees that lined the
roads approaching the site.
The canal banks, too, were to be
tree-planted.

The plinth, the equivalent of
Bari's mounded base, was not
piled up with earth. Instead,
what were in fact a sloping
concrete roof and more steeply
sloped walls, concealed several
levels of accommodation. As at
Bari, these included an internal
service ring road, store rooms,
lavatories for spectators,
changing rooms and other
facilities for players and
athletes. Here, though, this base
also included covered parking
for cars and emergency vehicles,
and the various access routes
to the seats in the lower tiers.

Site limitations meant that
on the east and west sides, the
plinth rose steeply from street
level, and on the north and south
slope more gently (as roofs over
car parking). Spectators would
have climbed the resulting
sloping parvises at either end
of the stadium to reach the top
of the plinth 12.5 metres above
street level. From here they
would have proceeded, via
bridges across an encircling
sunken court, to the ambulatory
in the open horizontal slot
between lower and upper tiers.
This would have commanded
an immediate view down on to
the playing field, and a counter-
balancing view outwards, not
of Apulia's Arcadian plain as at
Bari, but of the Parisian skyline.
The big bold forms and the views
would tend to give the stadium
a metropolitan scale and
connection, but Piano hoped
that when the stadium was not
being used for matches, the
parvises might be open to, and
used by, the local community.
He foresaw some of the activities

found in the Place Beaubourg in
front of the Pompidou Centre
taking place here, though it is
probably easier to envisage
skateboarders and roller-bladers
whizzing around the space.

Although, as at Bari, the
ambulatory rings the stadium
at this level, it would not have
been possible to walk around
it. This was because the
ambulatory and the seating
below and above were to be
divided into four sectors. Low
walls in the north and south
parvises would have guided
spectators from the point at
which they first presented their
tickets to their correct sector.
And although stairs would rise
from the promenade to the
upper tier, it would not have
been possible to descend directly
from here to the intermediate
and bottom tiers below.

Instead, the spectators in
the bottom tier would have
descended ramps set into the
parvises to reach the bottom
of the sunken encircling court
which served as a second
ambulatory, from where more
ramps led down to the seats.
Spectators in the intermediate
tier would use steps that
descended along the sides of this
encircling court from the
bridges across its top. Only the
ring of private boxes
immediately below the
ambulatory would be reached
directly from it, via stairs
placed against the glass
screens that subdivided the
ambulatory into sectors.

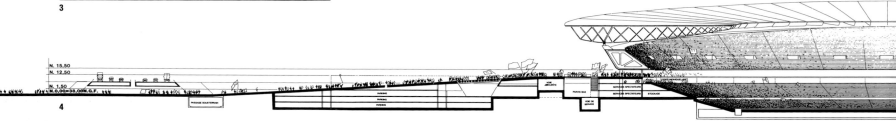

4

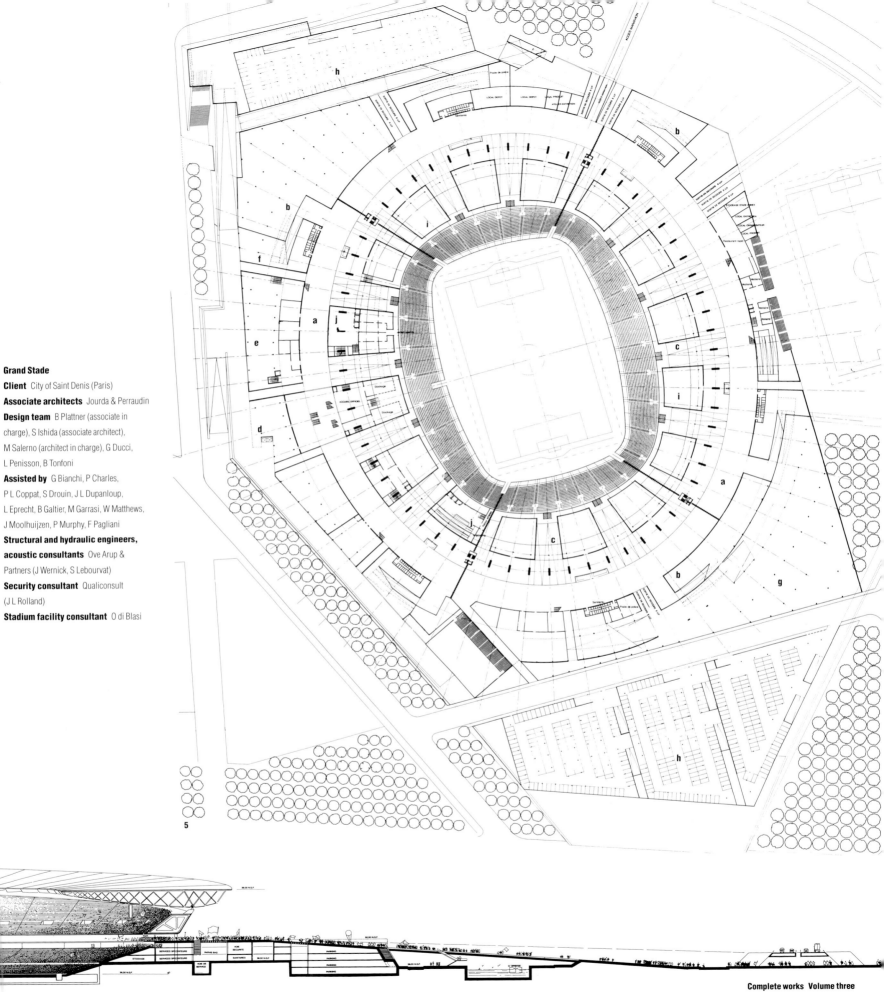

Grand Stade

Client City of Saint Denis (Paris)

Associate architects Jourda & Perraudin

Design team B Plattner (associate in
charge), S Ishida (associate architect),
M Salerno (architect in charge), G Ducci,
L Penisson, B Tonfoni

Assisted by G Bianchi, P Charles,
P L Coppat, S Drouin, J L Dupanloup,
L Eprecht, B Galtier, M Garrasi, W Matthews,
J Moolhuijzen, P Murphy, F Pagliani

**Structural and hydraulic engineers,
acoustic consultants** Ove Arup &
Partners (J Wernick, S Lebourvat)

Security consultant Qualiconsult
(J L Rolland)

Stadium facility consultant O di Blasi

5

118 **Grand Stade**

1 Location indicated by block model
superimposed on aerial photograph.
2 South elevation.
3 West elevation.
4 Plan at top of plinth **a** south parvis
b north parvis **c** north ticket zone
d west zone **e** south zone **f** east zone
g ambulatory **h** stairs to upper tier
i sunken courts **j** ramps to lower ambulatory
k stairs to intermediate tier **l** corporate and VIP
entertainment pavilion above.

The bottom tier of seats was on movable bleachers. These would be used only for soccer matches when they would extend out over the athletics track to the edge of the protective ditch that surrounded the pitch. The track and the playing field would be on an enormous barge, the top of which would be some 30,000 square metres in area. When used for soccer this would be 4.5 metres below street level. When the stadium was to be used for athletics, the bleacher seats would have been moved into storage under the intermediate tier, and the tank would have been flooded so that the 3-metre-deep barge would have risen until the playing field was level with the foot of this tier at a metre above street level.

Seats for press and television, officials and VIPs filled the western sector of the intermediate tier and were reached by a special entrance in the bottom of the plinth, off the Avenue Ouest and adjacent to the administrative offices. Boxes in this sector were to be reserved for sponsors who would enter in the same way, and could also use the bottom part of the western sector of the upper tier. The sponsors would also have had the use of the bar, dining facilities and roof terrace of a wing raised on pilotis above the western parvis. Access to this was up from the lower entrance, or by bridges across from a ring of bars and lavatories inside the structural bowl of the upper tier. Parking reserved for all these groups would be under the western part of the plinth.

Stairs to the raised upper tier ascended through its structural bowl between the trusses that supported the seats, through the soffit over the ambulatory and the forward-leaning outer wall, all of which were to be of precast concrete units. At their highest points, the trusses supported the pin-joints that are the sole support of each of the steel roof trusses. These trusses were stabilized only by secondary members that formed a series of concentric rings which linked all the top and bottom chords (the upper rings taking compression stresses and the lower ones tension), and by the cross-bracings that together made a beautifully organic pattern. This extremely elegant structure was designed with Jane Wernick of Ove Arup & Partners. The roof cladding was to be of translucent panels.

The top of the roof was not flat but curved, like the bottom of a cylinder with a radius of 1,300 metres. Nor was the roof level: like the top of the upper tier, it sloped down to the east. Apart from the fabulous formal finesse of this jauntily sloping, curving translucent roof capping the delicate steel trusses that reach out from the hovering bowl of the upper tier, this asymmetry would have brought functional advantages. It would have helped exclude blustery west winds, and both shade low afternoon sun and eliminate high-level westward facing seats. It would also have given the very topmost seats a view, through the trusses on the opposite side of the stadium to the trees across the canal to the east, making at least some connection with nature that is always so important for Piano.

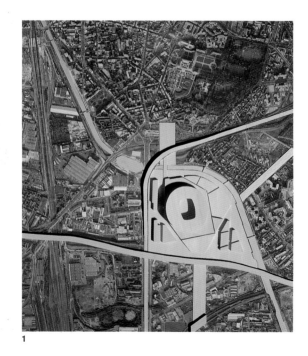

1

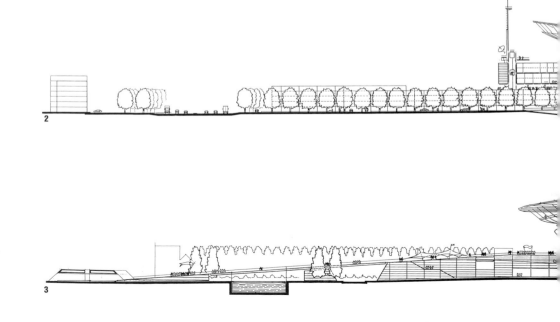

2

3

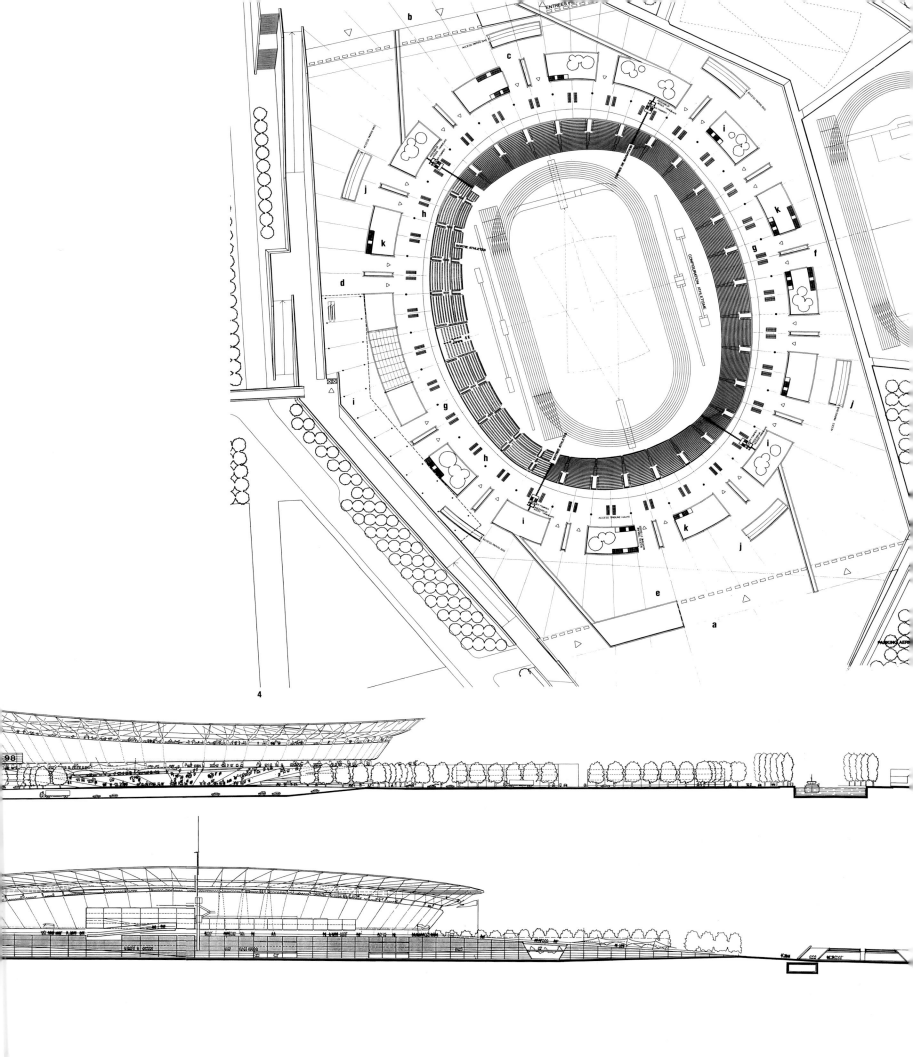

120

Saitama Arena Saitama, Japan 1994

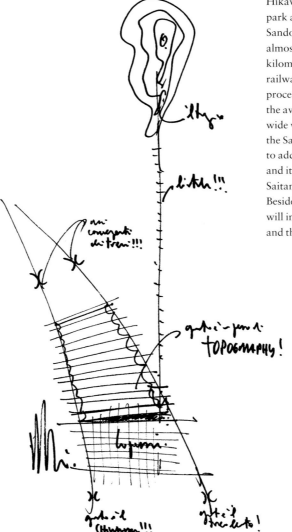

The unsuccessful competition entry for the Saitama Arena proposed a building that would have played a number of seemingly contradictory roles equally well. It would have been an extraordinarily flexible machine that could be adapted to any form of large-scale spectacle. Yet it would also have appeared to be semi-natural, a topographic feature that would play a key contextual role as counterpoint to a wooded park. Moreover, the building would be a civic monument, fronting and bringing intense around-the-clock life to a new piazza, the design of which had been decided in a slightly earlier competition.

Saitama is a dense urban sprawl of mostly small buildings. About its only distinguishing features are the Hikawa Shrine and the wooded park around it, and the Hikawa Sando Avenue that extends almost due south for nearly 2 kilometres, terminating near a railway line. (Once a processional route to the shrine, the avenue is now lined by a wide variety of activities.) So the Saitama Prefecture decided to add to both the city's amenity and its identity by building the Saitama New Urban Area. Besides government offices, it will include a new civic square and the multi-purpose arena.

The adjacent sites for the proposed square and arena are in a wedge of open land between two sets of railway lines, just south of where the Hikawa Sando Avenue terminates and above the tunnel of an expressway. To try and ensure imaginative design, both commissions were made subject to international competition. The design for the square was won by the American landscape-architect Peter Walker, with what he called the 'Sky Forest Plaza'. Both the name, with its mystic overtones, and the trees shading the square, evoke links with the park to the north and its religious purposes.

The competition brief for the Saitama Arena asked for a building that would be a symbol for the prefecture, where people of all ages from Saitama and the regions around would gather and interact. It was to host large-scale sport and music events. It should achieve additional flexibility with moving walls and ceiling, as well as by accommodating elsewhere other cultural and amusement activities, including a multi-media information exchange. The brief also drew attention to the fact that the new plaza was to be elevated so that there would be a raised as well as a real ground level.

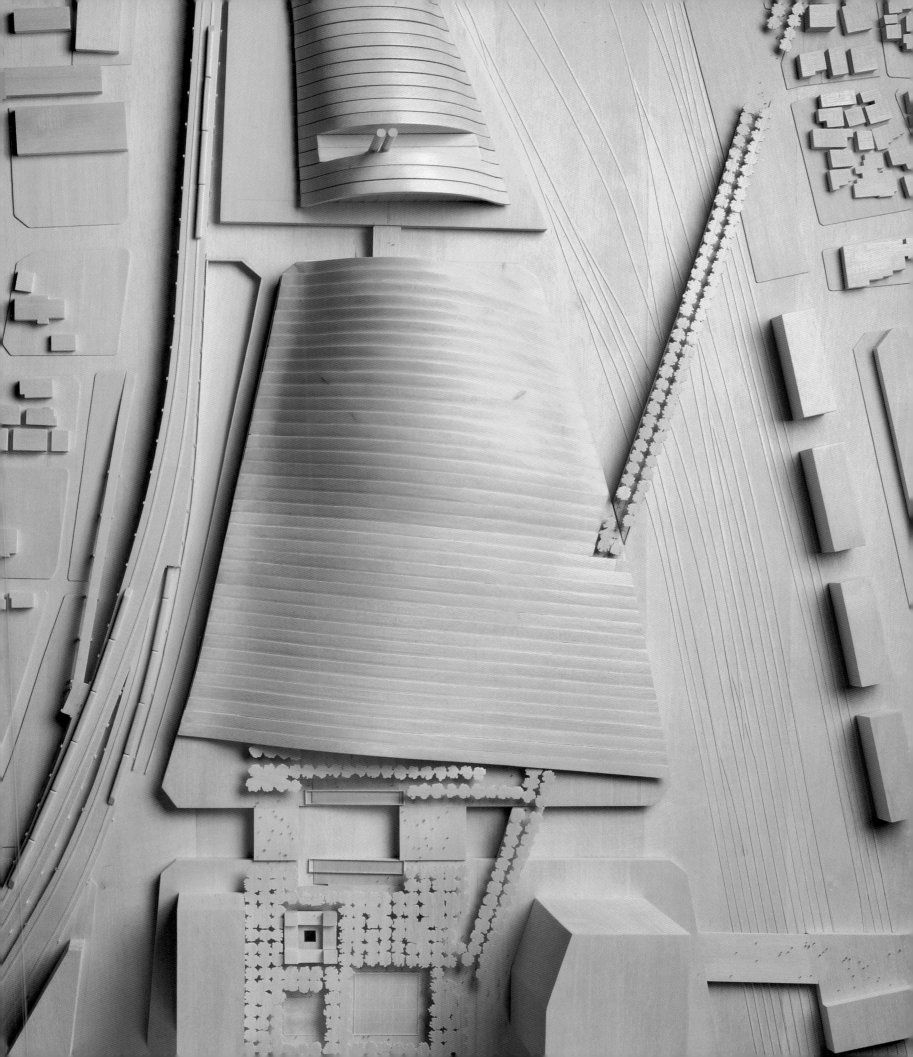

Saitama Arena

Previous page Plan view of model.

1 Site and roof plan: **a** Sky Forest Plaza
b Saitama Arena **c** district heating plant
d proposed bridge across railway lines to
Hikawa Sando Avenue.

2 Location plan: the arena was to form a hill-
like southern termination of Hikawa Sando
Avenue to counterbalance the park of the
Hikawa Shrine that terminates the avenue's
northern end.

3 Perspective showing erection and
cladding of roof trusses.

122

2

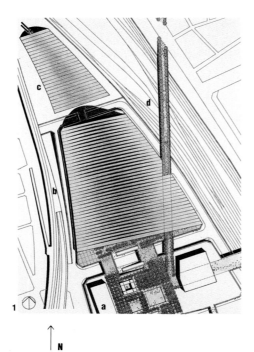

1

N

The Building Workshop's entry took some cues for its design from that of the plaza. It not only related to the plaza, but strengthened and clarified immensely the plaza's relationship to the park, while establishing its own relationship with the plaza. This strategy now seems such an obvious thing to do that it is unthinkable that Piano would not have echoed the park in some way, even without the plaza as precedent. Yet none of the other competition entrants picked up on any such possibility. Indeed, all the others except for one paid no attention whatsoever to context, merely designing self-contained structures that could have been plonked down anywhere.

Three basic contextual moves were elaborated on by the Building Workshop's design. Firstly, the building's roof was treated as a green hill-like mound, dubbed by Piano the 'Collina Verde'. This would set up a tension and enter into dialogue with the wooded park, with which it is almost equidistant from Saitama station and in the opposite direction. (Piano also proposed that the district heating plant, to be built immediately north of the site in the tip of the wedge between the railway lines, be roofed in similar fashion to complete the form of the mound.) Secondly, the avenue was extended across the railway lines by a bridge edged with trees, to then pass under the roof of the arena and terminate against the plaza. This linked both of them with the park and gave yet greater emphasis to the avenue. Thirdly, between the plaza and the multi-purpose arena, which Piano called the 'Colosseum', was a multi-level shopping, entertainment and information facility, which he called the 'Citadel'. It is this that would have related directly to the plaza, and brought constant crowds and life, to it.

The Collina Verde and the Citadel, together with the Colosseum, were the major elements of the building. The first of these, the roof (designed in collaboration with structural engineer Toshihiko Kimura), would have got its green colour from the patination of its copper cladding, and its shape from being supported by a series of independent parabolic truss arches that would span the Colosseum. (Where the roof extended to the sides of this, it was supported by lattice beams on slender columns.) The top and bottom chord of these truss arches were to be in the same vertical plane and, spreading from the pin-joint from which they both sprang, would diverge to a maximum of 6 metres. The middle chord was mid-way in height and a constant 4 metres to one side of the top and bottom chords; the arch trusses themselves were spaced at 6-metre centres.

The trusses were asymmetric in section because the upper part of the roof was a series of north-light monitors. Each sloping rooflet extended beyond the trusses in both directions: down from the middle chord to form a gutter between it and the next truss; up from the top chord to shade the windows just outside of the top and bottom chords. These windows opened outwards to allow natural

3

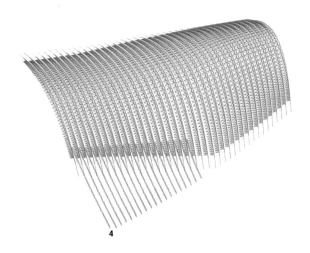

4

Saitama Arena

4 Roof structure of parabolic arched trusses with lattice beams extending to one side of these.

5–7 Computer studies of the shape of the roof defined by the arched trusses.

8 West–east section through 'Citadel'.

9 South elevation and section through bridges spanning to plaza.

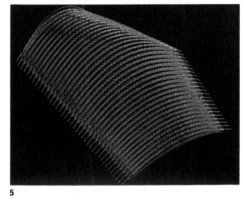

5

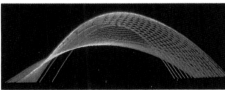

6

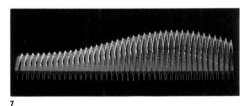

7

ventilation (the Collina Verde was to be less solidly enclosed than it appeared to be in some external views, exhaling stale air as well as admitting abundant natural light), while inward-opening panels inside of the windows could be closed to black out the volume below. The trusses also supported all sorts of equipment crucial to the flexible use of the arena.

Designed to be as big as it could be when squeezed between the confines of the Collina Verde's ceiling and the Citadel's edge, the Colosseum was asymmetric about both axes, with upper tiers only on the north and the south rather than ringing the arena. As with the Grand Stade, access to the seats was from ambulatories around the lower tiers, the lowest of which was again removable bleacher seating extending out across a floor that could be raised and lowered.

The upper ambulatory was at the top of the middle tier, the same level as the raised plaza outside. But lack of space meant that this ambulatory could not be a single continuous space. It flanked and was open to the arena only to the north and south, while on the other sides the foyers were screened by glass. But it would still have given those arriving from the plaza to the south, and also those in the foyers to east and west, an immediate view of the action of the sports floor below.

The second ambulatory was at ground level, on a level with the streets outside and the top of the lowest tier. Although it did ring the whole arena, it was not of constant width and overlooked the sports floor only at the corners, where it gave direct access to the floor when this was raised to the highest of its three possible levels. The arena floor could be adjusted in independent sections, so giving much greater flexibility than at Grand Stade. This was achieved by using twenty-seven jacks, a solution considered for the Paris scheme, and rejected as too complex and costly. The system proposed for Saitama, though, would have used the same jacks developed for and proven successful in Japanese shipyards.

Further devices used in conjunction with the adjustable floor promised immense flexibility. Movable partitions were to rise from the floor, which could then be used for up to four different events simultaneously. Several kinds of sports and other floorings (including grass) could have been quickly laid and removed. Also, hanging from the roof trusses were to be 102 multi-purpose grids from which would be suspended lights, speakers and roll curtains that could form a draped fabric ceiling. All of these, including the grids, were to be adjustable in position and height.

Sports events such as soccer and American football, or motor-cross races, could have used the floor raised to its maximum height and area, with up to 30,000 spectators in the middle and upper tiers. For other sports, the floor could be progressively lowered and increasing amounts of bleacher seating used; so athletics could command an audience of 33,000, while for basketball and boxing the distant upper tiers

123

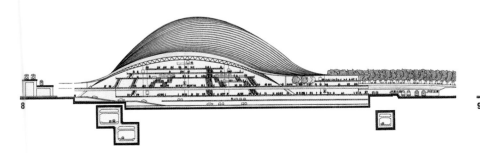

8

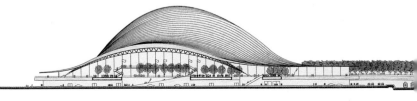

9

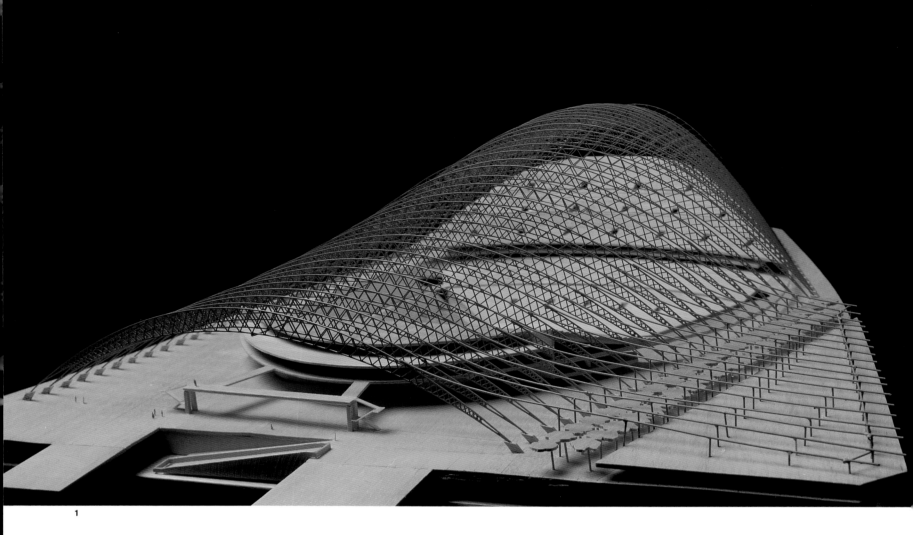

1

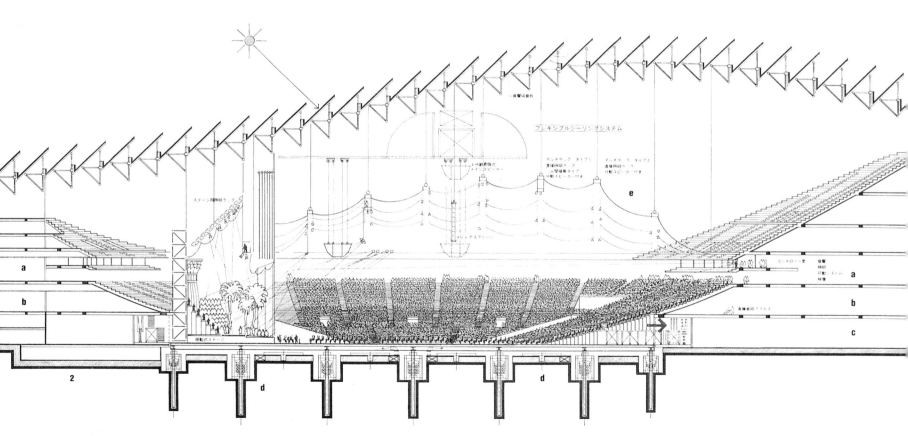

フレキシブルシーリングシステム

マルチラップ タイプ1
直接回顧タイプ
大型增幅タイプ
分散スピーカー付き

マルチラップ タイプ2
直接回顧タイプ
分散スピーカー付き

e

一音響可動板

ステージ照明用ラック

4分割昇降式
メインスピーカー

メインスクリーン

a
b

a

コントロール室

移動式ステージ

音響
照明
可動システム
音響

舞台衆用アラセス

b

c

2

d   d

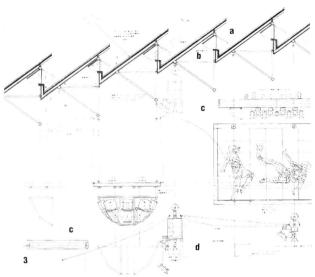

Saitama Arena

1 Model of arena and roof structure.

2 Section of 'Colosseum' showing devices that give flexibility of use: **a** plaza level **b** ground level **c** storage for retractable bleacher seating **d** jacks to raise and lower floor **e** adjustable fabric ceiling.

3 Detail section of arena roof with adjustable devices that give flexibility of use: **a** windows open for ventilation **b** panels close to shut out light **c** lighting gantries **d** fabric ceiling.

4 Model of four parabolic arched trusses with roof cladding.

5 Model of truss in more evolved form that tapers to and springs from a single footing.

could be closed and the audiences would be 27,000 and 30,000 respectively. For political conventions and rock concerts, a stage could be placed backed against the Citadel with up to 40,000 people seated in the other three sectors of the hall. By draping the fabric ceiling, the volume could have been reduced by differing amounts, and concerts and various forms of spectacle staged for audiences of 5,000 to 30,000.

This fabric ceiling would also have helped to reduce reverberation times, though the acoustics would be primarily controlled by sophisticated electronic means. Environmental comfort conditions were to be achieved by a combination of natural ventilation and air-conditioning, their mix depend-

ing on how much of the arena was in use, the heat loads from lighting and so on, and the external conditions.

The Citadel was not to be, as the name suggests, an isolated fortress. It was to be the opposite, a bustling multi-functional facility that was a filter between the plaza and the arena. Looking out on both of these for the excitement they offered, the Citadel's facilities also added another dimension to their events. Many of its activities and merchandise would have been tied in to events in the arena. Cafés and restaurants provided venues to meet before and after events, to which they might be themed, and the music and other shops would have sold CDs and goods related to concerts and other events.

Yet the Citadel, and especially that part known as the 'Antenna' Citadel, was also to have been tied in to the wider world, with Internet terminals and a gigantic Event Echo Screen hanging in the arena when not in use and reflecting world events, moment by moment. There also were to

have been a children's museum with interactive displays, a virtual-reality theme park, galleries for exhibitions and performances, a fitness club and sports bar (with non-stop sports coverage to enhance the image of the arena as a sports mecca), karaoke bars and a multi-screen cinema in the basement.

Ultimately, this was a scheme which combined ideals that were current at the beginning of Piano's career with others that are very contemporary. Here was promised a highly flexible, multi-functional entertainment and cultural machine, of the sort proposed by Cedric Price with his Fun Palace project and realized by Piano & Rogers' Pompidou Centre. Yet it also celebrates contemporary possibilities of instantaneous global linkages, as well as current concerns with appropriate contextual response and reciprocity with nature.

125

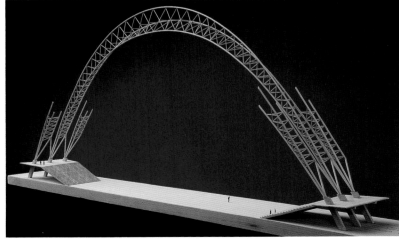

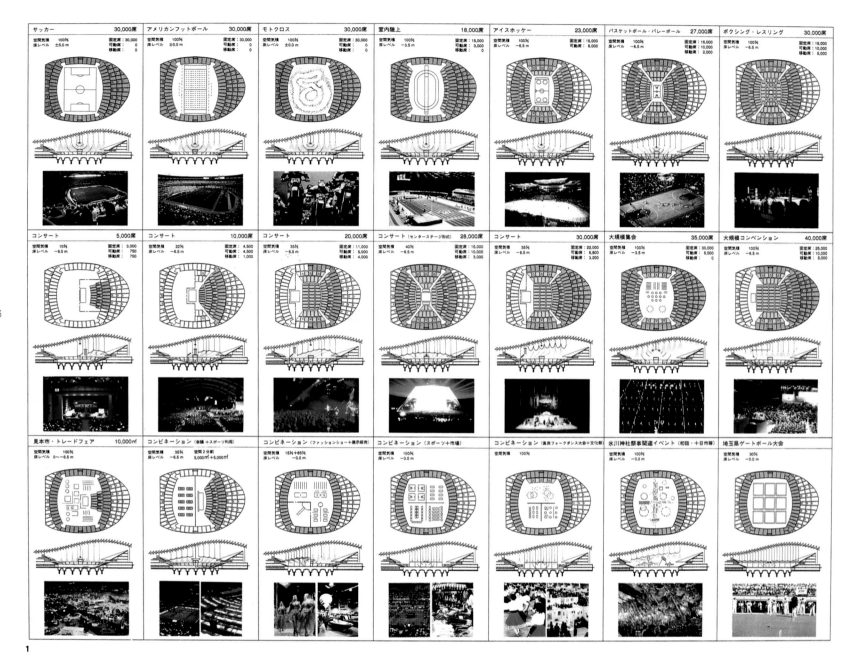

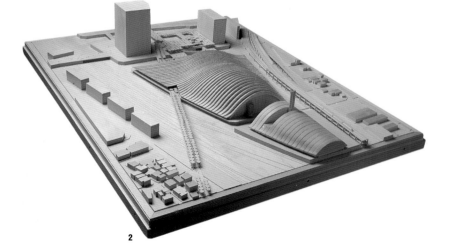

1

Saitama Arena

Design team R Piano, S Ishida (associate in charge), C Sapper, L Viti, A Zoppini

Assisted by M Carroll, M Palmore, V Truffelli, M Carletti, L Imberti

Modelmaker S Rossi

Structural engineers T Kimura with M Sasaki

Services engineers Manens Intertecnica

Acoustic consultant Müller Bbm Gmbh

Lighting consultant P Castiglioni

Consultants for movable elements in event space Hitachi Zosen Ltd

Consultant on amusement facilities Dentsu Ltd & Isaia Communications

Collaborating contractors K Gumi, S Kogyo, Turner Construction

2

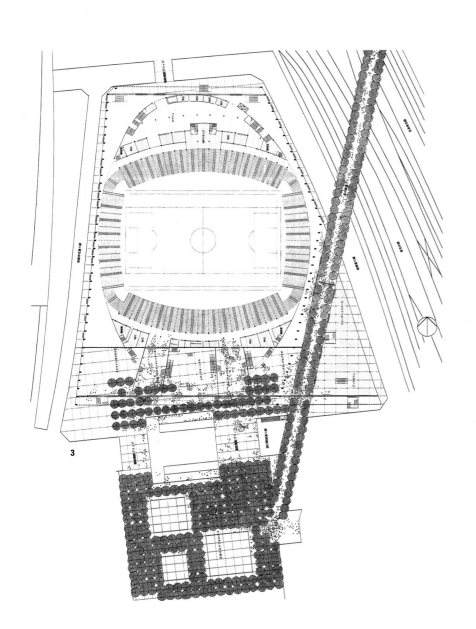

3

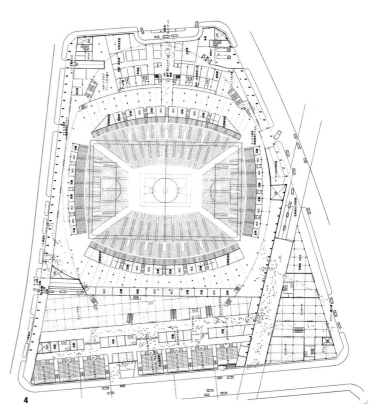

4

Saitama Arena

1 Table showing some of the different configurations of plan and section and their respective uses that the 'Colosseum' can adapt to.

2 Model of hill-like arena seen from north.

3 Plan at plaza level with floor raised.

4 Plan at ground level with floor lowered.

5 South–north section through 'Citadel' that overlooks plaza and 'Colosseum'.

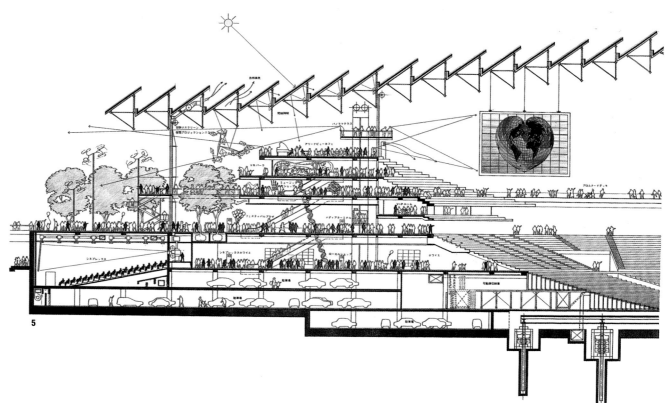

5

in collaboration with Nikken Sekkei and others

Kansai International Airport Terminal Bay of Osaka, Japan, **1988–94**

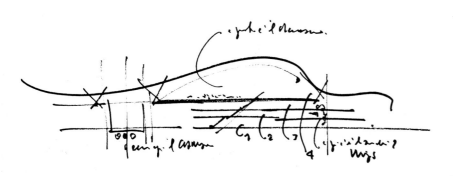

Kansai International Airport is on a specially built island in the Bay of Osaka. Because the flight paths of incoming and departing planes are entirely over the sea, the airport can operate twenty-four hours a day and so be a major new gateway into Japan and a hub for Southeast Asia and Australasia. The passenger terminal, a commission won in an international competition, stretches along one edge of the island. It is a novel type of terminal, with the international and domestic facilities sandwiched on different levels of the same central core, and all the planes docked along a single boarding wing that stretches out to either side. The immense length of the boarding wing makes this probably the longest building ever constructed, and the single interior space, which is 1.7 kilometres in length, is certainly much the longest 'room'. Yet this magnificent space, with its subtly tapering vistas, is only one in a breathtaking sequence of spaces that flow, one into the other, below a ceiling that billows like a forward-moving wave. These spaces include a multi-level hall called the canyon, encountered immediately on entry from the landside, and the international departures hall, between the canyon and the boarding wing.

However, the immense architectural significance of the terminal rests on far more than its innovative planning, vast size and extraordinary spatial sequence; or even the technical achievement of having built it very quickly and relatively cheaply on a typhoon-tossed and unstable island. In the history and evolution of the Building Workshop, this building is important for being the last collaborative effort of a group of team leaders who had worked together on many projects since first coming together as part of the team that undertook the design development of the Pompidou Centre. Alongside Renzo Piano, this core group of design leaders responsible for Kansai consisted of Peter Rice and Tom Barker, the structural and services engineers, respectively, of Ove Arup & Partners, and Noriaki Okabe, who was co-leader of the architectural team. (These were, of course, backed by talented and dedicated teams, each member of which made a contribution to the collaborative process that is Piano's ideal.) Sadly, Rice, whose collaboration with Piano is now the stuff of legend, died during the construction of Kansai; it was the last building he oversaw more or less the whole way through design and development. Barker, as one of Arup's directors, still supervises collaborations with the Building Workshop, but is no longer actively involved in design. Okabe left the Building Workshop to set up on his own following the completion of Kansai. So if Kansai opens a new era for architecture, it also closes a chapter for the Building Workshop.

Kansai is a fitting climax to this team's collaboration. The vast size of the terminal, and the great speed at which its design had to be developed, led the team to adopt the dictates of a stringent (if also tolerant) design discipline: the geometric solution that shapes the building's curves, to which all aspects of the design are subordinate. This innovative discipline and the formidable problems and pressures faced by the design team pushed the design into novel territory. The result is topical in terms of current debates about such things as 'bigness' as a contemporary condition, and the computer's contribution to architecture; but its significance goes much further. The building also finally realizes and fuses those, now, old ideals of an architecture that approximates the organic or the mechanical, though paradoxically this does not marginalize Man, but centres on him. Moreover, the design process developed here is remarkably analogous to developments in the new sciences, so that the building is almost certainly a herald for the architecture of the next millennium.

The terminal's exterior is as breathtaking as the internal spaces. Clad in a curving carapace of stainless-steel panels and dark glass, it seems to both embrace and almost lift off from the island, and is remarkable for how closely it follows the shapes of the spaces inside. When seen from the air in particular, the affinities between the building and the planes around it are striking, in that the latter almost seem like progeny against a vast mother ship. Like a plane, the terminal's shiny, symmetrical

form is strongly directional. This is not because the building will change location (though it will absorb considerable seismic and settlement movement), but because it is moulded closely around internal movement patterns, guiding the flow of passengers within it with the same unambiguous clarity that makes it obvious in which direction a stationary plane will fly. Some of these curves also guide the flow of air, although here it is not the flow of air over the outside that is crucial. Instead the flow of air inside, guided without closed ducts along the ceiling, determines the shape of the building's lightweight skin and structure.

These subtle and sensual curves, which are given definition and delicacy of scale by the repetitive rectangular stainless-steel tiles that clad the exterior, also steer the internal flows of space and structure. Passengers are urged forward by the asymmetric billowings of the ceiling in the international departures hall, which follows the tightening curve of the decelerating jets of air that ventilate this space, and by the continuous whiplash lines of the main trusses' lower chords that flow into the ribs of the boarding wing. Also encouraging passengers onwards are the vistas opening out before them to show clearly the building's organization and their destinations. The multi-level nature of the terminal, for example, is revealed immediately on entering the canyon, the planes come into view shortly

after, and then the boarding wing's tapering height makes clear the directions to and from the central core of the terminal.

As a consequence of the above, the terminal differs from the current norm for large buildings in several ways. The curves, especially the two-directional curves of the boarding wing, give the building an organic finiteness of form; it is no mere extrusion of a constant cross section of seemingly arbitrary length. Enhancing this very organic quality is the extraordinary degree of synthesis and integration achieved between the building's elements. Ceiling and roof, where not one and the same, closely parallel each other so that the outer skin is like a bubble blown out by the internal space, buoyed up by the flow of air it guides and the artificial light it reflects. The structure not only flexes with the line of the ceiling, but is shaped to emphasize this flow. So skin, space, services (air-conditioning and artificial light) and structure are all identically delineated and very intimately integrated.

This is the antithesis of most large buildings today, where structure, services and skin each follow their own disciplines and are only very loosely coordinated. In such buildings, you see flimsy finishes but not what supports them, and so cannot relate to the architecture with any depth: the architecture is literally only skin deep, restricted to a decorative external cladding and a slickly surfaced lobby. At Kansai, you can see and understand

everything, giving the building a compelling presence, and encouraging a special relationship between the user and the building.

A correlate of this integration of systems is the expanded role structure plays at Kansai, even in comparison with other Building Workshop designs. Structural components nearly always constitute the major characteristic 'pieces' that are intrinsic to the very identity of Piano's buildings; and as in this instance, they usually help people to relate to the buildings. Exposed structural elements furnish a comprehensible intermediary scale between the user and the vast spaces. These elements also tend to be shaped to elicit empathetic responses: their forms express visually the forces they carry and have a sculpted tactility that invites the eye, if not the hand, to linger.

What is unprecedented, though, is how Kansai's structure is a key element leading you forward through each space and on to the next. Some of the 'pieces' have even been designed so as not to emphasize their independence, but to stress their continuities. This can be seen in the way the main trusses elide into the ribs of the boarding wing. Also remarkable is how passengers seem almost complicit in the creation of the building as it unfolds before them, guiding their movement forward and the searching scan of their eyes, which, like the air-jets, seems almost to push out and upwards the billowing curves of

the ceiling. These roles played by the structure and the user make the terminal (despite its vast size and machine-like clarity and efficiency) a very humanistic building, in the Renaissance sense, having been conceived with Man at its centre.

All of these achievements are made possible, and are in large part the products of the innovative geometric solution devised to discipline the design's overall shape and various internal systems. Few architects today dare to make a big building as a simple unified statement, let alone can. Rather than risk being overwhelming or boring, they tend to fragment large buildings into contrasting elements, separate blocks or repetitive structural and spatial modules. (The last of these strategies was used by Sir Norman Foster and Partners at London's Stansted Airport, and now at Hong Kong's Chep Lak Kok Airport.) Kansai, though vast, is amazingly unified and understated in its external form. The whole is contained in a single shell which fuses the curves of a toroidal ring of immense radius, enclosing the boarding wing, with arcs of cylinders of differing radius that roof the central terminal. The curves all flow seamlessly into each other and are clad only in rectangular, flat stainless-steel tiles and frameless dark glass panes.

The result is far from boring. Seen from the airside (it is impossible to see the whole of the terminal from the landside), it combines a thrilling boldness with a subtle grace and

poise, and even mystery. A supreme statement of technological control, the terminal also calls up such naturalistic associations as a cloud bank or glistening wave, and is teasingly ambiguous in both its scale (it is difficult to judge how many floors it contains) and, because of the curves, in its perspective views. Photographs cannot capture the constant changes with the light, weather and position of the viewer, nor the sense of the building's awesome size.

Like the overall form, the detailing is remarkably restrained; even tiny touches are telling, such as the way the ends of the curving rafters which support the lowest roof tiles form highlights against the dark shadow below. Yet within and exactly conforming to this simple envelope is a richly modulated interior, where the grandeur of the whole can be appreciated because, at the small scale, undue cluttering distractions, with the exception of some occasional lapses, are kept few and low in height.

There were more reasons for adopting the overriding geometry than the extraordinary integration and aesthetic grace it achieves. Although the shell and structure are subordinate to the dictates of geometry, nothing has been compromised. The shell fits the spaces below it as tautly as a surgical glove, and both the repetition of components and the efficiency of the structure have been maximized. This, together with the sense of

inevitability that the design projects, are arguably the greatest triumphs of the geometry. But its significance extends further.

Most of the really crucial aspects of this design could only have been devised with the aid of the computer: the geometry of a shell clad entirely in identical panels, and yet tightly tailored to the spaces below; the efficiencies of the boarding-wing structure whose ribs curve to minimize bending moments and act synergistically as a shell structure with the other components; and the extraordinary synthesis whereby all the building's systems accommodate each other without compromise, as if they were the product of the long and interactive refinements of evolution.

At Kansai, the Building Workshop has revealed much of the real promise of the computer in generating architectural form. This is not to facilitate whimsy, but to let designers devise and adopt more stringent disciplines, such as new conceptual topologies, that bring new levels of efficiency and economy. Perhaps inevitably, these new worlds of form are the same ones that the computer is revealing as underlying much of nature, such as the toroid, to which the geometry of the boarding wing conforms and which pervades nature, shaping the earth's magnetic fields, convection and ocean currents, and many fruits. Though the toroid was not chosen for this reason, this happy coincidence fits well with Piano's quest for a natural architecture:

for construction which is seemingly uncontrived in form and that coexists harmoniously with and even emulates nature. With a large building like this, he seeks an industrial equivalent of organic order, one compatible with machine manufacture. Here the maximum repetition of identical components is the equivalent of nature's differing-sized elements (such as scales or leaves) all grown from the same genetic template.

As already noted in the introductory essay to this volume, there are strong and significant parallels between what has been achieved at Kansai and the revolution the computer has brought to the sciences. Until recently a science like biology was concerned largely with the classification of species and their parts. But the computer has changed all this, and has made possible the study of dynamic processes and not just static products. It can make visible what was previously invisible, by charting and slowing down processes and also by creating conceptual models as exploratory and often very revealing analogues of natural processes. Thus these sciences are changing from a concern with taxonomy to the study of emergence, with how forms arise and how they transmute into others. The Kansai terminal is the first building to be created by what might be thought of as an inversion of that process, as if it had been generated by its own internal laws and disciplines, and by the multiple mutual

accommodations of its various systems in settling on a form that best suits them all.

Such a notion encapsulates Piano's essential design ideals. For him, design is a collaborative process bringing together the input of various disciplines in a way so thoroughly synthesized that it should be impossible to say afterwards who contributed what to the design. Design is not a product of wilful imposition of form, but a process of slow sedimentation as it is explored from several directions simultaneously starting from both the general and the particular, and from both abstract speculation and the very physical manual manipulation of materials.

Not only are Kansai's forms subject to the overall geometric discipline, but the design has a very clear internal logic of its own which helped fuse into an organic whole the contributions of consultants and collaborators. Where these internal rules have been followed, the result is a triumph. Such rules, however, are not forgiving. Where cost cutting has forced compromises, or worse, where nervousness about the scale and restraint of the building has led to resurrecting details from earlier buildings by Piano, the results seem out of place. Even these lapses, though, might have a virtue. Like the deliberate mistakes in a Persian carpet, included because only Allah can create perfection, they highlight just what has been achieved in a design that otherwise seems so

extraordinarily uncontrived, even inevitable.

Kansai at last achieves and marries a pair of ideals that has persisted since the nineteenth century: to create a building that approximates the perfect match between form and function found in a machine or organism. Some have argued that these ideals are unachievable and inappropriate because architecture, unlike a machine or organism, does not move. So it is most fitting that this ideal has been achieved in a building shaped by flows of people (on foot or shuttle), baggage and air inside and by the planes, trains and motor vehicles that circulate around and stop against its exterior – and also accommodate very considerable movement caused by seismic action and settlement.

This vast machine-organism heralds the next century in its pioneering use of the computer and it reflects an age in which technology approximates the natural (in performance if not in form) and, conversely, nature is increasingly engineered (from agri-business farming to genetic engineering). Yet if this consummation of the bio-mechanical tradition, which first found expression in the Neo-Gothic and then Art Nouveau, appears in its forms and synthesis to approximate a Gothic for the space age, the spirit of the building recalls that of the Renaissance, whose artists' and architects' studio-workshops were a major inspiration for Piano's notion of the Building Workshop.

Background and design development

The island

Kansai, with its 20 million inhabitants, is Japan's second most populous region. Important both commercially and culturally, it includes the two big commercial ports of Osaka and Kobe, and the two historic cities, Kyoto and Nara, which are custodians of different aspects of the country's traditional culture and religions. The region attracts millions of business travellers and tourists each year, mainly from Japan, but also from abroad.

Despite its importance, Kansai has in recent decades fallen steadily behind the Tokyo region. This is largely because so many enterprises want to be near the seat of government. Tokyo's port, Yokohama, has for instance overtaken Osaka as Japan's second city. The need to correct this imbalance has now been recognized, and the Kansai International Airport is the first in a series of planned major investments in the region, which will in turn attract further investment. Besides new transport connections (these are not just to and from the airport, but include such things as a major bridge over the Akashi Channel), these will include the new Kansai Academic City dedicated to scientific research, a synchrotron and teleport.

Osaka's Itami was the only airport in the region. Last upgraded for Osaka's 1970 World Expo, its runways and terminals had become severely overstretched. Already dangerously hemmed in by the surrounding city, Itami could neither expand nor extend its restricted hours of operation. Yet there was nowhere else to build the new airport: though there are still pockets of intense agriculture, most of the flatter land between the forested mountains (which, as elsewhere in Japan, make up most of the natural landscape) is now heavily built up in a more or less continuous megalopolitan sprawl.

Official investigations into the need for a new airport, and its possible sites, were initiated some three decades ago. More than fifteen years ago it was already recognized that the most viable option for a new airport lay in constructing an artificial island in Osaka Bay (much of the edges of which had already been encroached upon by land reclamation). Here it could be sited and angled so that landing and take-off paths were entirely over the sea. The enormous costs of building the island and its connecting infrastructure would be offset by setting it up as Japan's only twenty-four-hour airport, and thus as a major hub for

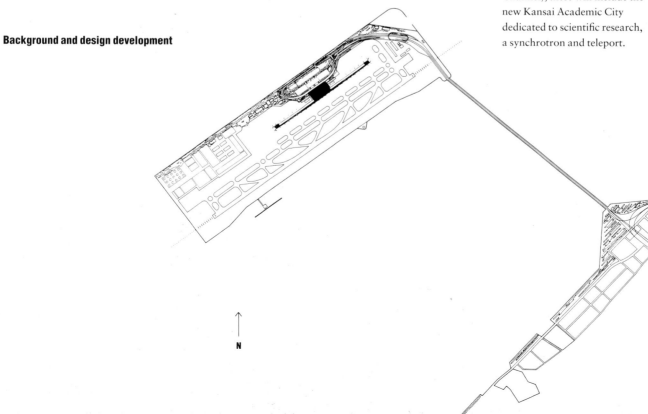

N

Southeast Asia and Australasia, with all the consequent commercial spin-offs.

By building in the sea, it would also be possible to expand the airport by enlarging the island or, as is now thought more likely, by building another (served by its own terminal) alongside the present one. Crucially too, this option would not provoke protests by dispossessed landowners, local farmers and environmental activists, like those who had harried construction of Tokyo's Narita Airport, and it would make effective action of this sort very difficult. To investigate and implement construction of such an airport, the Kansai International Airport Company was set up. Most of the members of this client body were seconded from the Ministry of Transport, with which the client continued to collaborate closely.

Eventually it was decided to build the island 40 kilometres south-west of the centre of Osaka and 5 kilometres off-shore. As well as providing new transport connections to the island, those of the whole region

were to be upgraded and better linked into the national system. Though the island has only a single runway, it can handle 160,000 flights and 25 million passengers a year. Connecting the island to the mainland is a 3.75 kilometre double-decker bridge. On top is a road and below is an independent pair of railway lines for each of the two companies that operate services to the airport.

Both the railway companies, Nankai and Japan Railways West, offer express services to the airport and have extended their local services out to it. The latter's new Haruka express service connects the airport to the southern edge of central Osaka (Tennoji) in just under half an hour, then runs on to connect twenty minutes later at Shin-Osaka with the main routes of the Shinkansen (the bullet trains), and eventually terminates at Kyoto only seventy-five minutes after leaving the airport. (There are check-in facilities for all the airlines at both Shin-Osaka and Kyoto.) Nankai's new express service, the 'Rapi:t', connects the island directly with Osaka's Namba station in thirty minutes.

The six-lane road over the bridge connects to a new motor-

way around Osaka Bay that is part of the national network. From the harbour in the chamfered northern corner of the island, frequent hydrofoils cross the bay to Kobe in thirty minutes. Others run to Osaka harbour and to Awaji Island that lies across the mouth of the bay, and is a natural resort with holiday attractions.

Constructing the 4.37 x 1.25 kilometre island was an immense feat of civil engineering, in which neither the Building Workshop nor Ove Arup & Partners played any part. It took five years to complete. Not only was the island built where the sea was some 18–20 metres deep, but below the water was another 20 metres of very soft, squishy clay. (The option of a floating island was also studied in considerable detail. Though local ship builders had ample experience of oil tankers more than 500 metres long, a 5-kilometre floating island was felt to raise too many imponderable questions of performance and maintenance.)

Before building up the island with landfill, the soft clay had to be stabilized and compacted by squeezing the water from it, mainly by using what are known as sand-drains. To do this, one million sand piles, each 0.4 metres in diameter and 2.5 metres apart, were sunk through the clay, over which was laid a metre of sand. Layers of earth were then dumped on

top of this, their weight squeezing the water from the clay and into the sand piles, and then up these and horizontally outwards through the top level of sand. Over time, what was the sea bed will sink by some 8 metres, and the top of the island by 11 metres. So the height to be filled included this 11 metres as well as the original 20-metre depth of the sea, and the island's eventual 5-metre elevation above sea level.

Steel caissons were sunk to create the perimeter of the island. Two mountains were razed and a nearby island quarried for the infill of crushed rock. Huge barges transported this, each guided to deposit its load in exact position by computers linked to satellites. Outside the caissons and beneath the sea, the earth steps out in shelves to the sea bed so as to form new breeding grounds for fish. These have apparently already resulted in increased catches for the local fishermen, who had also been handsomely compensated for the disruption to their livelihood and for ferrying people and goods to and from the island. (At the insistence of the fishermen, the bridge remained closed throughout the construction period.)

The part of the island where there are now buildings was

138 **Kansai International Airport Terminal**
Previous page Satellite photograph shows new airport island off the Bay of Osaka's east coast. Osaka is around river mouth to north-east and to the west, almost closing mouth of bay, is Awaji island.

1–5 Island under construction:
1, **2** securing the perimeter with steel caissons; **3–5** infilling the island.
6 Aerial photograph of the completed island with terminal under construction.
7 Size comparison between island and terminal building of Kansai and the whole of Venice.

1

2

3

filled first so that construction could get underway while much of the island had yet to appear. However, construction of the buildings had to be delayed because the submarine clay compacted more than had been predicted, thus necessitating extra fill. This led to razing a third mountain, and a year's extra work. When the construction of buildings began, the island was still subsiding, and it will continue to do so for several years. This, of course, has brought considerable technical problems, to add to those of typhoon and seismic activity, and the tidal waves (*tsunami*) caused by the latter – and so to higher building costs. But these extra costs have been more than offset by the revenues gained by opening the airport as quickly as possible.

4

5

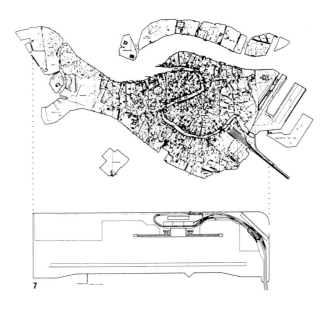
7

139

6

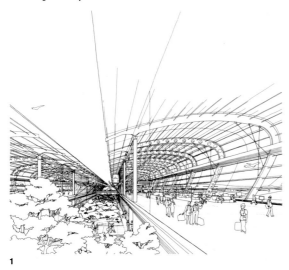

1

Kansai International Airport Terminal
Competition-winning scheme.

1 Perspective of double-sided boarding wing
with central tree-planted 'canyon'.

2 Model with trees invading the building from
the landside and extending along boarding
wing 'canyons'.

3 Section through station, main terminal
block and boarding wing.

4 Section through boarding wing with main
terminal block in elevation.

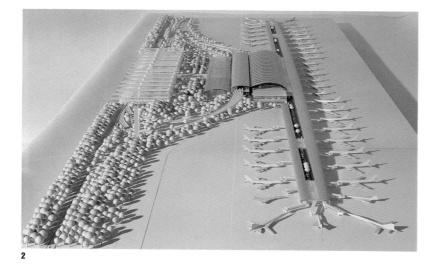

2

The competition

Once committed to building the island, the Kansai International Airport Company asked six of Japan's largest architectural/construction companies to make proposals for the design of the airport terminal. Of the resulting designs, that of the architectural and engineering giant, Nikken Sekkei, was preferred. This was a conventional bi-polar solution with separate but linked domestic and international terminals. It was sent to leading airport authorities around the world, from whom comment and feedback was requested. Most of these merely drew attention to what they saw as potential problem areas, though some suggested how they might be revised.

However, a much more radical reply came from Aéroports de Paris. Besides running the Paris airports, the firm is also a huge design consultancy run by Paul Andreu, and is busy building airports around the world. Instead of offering detailed criticisms of Nikken Sekkei's scheme, Andreu sent a sketch design of a totally different and new kind of terminal. This multi-level rather than bi-polar solution handled domestic and international passengers on different levels of the same central terminal, and docked all aircraft along boarding wings that extended far beyond the two sides of the terminal.

Matching a long, narrow and layered terminal to the elongated rectangle of the island brought obvious efficiencies in the use of land and taxiways. The client was impressed also by the very direct transfers between domestic and international flights, not only for the resultant convenience, but also because it was felt to signal the outward-looking Japan of the future. It was decided immediately to proceed with such a solution, but both Nikken Sekkei and Aéroports de Paris were somewhat rebuffed: the former by not being asked to prepare a new design along these lines; the latter by not being appointed the architects to work up and build its proposal.

Instead, the client, now wanting to ensure that the terminal would be of an architectural quality commensurate with the engineering feat and enormous cost of the island, opted for a high-profile international competition. An announcement invited architects wanting to compete to submit documentation, and Aéroport de Paris, acting as consultants, helped formulate the brief. Eventually fifteen practices were invited to compete, a deliberate mix of those which had airport experience, and others with none. The Renzo Piano Building Workshop had built no airports, but were probably invited – as well as for its international standing – because two of its key associates, Noriaki Okabe and Shunji Ishida, are Japanese. Also, the Building Workshop's Paris office had already had dealings with Aéroport de Paris, who had made the transport studies associated with the aborted scheme for Expo '89, which was to have been part of the Paris celebration of the bicentenary of the French Revolution.

When invited to participate in the competition, Renzo Piano and some of his associates were very reluctant to enter. The Paris office had recently invested heavily in competition-winning schemes, such as the Grenoble Synchrotron (Volume one p 200) and Lyons' Cité Internationale (p 74), from

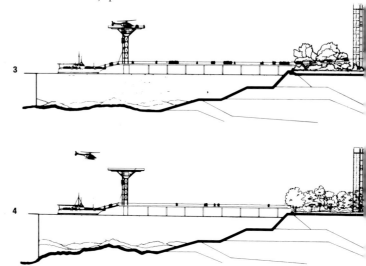

3

4

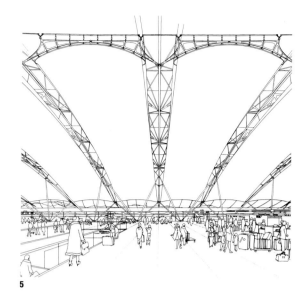

Kansai International Airport Terminal

5 Sectional perspective of international departures hall with air scoops attached directly to brackets cantilevered off primary trusses.

which no commission had as yet materialized. Moreover, in contrast to these French schemes, the airport seemed too far away, and the outcome of the competition too unpredictable for it to be sensible to pursue. Noriaki Okabe, however, who was then one of the associates in charge of the Paris office, was determined not to miss the chance of such a prestigious commission in his homeland. First, he got Peter Rice to agree to collaborate, and together they prevailed upon Piano. Eventually, in the summer of 1988, Okabe and an initially tiny team moved into separate premises in the rue Renard overlooking the Pompidou Centre, where they could work undistracted by day-to-day office business.

Most of the other architects in the competition got financial and technical support by forming joint ventures with

big Japanese construction companies, who stood to back a winner and thereby land the building contract. Although dependent on the technical support of Ove Arup & Partners, led as so often before by Peter Rice and Tom Barker, the Building Workshop otherwise retained its independence. Lacking the financial backing of a contractor, it deployed only two other architects, Olivier Touraine and Ken McBryde, to work with Okabe for the first half of the six month competition period; though, of course, there were regular meetings with the consultants and Piano. However, members of the team who had worked with Okabe on the Bercy 2 Shopping Centre (Volume two p 16) and were now supervising its construction, including project-architect Jean-François Blassel, would drop in in the evenings to help. Then, for the final two months an expanded team worked long hours, seven days a week, finalizing the design and preparing the presentation documents.

An unusual aspect of the competition was that it involved designing for a site that had not as yet come into existence. For many architects, this and the *tabula rasa* of the artificial

island would probably have suggested the appropriateness of an entirely abstract and mechanical architecture. However, for Piano, for whom the *genius loci* is a crucial influence on architecture, a design should respond to much wider contextual influences than the character of its immediate site. Besides reflecting the spirit of the place, it might be shaped by such factors as the climate and its moods, and local building traditions. Piano always seeks to reconcile his buildings with nature, in whichever of its multifarious forms it might be present, introduced into or even suggested by the architecture.

Piano, Rice and Okabe first visited the site together in September 1988. By then the island's 11-kilometre bounding walls were largely in place, revealing its size and shape to the three men sitting in the boat, where the island had otherwise yet to appear. (Lingering traces of the forms of the waves, the glistening of the sun on the water and the lightness of

141

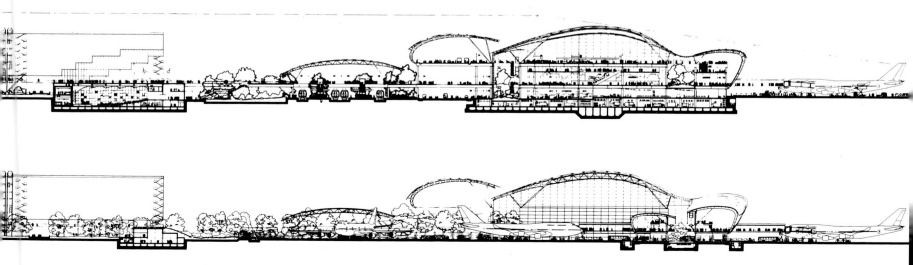

scudding clouds might perhaps be detected in the final building.) Here, as Piano has related, 'the Italian, Irishman and Japanese, each with a very different sensitivity and intelligence, yet deeply familiar with each other's ways of thinking from long experience of working together', mused on the broad essentials of how to approach the design of the terminal. Piano's instinct, endorsed by the others, suggested that the correct response to the vast flat datum of the future island's top, where only the distant mountains separated the sky from the horizon, had

to be some immense semi-topographic element. He imagined something that was both a seeming fact of geography and yet of immediately recognizable identity, with its own distinctive curving profile clearly contrasting with those of the mountains.

Rice's speculations reinforced this image: though concerned with very physical engineering problems, such as seismic action and settlement, he talked of the resultant undulatory movements of ground and waves. All three also pondered on what sense the building might be Japanese. Though determined to avoid anything mimetic or sentimental, they felt the building might reflect Japanese tradition by exposing a hierarchy of distinctive structural components and through its sensitivity to the character of materials, though these would now be industrial rather than natural.

Impressed by the grand gesture of building this artificial island, Piano later pondered how to make the most of the potentially magical experience of landing and flying from an island. He wanted the terminal to invest contemporary air travel with some of the drama and dignity that nineteenth-century stations gave to both train travel and to arrival and

departure in a particular city or country. But, if dramatizing arrival into a particular city poses some design problems for out-of-town airports, then achieving a sense of arrival in a country or one of its regions might be yet more problematic when landing on an artificial island. Piano felt it was necessary to temper the island's abstract and arid artificiality so that passengers would feel they had actually *landed* in Japan, making contact with *terra firma* and Japan's abundant vegetation. To give it some of the character of a natural island, he proposed dense planting of indigenous trees along the whole edge of the island behind the terminal. He also envisaged these trees as invading the terminal so that everywhere within the building travellers would be accompanied by vegetation, and greeted with it immediately on landing.

142

1

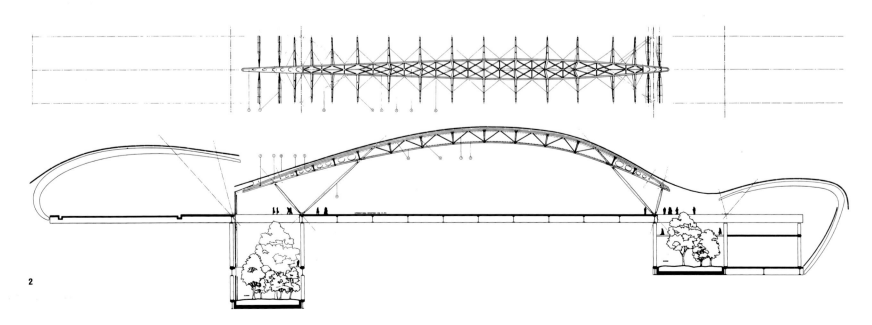

2

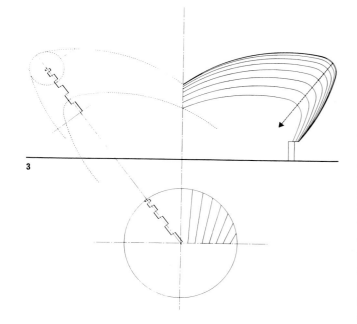

Kansai International Airport Terminal

Competition scheme: roof structure and geometry.

1 Model of a slice through the main terminal block showing how arched main trusses and bowed ribs of boarding wing and departures level road are still independent of each other rather than integrated.

2 Plan of main truss with cantilever brackets and section showing discontinuities between main structural elements.

3 Early study of toroidal geometry of boarding wing.

4 Later study showing revised shape of rib and how passengers can view planes from various parts of interior.

To celebrate the drama of flight, Piano envisioned the terminal as emerging from, and stretching out in front of the trees, poised as lightly and gracefully as a glider. Within the light and airy interior, he imagined being aware simultaneously of land and nature in one direction and machine-borne flight in the other. As well as the machine metaphor of the glider, he imagined the terminal's exterior might conjure further natural images, such as a dune spread before the trees, or a wave or silver-grey cloud bank rolling off the sea. All this was consistent with the already made decision to use curving roofs. The dense planting reinforced the original concept behind the curving roofs: that of 'naturalizing' the island. Just as the harbour of a natural island is often its major topographic feature, so this terminal would seem to be a semi-natural feature to which planes would come and go as naturally as boats to a harbour bay.

The brief proposed that entrants should follow Aéroport de Paris's schematic solution, which seemed to lend itself to a design consistent with what Piano and Okabe envisioned. So Olivier Touraine was assigned immediately to undertake a painstaking analysis of the very detailed competition brief. This continued after design had begun, and eventually took three months to complete. But it very quickly confirmed the basic soundness of Aéroport de Paris's proposed solution, and so the Building Workshop stuck with it, one of only two entrants to do so more or less entirely. This is yet another good example of the Building Workshop's reluctance to impose unnecessarily on received situations, be these existing buildings, context, nature or the sound proposals of others. (Piano and his associates are refreshingly free of most architects' compulsion to stamp their ideas and idiom on all aspects of a scheme, an egotism, which besides betraying insecurity, also isolates these architects from an appreciation of the full and subtle complexities of a situation.)

Aéroport de Paris's proposal did not split domestic and international flights into separate terminals, or into opposite ends of the same one. Instead, it had a single multi-level main terminal block. In this, departures and arrivals halls for domestic flights were side-by-side on a middle level, sandwiched between an international departures hall on the top level and international arrivals on the ground. All flights were then boarded from lounges in the same immensely long boarding wing that stretched out to either side from the airside edge of the main terminal block. Domestic flights used the central portion of this wing, directly in front of their terminal facilities. International flights used the rest of this, with arriving passengers transferring to a walkway one level up and within the volume of the wing, and then descending to the ground floor once within the main terminal block. Running outside the landside of the boarding wings, a shuttle transit system took passengers to and from the international gates. Those gates immediately on either side of the central domestic gates were organized to serve domestic or international flights, thus providing a flexibility in gate allocation to match the varying demand throughout the day.

While the appraisal of the proposed solution in the brief continued, design discussions started, drawing on the very considerable collective experience of the architectural team and its consultants as users of airports. One issue immediately emerged as paramount: clarity of orientation. In contrast to other airports, there were to be no confusing and claustrophobic corridors. Passengers must be able to orient themselves without signs, no matter where they are in the building. Everywhere it was to be immediately obvious, even without thinking, in which directions are the land and airsides and whether one is walking away or towards one's plane. This was to be achieved by a combination of transparency (with views through to the planes from all parts of the building), a flowing sequence of

143

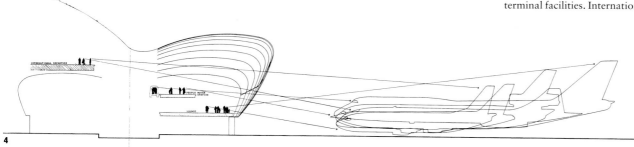

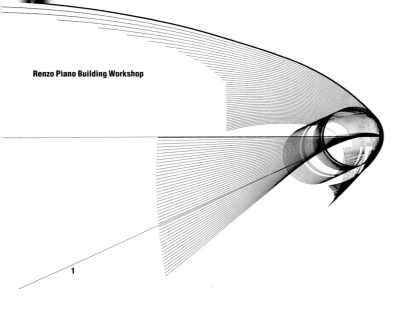

1

146   **Kansai International Airport Terminal**
Previous pages Upper part of gable end of
main terminal block. Curving end truss is
doubled up so that glazing can extend up to the
roof and deflections in truss and glazing are
easily absorbed. Secondary structure
oversails the truss to create broad sunshading eaves.

1 Study of geometry of boarding wing.

Competition scheme.
2 Section through station, access roads,
main terminal block and boarding wing.
3 Landside elevation of main terminal block.

spaces, which are wide open one to the next, and by the shapes of the exposed structural elements.

The concern with orientation and transparency led to two new elements being introduced as improvements to the brief's schematic proposal. In the main terminal building, all concessions such as cafeterias, shops and duty-free shops were moved to an additional level sandwiched between the international departures and domestic floors. Free of the concessions, these latter levels could be kept relatively open so as to allow views across them and the boarding wing, and so out to the planes. Contributing further to the transparency was another advantage brought about by this arrangement: by gathering together all high-fire risks where they could be doused with sprinklers and closed off with fire doors, the usual requirement for fire compartmentalization between the principal spaces was obviated.

The second improvement was to insert a narrow hall on the landside of the main terminal block, extending its full width

and height. The entrances from the station and those from the roads, above and below it, were directly into this hall. Here, the scale and multi-level organization of the terminal were to be impressed immediately on those arriving, who could then proceed via conspicuous escalators to the level they required. This hall was to be invaded by trees, an inward extension of those outside: hence the name given to the hall, the canyon. Echoing this, and extending the presence of planting all the way to the aeroplanes, a second canyon stretched up the middle of the entire length of the boarding wing.

Right from the start, Peter Rice proposed that the structure should aid orientation by being strongly directional, with a pronouncedly oblong rather than square grid. The model to be avoided was that of Foster Associates' Stansted Airport, which also exploits transparency to facilitate orientation. A tiny building by comparison, Stansted's structure offers identical views in whichever direction one looks, which

would disorientate the traveller in a building as vast as Kansai.

From early on, too, it was apparent that the roof structure would be steel: it is easy to fabricate off site and assemble into long spans, and is relatively light and cheap. For structural efficiency some form of arched truss would be used, a form that further contributes to the directionality of the structure, and the sense of lightness the Building Workshop seeks. This could result in the semi-topographic forms conjured up in Piano's mind when first boating around the site.

The arched truss, which produced a lofty space that was nevertheless quite low towards its edges, helped meet a crucial constraint: that the tails of all aircraft should always be visible from the control tower. Designed by specialists, the tower was to stand on the landside of the terminal, towards the island's edge, where it could also serve the extension of the airport that will one day be built in this direction. Visibility from the control tower required that no part of the

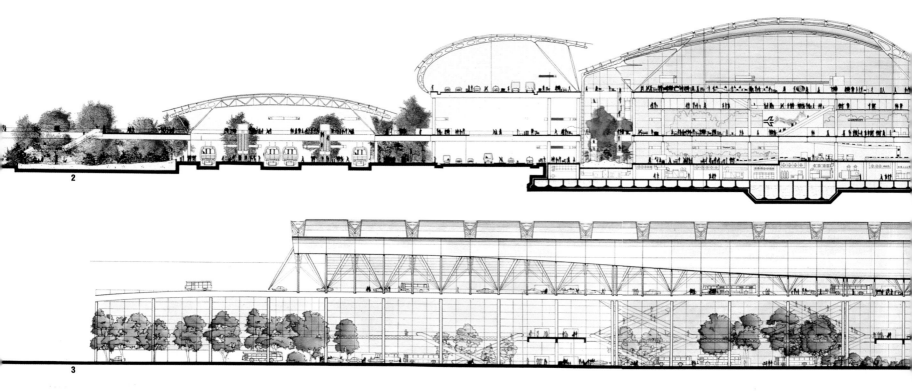

2

3

building could protrude above a segment of an imaginary cone that flared downwards from its apex in the tower. A model was made early on of the volume within which it was permitted to build. It was studying this model which first suggested that the roof of the boarding wing be curved in the longitudinal direction, tapering from a central portion, which had to be high enough to allow views out from the international departures hall, downwards in height towards its ends.

But the boarding wing was to be curved in the transverse direction too, partly to be sympathetic in form with the curved roof over the terminal building, and also to furnish a forward lean that would shade the huge stretch of glazing along the airside. What was required was a two-directional curve, and Rice and the architectural team realized that here was the perfect opportunity to use a true toroidal form, that could be generated in the same way as the geometrically fudged curves of the shell of the Bercy 2 Shopping Centre. (A toroid is formed by the rotation of a constant curve. If this curve is a circle, then the resultant form is a ring or torus – but this is only a special case. Most toroids, such as those from which Kansai's roof is cut conceptually, are not generated from pure circles.)

The adoption of such curves, which were generated graphically by taking a constant curve (made up of tangential arcs of circles of differing radii) and shifting it progressively backwards and downwards in section, had allowed the shopping centre to be clad entirely in rectangular panels. There, however, the complex curves dictated by the shape of the site and the relatively small size (compared to Kansai) of the project, had resulted in some thirty different sizes of panels being required. But the huge scale and more gentle, pure toroidal curves of Kansai could be clad entirely in a single size of panel.

Use of the toroidal curve, which persists as one of the most significant features of the much revised, executed design, was a relatively early design decision.

Considerably later, the resolution of another problem was to deform the symmetry of the arched truss of the main terminal block roof. Seeking a solution to air-conditioning the vast space of the international departures hall without hanging a clutter of heavy ductwork from the exposed structure, Arup's Tom Barker proposed a solution which had never been tried on this scale nor been used to generate the form of a building. This was to blow a jet of air from the landside and let this be entrained against the ceiling that would be shaped to follow the natural curve of the decelerating air. The progressively tightening curve resulted in an asymmetrical arch, which Rice readily accepted, not least because it made the structure even more unambiguously directional.

The resulting structural solution was suggestively zoomorphic. Triangular sectioned trusses were supported towards each end by leg-like splayed props, and at regular intervals along both sides of the trusses were rib-like cantilevered wing-brackets.

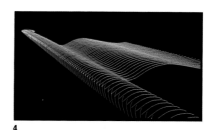
4

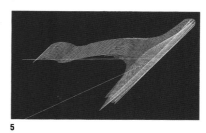
5

147

Kansai International Airport Terminal
4, **5** Studies of alternative geometric solutions for executed design. **5** shows an attempt to sweep roofs of boarding wing and main terminal into each other in plan as well as section.

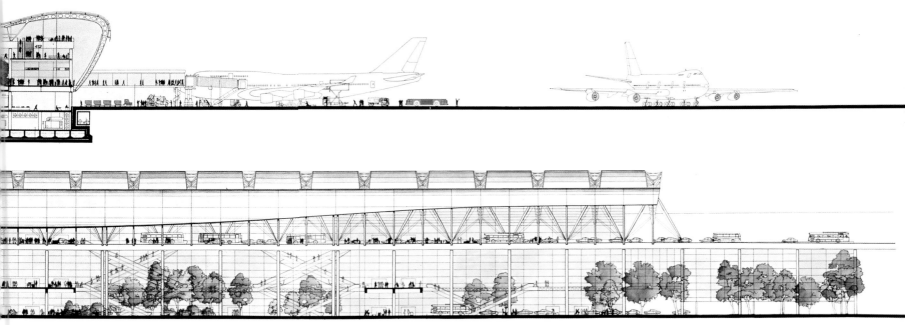

148

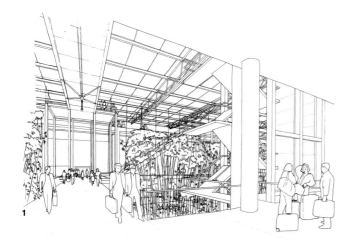

1

2

Fixed to the undersides of these brackets were huge scoop-like ceilings that would entrain the jets of blown air. Over the tops of the trusses were rooflights. Despite these, there would be less light in the central international departures hall than in the canyon and boarding wing, both of which were abundantly lit through the glazing on their sides. These contrasts in intensity of natural light would also aid orientation, with the land and airsides more brightly lit than the multi-levelled centre, a contrast that would be emphasized by the lighter structure in the perimeter parts. At night, these contrasting light intensities would be reversed, with the multi-level section brighter lit than the peripheral spaces.

Covering the complete airport complex was a series of independent curved roofs. The airside was fronted by the toroidal roof of the boarding wing; and those parts of the boarding wing on the landside of its central canyon were enclosed by a lower roof, curved in only one direction. Both roofs were supported on huge curved ribs, as was another roof sheltering the drop-off areas on the elevated road on the opposite side of the main terminal block. Beyond this the roof of the station was supported on symmetrically arched trusses. Of all these, the only roofs joined together were those of the main terminal building and the front of the boarding wing: the contrasts between their geometries were fudged by the complex concave curves of the glass roof which joined them. Okabe and Blassel knew this solution to be problematic, but felt its resolution could wait until the competition was won for certain. Rice had also already conceived of treating the boarding wing as a light shell structure rather than heavy independent ribs, but similarly postponed the complex computer analysis required to resolve such a structure.

The Building Workshop submitted by far the most seductive competition entry. Its curved roofs and the interweaving of architecture and vegetation evoked the vision that underlies all of Piano's mature work: that of technology emulating, and in harmony with, nature. It was also the scheme that functioned best because it both followed and improved upon the proposals of the brief. Judged the winner at the end of 1988, the jury applauded the conjunction of architecture and nature. The ecological vision encapsulated by the design was deemed apt as it was intended that the Kansai terminal should herald the architecture of the next century. The jury commented on how the delicate forms of the structure blended with nature without overwhelming people. Instead, they wrote, 'the design allowed people to experience a drama of changing space, light and sights, creating a familiar space as well as bold revelations of the future'.

On the announcement of the winning design, some local environmentalists queried what the jury had seen as an ecological vision. They were worried that the dense tree planting between the terminal's landside and the island's edge would attract birds that would have to be exterminated as a hazard to the aircraft. (After investigating such solutions as radio-controlled mechanical hawks, it was decided to use only tree species that were unattractive to birds. Though the budget did not allow for these to be planted immediately, money is being raised from a variety of sources to realize this aspect of Piano's original vision.)

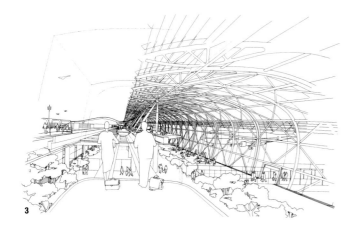

Kansai International Airport Terminal

Penultimate design: interior perspectives.

1 Bridge from domestic flights hall crosses canyon to entrance from station.

2 Ground floor of canyon.

3 Domestic boarding lounges seen from international arrivals walkway. Transition of main truss into boardig-wing rib is still not as simply resolved as in the final design.

4 International departures hall.

5 View from departures level drop-off under cantilevered eaves across canyon and into international departures hall.

Development of final design

Having won the competition, it was now necessary to revise, develop and execute the design of this huge and complex building in a very short time. To do this, the client had the Building Workshop set up a consortium with other powerful players, each of whom was very different, not only in expertise, but also in organization and working methods. So the first three months were spent working out how to orchestrate the joint venture, and what were to be the roles and responsibilities of each member and the modes of interaction between them.

As eventually formulated, there were four major partners in the joint venture. The Renzo Piano Building Workshop remained in charge of both design and coordination, and Piano himself was the chairman of the consortium; but the architectural design and engineering was done by both the Building Workshop, with whom Ove Arup & Partners collaborated together forming a single partner, and Nikken Sekkei, who are engineers as well as architects. Aéroport de Paris was responsible for devising the basic zonings and circulation patterns and for the design of such things as the transit shuttle and baggage-handling systems. The fourth partner, Japan Airports Consultants Inc, took charge of the airside planning and the tough negotiations with the various government departments (particularly in relation to customs, immigration and quarantine facilities), as well as with the civil aviation authorities.

Initially, it was intended that the design and construction documents be ready to start on site within two years, with about a year allocated to revising and finalizing the basic design and another year to its detailed development. Construction was then to take only a further twenty-eight months. However, delays due to settlement of the island resulted in this finally being thirty-eight months.

The three months of negotiations setting up the joint venture left only nine months to revise the basic design and bring it to maturity. Though the Building Workshop had already opened an office in Osaka run by Okabe (the Renzo Building Workshop Japan, a locally registered company), Piano decided to bring safely to term the basic design, now known as the baby, in Genoa where it was under his wing and removed from undue interference. So he moved key members of the competition team, Ken McBryde and Olivier Touraine (to be joined later by Jean-François Blassel who was completing the Bercy 2 Shopping Centre), from Paris to the office in the Piazza San Matteo, where he could also keep close watch and be immersed in every aspect of the design development.

Once there, the team was also expanded into a youngish, thoroughly international group that was devoted exclusively to this project. Key new members of the team included Mark Turpin and Kenny Fraser. During this period the contribution of Shunji Ishida, who dedicated most of his time to this project, was especially important. It was he who mainly interacted with the Osaka office, and who made many of the numerous key drawings, the latter a process that inevitably involves making or refining

149

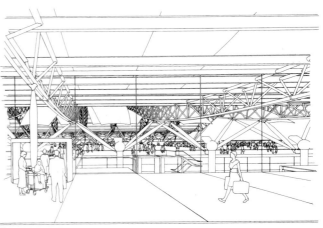

5

1

Kansai International Airport Terminal

Members of the design team.
1 Yasuji Sugimoto and Takayuki Inakura
(both of Nikken Sekkei), Renzo Piano, Olivier
Touraine and Marion Goerdt.
2 Kohji Hirano, Peter Rice, Renzo Piano,
Noriaki Okabe and Jean-François Blassel.
3 Peter Rice.
4 The Genoa team: Geoff Cohen, Randy
Shields, Stig Larsen, Barnaby Gunning,
Alessandro Montaldo, Shunji Ishida,
Ken McBryde, Jean Marc Weill, Chris Kelly,
Stefan Oehler, Tomoko Komatsubara,
Simone Medio, Kenny Fraser, Ariel Chavela
and Ivan Corte.

2

3

4

countless crucial design decisions. Later, Ivan Corte played a crucial role in working out how to set up the complex geometry on the computer, while the mathematical skill of Ariel Chavela, a young student temporarily in the office, was invaluable in deriving and refining the exact geometry.

Throughout, though, Okabe remained in charge of the project, along with Piano. Thanks to modern information technology, Okabe was in constant touch with the Genoa members of the team, with whom he spent some days each month. The rest of the time, he (along with some architects who were transferred from Paris, and a Japanese staff hired by the Building Workshop) was in immediate contact with the client, the relevant regulatory authorities and Nikken Sekkei, as well as with local contractors and manufacturers, and could offer instant feedback from them.

Hence the design and its development were advanced in both offices simultaneously. At the end of each working day in Genoa, all new ideas, revisions and refinements were summarized graphically and faxed to Osaka, and vice versa. By early the next day Okabe would have telephoned or faxed through not only his comments, but those of the relevant collaborators or authorities. While reworking the basic design, the Genoa office was dominant, but gradually more of the detail design development was done in Osaka. Some of the Genoa team (including Touraine, Blassel, McBryde and Fraser) joined Okabe there for differing periods of time. Among the local members of the team helping Okabe were Akira Ikegami, Tetsuya Kimura and Taichi Tomuro.

As well as being in touch by fax and telephone every day, a few members of the Genoa and Osaka offices met regularly face to face. This happened at the intense three or four day working sessions held every month, alternately in Genoa and Osaka, and attended by the key members of each group: the Genoa and Osaka offices of the Building Workshop, Arups, Nikken Sekkei, Aéroport de Paris, Japan Airports Inc and the client. To provoke and facilitate the most productive interchange, these meetings employed what is the conventional format for the Building Workshop. Everybody sat at the same round table, as equals who could see all the others equally well, in a room with floor-to-ceiling pinboards covered with the drawings of the latest scheme or developments. As well as showing the latest design developments, the results of studies on functional and technical options were reported on. This all led to a lively exchange of views and either approvals by the client or agreement among members of the consortium as to how alternatively to proceed.

Inevitably, the competition design needed much revision. The only major criticisms of it

5

Kansai International Airport Terminal

Members of the design team.

5 Tatsuya Yamaguchi, Akira Ikegami, Renzo Piano and Noriaki Okabe.

6 Tetsuya Kimura, Norio Takata, Taichi Tomuro, Renzo Piano, Noriaki Okabe and Jean-François Blassel.

7 Khoji Hirano, Jean-François Blassel and Taichi Tomuro.

8 Noriaki Okabe and Renzo Piano with representative of client.

6

7

offered by the jury and the consultants were that the boarding-wing lounges and canyon were both too narrow. As the space between the landside roads and airside docking apron was fixed, the only way to widen these was to omit the canyon from the centre of the boarding wing. Cost savings would have necessitated this loss sooner or later, in any case, and it was partially compensated for by widening the canyon on the landside of the main terminal building. Other changes arose because Aéroport de Paris and the Kansai International Airport Company had continued to reappraise and refine the programme during the period of the competition, and indeed continued to revise such things as baggage handling through much of the basic design period.

And there were several aspects of the competition design that the Building Workshop were well aware were problematic or could be much better resolved.

For instance, it had already been realized that the structural solution, with its cantilevered brackets, was too rigid to cope with the lateral stresses characteristic of seismic action. A geometric form, which would allow the main terminal building roof to sweep smoothly into that of the boarding wing, was preferred to the fudge of glazing used in the competition scheme. While reworking the structure and geometry, it was intended that the structural members of the roofs of the main terminal block and boarding wing should also somehow run into each other to stress the spatial fluidity that was being sought. With the station now a separate design contract outside of its control (and so not covered by one of the family of curved roofs), the

Building Workshop also decided that all parts of the terminal should be unified under a single roof whose complex curves would flow seamlessly into each other. The separate roof over the departures level drop-off was to be omitted and shelter provided instead by cantilevering out the end of the main roof.

To make the best use of the working sessions and the expertise of the people present, the nine-month basic design 'baby' evolved through a series of bimonthly babies, each named after the month they were prepared for. The May Baby (May 1989) marked an initial attempt to fuse the spaces, structure and roofs together. The July Baby sought ways to reduce costs and the September Baby attempted to integrate a revised baggage-handling and circulation system, and in the process revealed serious functional conflicts. This strained relationships within the consortium and led to an intense working session of more than a month in Genoa, from which came a radically revised and better integrated design – and the need for a total recalculation of the roof design by Ove Arup.

8

Detail design

Although the Building Workshop prepared the revised overall basic design, in constant consultation with its partners, the building was split up for detailed development. The Building Workshop was responsible for the canyon, the international departures hall and the boarding wing, for the roof structure and its exposed steel supports, and for the cladding and glazing. These constitute the whole exterior and all the major spaces, which are each shaped by the exterior and its structure, and give the terminal its very particular character. Within the curving skin and structure of this outer building is the trabeated inner building developed by Nikken Sekkei. This contains the international arrivals' baggage handling and customs, the domestic departure and arrival facilities, concession floor and the service basement.

Nikken Sekkei were also responsible for the measures taken to deal with differential settlement, and for the overall coordination of technological matters and cost estimates. The Building Workshop, Arups and Nikken Sekkei collaborated on negotiations with the fire authorities, while other negotiations, such as with the Ministry of Construction were undertaken by Nikken Sekkei on behalf of the consortium. Nikken Sekkei also built the adjacent station and the office buildings for airline administration departments.

During the most intense period of detail design development, the Building Workshop had more than one hundred people, including members of Arups, in the team committed to the terminal. Coordinating such a large team based in Genoa, Osaka and London presented its own logistical problems; these were further compounded because nearly ninety percent of the team were not Japanese, the language in which all construction documents were to be issued. So one of the tasks undertaken by the Genoa and Osaka offices of the Building Workshop was to create a glossary of standardized technical terms, that were translated into Japanese as the Kansai International Airport glossary. But the most tricky problem during the detailed design phase was to get an accurate estimate of costs, particularly in a period of runaway economic boom and on a site that might present unforeseen problems. This resulted ultimately in the Building Workshop team undergoing a highly pressured period of frantic and ruthless cost cutting necessitated by some very high tender bids.

Kansai International Airport Terminal

The enormous length and glider-like form of the terminal is evident in this aerial view, as is the contrast between the two-directional toroidal curves of the boarding wing and the one-directional curves of the central terminal block. The shuttle tracks can be clearly seen on the landside of the boarding wing.

1

2

154 **Kansai International Airport Terminal**

Manufacture and assembly of structural elements.

1 Welding sections of the main trusses in rotating jig in Japanese steel works.

2, **4** Manufacture in Britain of boarding-wing ribs.

3 Checking angle at base of boarding-wing rib.

5 Delivery of site of portion of main truss and

6 assembly.

7 Manufacturing process of main trusses; from top to bottom: robot welding of tubes into required lengths; bending tubes to required radius; positioning upper chords and welding secondary structure; assembly of sections of truss; welding in rotating jigs; test assembly and checking.

8 Construction view brings home the immense scale of the boarding wing.

3

4

5

6

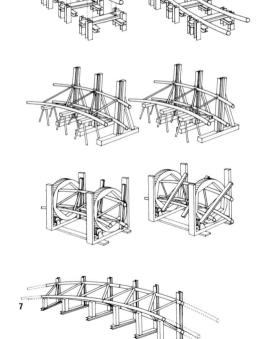

7

Cost cutting and construction

To estimate the costs accurately is very tricky for an architect working in a foreign country. This is especially so in Japan, where no large building had been built by a non-Japanese team of architects and engineers, and with a design that pushes a reluctant building industry to its limits, insisting on many changes in their conventional methods of operating. Many of the crucial factors determining cost in such circumstances are as much psychological and cultural as technical and economic. Moreover, Japan was then at the peak of an economic boom, the so-called 'bubble', with over-full order books and costs escalating unrealistically. So it is perhaps unsurprising that initial tenders, which had been called for only from local contractors rather than internationally, as had been agreed with the client originally, were over budget. Cutting costs necessitated a rushed process of revision and some compromises to the design, a few of them especially regrettable, while fighting to keep its essence and integrity.

The glazing had to be reduced considerably in area. Much of the landside glazing went: that below the top floor of the canyon, and all but a narrow strip at the head of the wall where the boarding-wing edges the shuttle track. In the central part of the boarding wing, the roof was extended downwards, lowering the head of the airside glazing by 4 metres. The rooflights over the international departures hall went too, despite calculations by Ove Arup & Partners to show that, over time, the savings in electricity for lighting would have paid for them. All this also reduced air-conditioning loads and so led to further savings on plant. The result is not just a loss of some of the building's intended lightness and trans-

parency, but also of views that
are crucial to immediate
orientation and understanding
of the terminal's workings: those
of the escalators from the
landside approach, of the
shuttles and external structure
from the boarding wing, and of
the planes from all parts of the
international departures hall.
Though the last of these considerably compromises one of the
fundamental concepts that generated the design, the architects
accepted this change without
too much reluctance because
it helped the exterior of the
boarding wing read better as
a single volume. Also to save
costs, the boarding wing's
intended fenestration on the
landside below the shuttle
track and on the airside ground
floor was replaced with
standard windows.

First tenders for the structural
steelwork came in particularly
high. This resulted in
considerable pressure to
simplify the design, especially
the toroidal geometry and
leaning ribs of the boarding
wing, as well as the way that the
tie-bars were secured to heavy
plates, which pass through, and
were welded into cuts made
through both sides of the
tubular curved ribs. However,
the Building Workshop and Ove
Arup were adamant that all
these features had to stay.
Eventually Arups persuaded
both the joint venture companies and their steel subcontractors (Nippon Steel and
Kawasaki) to put the steelwork
of the boarding wing out to
international tender. After
negotiations with Eiffel of
France and Watsons of Britain,
the latter won the contract with
a tender that was almost exactly
that estimated by quantity
surveyors, Davis Langdon

8

156 **Kansai International Airport Terminal**
Constructing the central terminal block.
1–7 At work on the international departures hall.
8, 9 Internal ductwork of jet nozzles delivered to site.

Everest (who were consultants to the Building Workshop), and about a third of that of the Japanese subcontractors. So, after Japanese experts had visited and approved the factory in Bolton, the steel of the boarding wing was fabricated in Britain and shipped to site. The contractors found that, once they properly understood the geometry, these elements were not so difficult to erect.

However, the cantilevered ends of the main trusses and overhanging roof they support over the departures level road were shortened by 4 metres. This necessitated cheaper but fiddly little canopies across the road to shelter arriving travellers. Also, the flanged, box-sectioned secondary structure over the main trusses has been replaced with standard I-sections and extra cross bracing, all hidden by a suspended ceiling; a solution the architects now prefer.

The stringent budget led to many of the internal finishes, and external finishes on the landside, having to be of the cheapest sort. Much of what is now plasterboard was intended to be flat aluminium panels. The artificial stone floor that was to be used throughout, now gives way to rubber beyond the security controls on each level so that the whole boarding wing is floored in rubber. The windows used on the lower levels along both sides of the boarding wing are not only in awkward standard sizes, but are in a too-pale standard colour. Internally, light fittings and public address speakers are off-the-peg items, the latter again in a less than ideal, standard colour.

Because of its immense size and the inherent difficulties of building on the island, the terminal cost a lot of money. However, if its cost is measured per square metre, or especially per cubic metre, then it is not at all expensive. But the huge cost of building the island, and then the unforeseen cost of the extra landfill due to greater settlement than predicted, led to pressures to make savings wherever possible on the terminal. The stainless-steel skin, the sinuously formed structure, the vast abundance of flowing space all remain magnificent; but here and there are details and finishes that are not of equivalent standard.

A casualty not of cost cutting, but of omission from the original budget, was the tree-planting outside the terminal and along the edge of the island. However, the idea of the trees has caught the imagination of both the client and the public; the local prefecture has donated money for the trees and a number of local campaigns are steadily raising more.

To construct a building like Kansai's passenger terminal is an epic undertaking. It is especially so on a typhoon-lashed, unstable island to which all deliveries had to be made by sea, including the workers. An average of about 4,000 workers (employed on all construction on the island, not just the terminal), rising to a maximum of 10,000 were ferried out and back each day, and fresh lunches were ferried to them each noon. At one peak point, 5,000 workers were busy on the passenger terminal alone.

Moreover, the construction of such a vast building was beyond the resources of any single contractor. So two consortia were formed, the North and South Joint Venture Companies led by Obayashi and Takenaka corporations respectively. Besides those that led them, each joint venture included nine other huge contracting corporations, including in each of them an American contractor (Fluor Daniel and Bechtel respectively). The building was split between the consortia, not as might be expected into, say, main terminal block and boarding wing, but in exact halves meeting in the middle of the main terminal block. The differences in the ways that the two joint venture companies set about both the making and the assembling of the components of what would eventually be identical halves of the same building could not have been more striking. One, for instance, used masses of scaffolding to erect the boarding-wing ribs; the other, hardly any.

Yet the collaboration ran smoothly and without friction. And so well organized was every contractor and every aspect of the building process that, despite all the difficulties to be overcome and the 10,100,000 man-hours worked, there was not a single serious injury on the site.

2

1

3

4

5

6

8

7

9

Renzo Piano Building Workshop

1

2

3

158 **Kansai International Airport Terminal**

Construction.

1 Junction of primary and secondary structure of boarding wing.

2 Protection against fierce sun as well as the rigours of the work.

3 Pouring concrete of apron for docking aircraft.

4–6 Along immense airside length of building, different phases of construction proceed simultaneously, from raising of the ribs with their already-tensioned ties, **4**, to glazing in bottom right of **6**.

7 Assembly sequence of roof structure.

Roofing and glazing.

8–10, **14**, **15** Applying bottom layer of inner roof that was delivered to site as individual trough-shaped elements.

11, **12** Glazing airside of boarding wing.

13 In foreground are fin-rafters for overhanging eaves. Behind, roof tiles have yet to be affixed along the expansion joint.

4

5

6

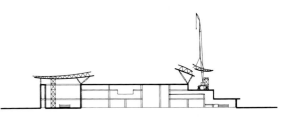

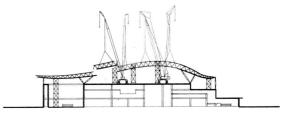

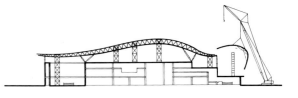

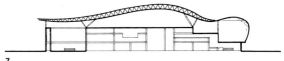

7

8

9

11

10

12

13

14

15

160

Elements of the final design

Circulation

The terminal's design is shaped by the disciplines of moving and docking around its perimeter not just planes, but also trains and motor vehicles, and then transferring passengers and baggage between these by different routes threaded through the building. The clarity of the various circulation patterns, and the fluidity and forms of the spaces and structure that guide them were crucial determinants of the design.

On the airside, all planes are disembarked via the same boarding bridges to the same level – the first floor. But the landside is entered at three levels. Roads drop off passengers and visitors on the top level outside the international departures hall and on the ground level outside the floor of the canyon and the international arrivals level. Most people, though, arrive and leave by train, exiting the station via footbridges that span the ground-level road and enter the building at first-floor level. Passengers for domestic flights proceed straight ahead on this level. Those for international flights, or domestic passengers who have arrived by bus or car use the escalators or lifts in the canyon to change to the level they require.

Passengers to and from domestic flights use check-in and baggage-collection facilities on the first floor and wait in, or pass through, the vast boarding lounge on the immediate airside of these. Passengers for international flights check-in on the top floor and pass through immigration on the airside edge of this hall. They then descend to the concessions level on which there are duty-free shops, bars and restaurants, and on the airside of these, a transit lounge. Proceeding to the airside corners of this lounge, they board the automated shuttles, or, if using one of the closer gates, descend a level by escalator to the floor of the extended boarding wing, in which there are the international departure lounges.

From the main terminal block, the three-coach automated shuttle runs on tracks along the landside edge of the boarding wing to stations midway along it and at its far end. Leaving every two minutes and travelling at up to 35 kilometres per hour these reach the midway station in 60 seconds and the wing-tip station in 120 seconds, carrying up to 2,300 passengers every 10 minutes. From the stations, escalators lead to the floor of the boarding wing. Passengers walk along its landside edge to the lounge beside the gate they require.

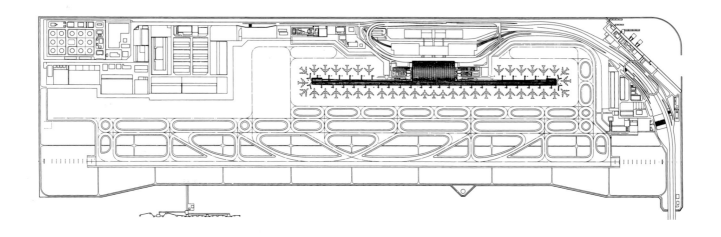

Those arriving by international flights pass between these lounges and immediately take an escalator or lift up to a walkway which projects into the boarding wing on the level above. Once on this, they proceed to the nearest shuttle station to take a shuttle to the main terminal block. Here, more escalators take them down a level to the immigration halls set in the corners of the domestic flights level, and then down to baggage reclaim and customs on the ground floor.

At this level, the landside of the main terminal block is given over to baggage handling, which, because of the building's multi-level organization, is mechanically transported up and down through more levels than is usual in an airport. In many countries the client would have been nervous about such a solution, and might have required extra or alternative systems as a back up. However, Japan's high standards of maintenance meant the dependency on mechanical systems for moving baggage and passengers in no way perturbed the client.

The varying proportion of domestic to international flights throughout the day has meant that a considerable flexibility has been provided for in the allocation of boarding gates. A number of them, immediately to either side of the domestic boarding lounge in front of the main terminal block, can be switched to serve either type of destination; the 'swing gate' system is used that was devised by Aéroport de Paris and improved upon by the Building Workshop. When these gates are being used for domestic flights, departing international passengers proceed above them, along a walkway parallel to that for those arriving, before descending to the floor of the boarding wing at a point beyond these gates. This simple solution clearly works well, but the intrusion of the walkway close to the airside glazing frustratingly blocks what could have been incredible vistas down the whole length of the boarding wing.

162

1

- ■ International departures
- ■ Domestic departures/arrivals
- ■ International arrivals

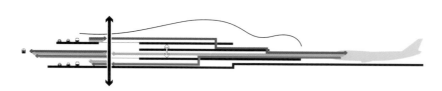

2

3

International departures area

Domestic departures/arrivals area

International arrivals area

International departures

Domestic departures/arrivals

International arrivals

Kansai International Airport Terminal

Circulation.

Page 161 Temporary security arrangements control access to check-in counter at north-eastern end of international departures lounge.

1, 3 Ground floor views of the canyon where passengers immediately orient themselves and change to the level they require.

2, 4 Circulation diagrams.

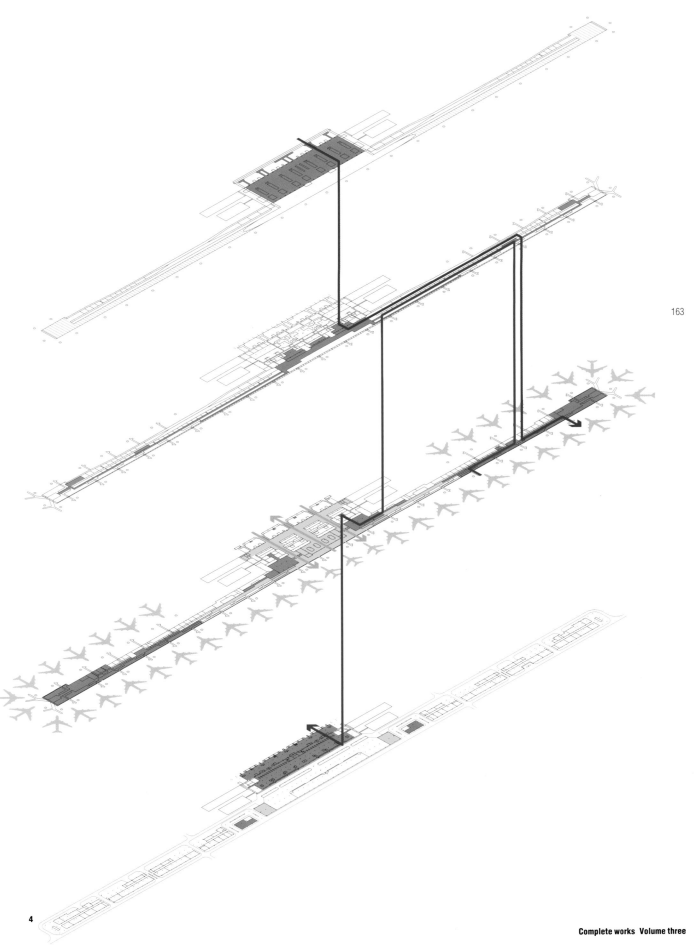

4

1

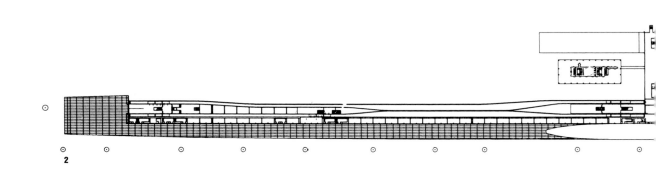

2

164   **Kansai International Airport Terminal**
Elevation and plans.

1 Landside elevation.

2 Third floor plan of international departures
hall: **a** departures drop-off **b** void over canyon
c check-in desks **d** escalators to shopping
level **e** security checks and access to
lower levels.

3 Second floor plan of concessions,
international arrivals walkways and shuttle:
a void over canyon **b** concessions
c immigration (international departures)
d duty free shops **e** transit lounge
f shuttle station **g** customs, immigration and
quarantine administration building
h airlines' administration building.

4 First floor plan of domestic arrivals and
departures and all boarding: **a** arrivals from
station **b** void over canyon **c** domestic check-
in desks **d** domestic departures security
e domestic boarding lounge **f** baggage
collection **g** domestic arrivals lobby
h escalators to concessions level
i immigration (international arrivals)
j quarantine **k** international departures
lounges **l** 'swing gate' boarding lounges.

5 Ground floor plan of international arrivals
and baggage handling: **a** arrivals pick up
b canyon floor **c** customs **d** international
baggage collection **e** international baggage
handling **f** domestic baggage handling
g customs, immigration and quarantine
administration **h** airlines' administration
building **i** domestic bus lounge **j** international
bus lounge **k** airline offices **l** garage for
ground support vehicles.

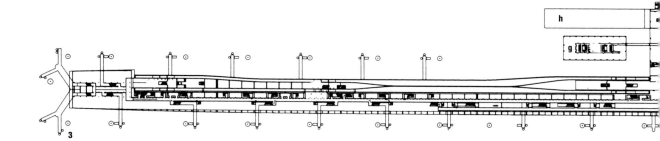

3

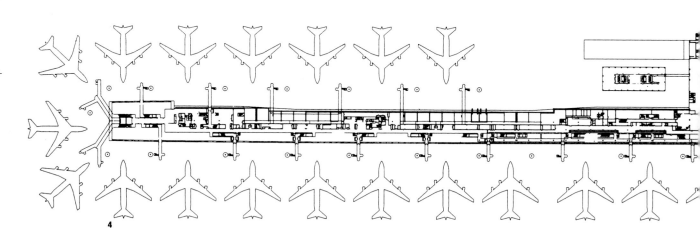

4

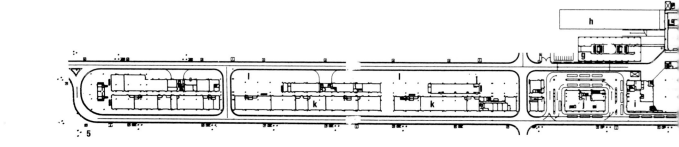

5

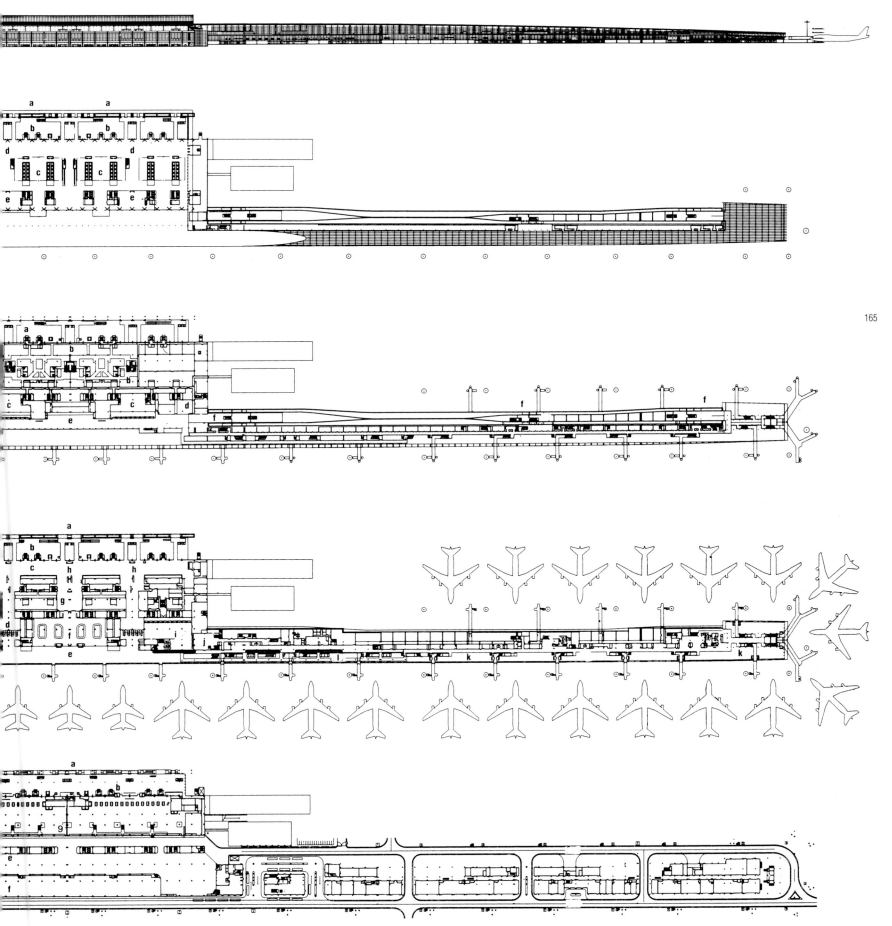

Geometry

The most immediately striking aspect of the Kansai terminal, inside as well as out, is the softly billowing curves, which give it grace and poise, stressing both the fluid continuities and the finiteness of its form. In the introduction to this project, it was discussed how the curves were adopted for more than formal and aesthetic reasons: the main trusses are arched for structural efficiency, and are asymmetric so as to entrain the air-jets blown into the international departures hall (p 000); the curves also ensure that sight lines from the control tower are not obscured, as flight controllers must be able to watch all planes wherever they are. The downwards sweep of the main terminal block roof towards the airside helps achieve this, as do the downward curves along the length of the boarding wing (where the view at the north wing tip is the critical constraint).

The curves bring further benefits, not least in giving the directionality of form that aids orientation inside. But even more important than the curves' contribution to the design solution, is what is achieved by the geometry devised to generate them. This provides the discipline that allowed all aspects of the building (skin, structure, space and services) to be so extremely tightly integrated, and for an extraordinary degree of standardization of components.

The geometric solution finally adopted evolved from that of the competition scheme. It combines uni-directional curved surfaces (derived as tangential arcs of cylinders of differing radii) and toroidal two-directional curved surfaces (derived from the rotation of a curve, that is again made up of tangential arcs of differing radii). But unlike the competition scheme, which was covered by a series of independent roofs each with their own structure, the final design is covered by a single roof in which the differing geometries sweep seamlessly into each other, as do the supporting structural systems.

A crucial problem lay in marrying the two-directional

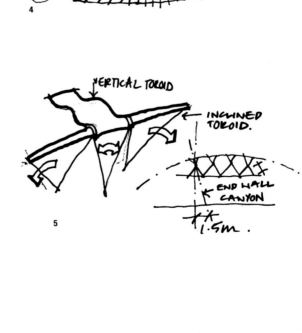

VERTICAL TOROID

INCLINED TOROID.

END WALL CANYON

1·5m.

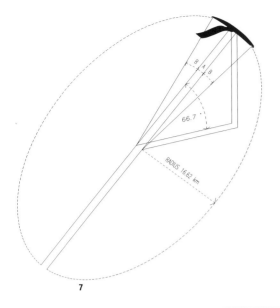

7

Kansai International Airport Terminal

Geometry.

1 Diagram showing curves of roof and structure generated as arcs of different radii.

2–6 Diagrams of evolution of geometric solution: **2** competition scheme with boarding wing as part of toroid and other parts as constant-section extrusions of single-directional curves, but no integration between systems **3** boarding wings generated by rotating and trimming a constant section, but warped surfaces and no repetition of cladding panels **4** single toroid, but each end of canyon 3 metres off grid **5** two tangential toroids, but outward lean of gable-end glazing and differing lengths of structural props **6** final solution with central portion as constant-section extrusion and toroidal boarding wings.

7 Diagram showing how boarding wing is generated as top of sloping toroid of enormous radius that barely emerges above island.

8, **9**, **12** Stills from computer animation showing derivation of geometry.

10 Computer perspective of final roof geometry.

11 Computer study of aborted geometric solution in which roofs of boarding wing and main terminal block sweep into each other in plan as well as section.

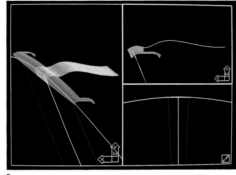

8

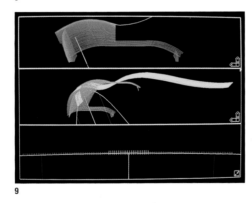

9

curves of the boarding wing with the uni-directional ones of the main terminal block. This problem was not made any easier by the fact that the structural ribs of the boarding wing all lean at different angles as they radiate from the common centre from which the toroid is generated. Various solutions were attempted before eventually settling for what now seems like the sole obvious and inevitable one.

One early solution attempted was that the middle part of the building should be generated pretty much as it is in the final scheme: both the main terminal block and the central portion of the boarding wing under a single roof formed from tangential arcs of cylinders. The boarding wing then swept away from this in plan and section, its form generated by rotating a constant curve (itself made up of tangential arcs), rather than progressively sliding such a curve against horizontal and vertical axes, as was used to generate the toroid. However, this complex form proved impossible to rationalize and clad with repetitive units, and so was soon abandoned.

Then an attempt was made to generate the whole roof, that of the main terminal block as well as the boarding wing, as part of a single inclined toroid of rather complex outer profile. This presented several major problems. Not only the wing ribs, but the primary trusses would have had to lean too. And within the 150-metre depth of the main terminal between the airside and the landside of the canyon, the structural grid would have been radial too, with the canyon being some 3 metres shorter than its equivalent stretch of the airside.

The next solution tried used two toroids, the boarding wing generated by an inclined ring and the main terminal block by a vertical one. Nevertheless,

there were still problems. The primary trusses were now parallel again, but they still leant at different angles so that each inclined prop would have had to be slightly different. Also, the gable-end glazing would have had to slope outwards towards the top, and yet also take up huge deflections.

Eventually it was decided that the roof of the main terminal block should continue to be generated geometrically as portions of cylinders of differing radii, and that the central section of the boarding wing in front of the main terminal block should be constant in section. The extensions of the wing on either side of this would remain toroidal. This may sound like a bit of a fudge, but visually, as resolved and built, it works brilliantly. Seen from the airside and on the ground, the slow curve over the immense length of the boarding wing seems almost to be an illusion, some trick of perspective. The contrast of the flat ridge of the central portion gives some definition to the curve, and also provides some relief in its relentless progress.

Conceptually, the boarding wing is cut from the top of a ring of 16.4-kilometre radius and inclined at 68.2 degrees to the horizontal, that barely emerges from the surface of the island. Strictly speaking, this ring has been bisected in the vertical plane and its two halves slid apart by 300 metres to make way for the extruded non-toroidal portion in front of the main terminal building. The uni-directional curves of the roof, from that of the landside overhang to that over the airside of the boarding wing, are defined as tangential arcs of

167

10

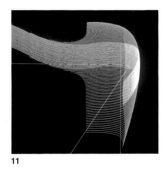

11

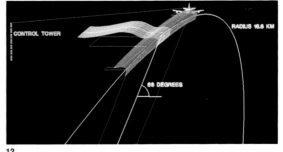

12

1

Kansai International Airport Terminal
Geometry.

1 Swooping curves of roof and structure seen from departures level road.

2 Sydney Opera House by Jørn Utzon: precedent of a design disciplined by repetitive geometric units, though here the spherical geometry results in mismatch between external form and internal space.

3 Curves of boarding wing and main terminal block are entirely clad in identical rectangular tiles.

4 Early study of geometry of boarding wing seen end-on.

5 Section shows tight integration of skin, structure, space and services achieved by geometric solution.

eleven different radii, and that of the airside glazing as another two arcs. The cross section of the toroidal curve, to which the boarding-wing ribs conform, is generated as arcs of four different radii. This constant curve is progressively slid downwards and backwards against conceptual vertical and horizontal axes to generate the two-directional curve.

The geometric discipline of the curves and their cladding has its origins in the Sydney Opera House, on which Rice had worked as a young man. Here, Arups had to find a geometric discipline for the forms of Jørn Utzon's shells that would allow them to be cast and clad in repetitive units. Rice, who was a good mathematician as well as a brilliant engineer, remained fascinated with novel and exotic geometries throughout his life. Also working on the opera house was a Japanese architect, Uzo Mikami, whose writings about this experience had made a great impression on Okabe before he left Japan. For Mikami, architecture and engineering draw on both the well of personal genius and the ever increasing wealth of common knowledge. Of particular importance, he predicted, would be new discoveries in mathematics, particularly those

that could generate complex forms through the repetition of simple units.

Another influence on Piano, Rice and Okabe's interest in geometry was the experience of working on the IBM Travelling Pavilion (Volume One p 110), when they came into contact with the work on fractals by Benoît Mandelbrot, then still a relatively unknown researcher at IBM. (Discovering fractals and debating their relevance with Rice, as well as with musician friends, provided intellectual confirmation for Piano of his instinctual tendency to provide perceptual richness and grain by composing buildings with elements, sometimes with a degree of 'self-similarity', at a whole hierarchy of scales.)

The geometry of Kansai owes nothing to fractals (though at one stage during the competition Okabe tried to use a series of diminishing roofs inspired by fractals, an idea that did not appeal to Piano), but Okabe claims that knowledge of this work freed up the design team to exploit a discipline that conformed to new understandings of the geometric order of nature. Significantly, toroids, to which magnetic fields, convection currents and many fruits conform, are among the most pervasive forms in nature. Though the form was not selected for this reason, it confirms, at some instinctual level at least, the soundness of the approach applied here and resonates with Piano's constant dream of bringing technology and nature into a profound and complex harmony.

Though both the Sydney Opera House shells and the Kansai roofs are rigorously

disciplined geometrically so as to be constructed and clad in repetitive units, there is a crucial difference between them. In Okabe's words: 'The geometry of Sydney is rigid; that of Kansai is soft.' The rigid spherical geometry adopted at Sydney resulted in a very considerable mismatch between internal space and external volume. But Kansai's more tolerant geometry could be adjusted to result in a roof that conforms so exactly to the spaces inside that it seems draped over them, or perhaps, more accurately, pushed out like the skin of a balloon by the swelling spaces inside.

Moreover, the basic geometry was easily adjusted, with no loss of discipline, to required changes, such as when the roof had to be lowered by three metres to improve the view from the control tower. The tolerant geometry also allows the lowest rows of roof tiles on the airside of the boarding wing to peel away from the glazing, which also conforms to the toroidal geometry, so as to project and shade the glass. Softness, gentleness, lightness, along with discipline, are key qualities always sought by Piano. All of them are beautifully realized by Kansai's geometry.

The geometry also achieves a goal that originated with the very first visits to the still non-existent site: that the flat-topped artificial island should not be married with an equally abstract building. Though obviously artificial and man-made, the building would also somehow seem organic, thus inverting the normal process of placing an artificial building on a natural site. In retrospect, the analogy for Okabe is of placing an organic sculpture on an abstract plinth. The sculpture he associates with it is Brancusi's *Bird in Flight*, its spare curves giving the same sense of graceful soaring as those of the terminal.

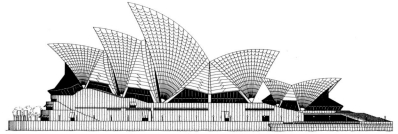

2

3

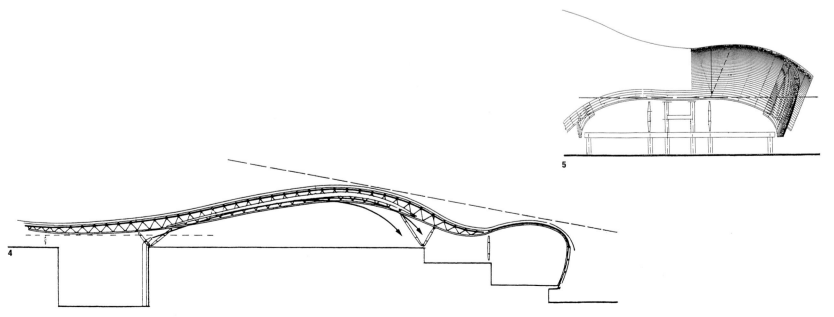

4

5

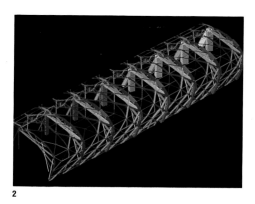

2

Structure

Kansai International Airport Terminal

Structure.

1 View from transit lounge up into international departures hall. Sloping props support main trusses, between which are suspended by the scoops that entrain the blown air that ventilates the space.

2 Computer analysis of forces in structure of boarding wing. Colour denotes type of force, and width its intensity.

3 Model of structural bay shows how main trusses, supported on sloping props, sweep into ribs of boarding wing. Over these is a secondary structure of purlins and cross-bracing.

4 Section of international departures lounge looking towards airside.

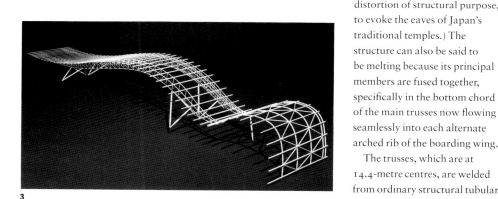

3

Despite the dramatic curving shapes and the huge spans of the main trusses with their shapely props, most of the structure is, in engineering terms, fairly conventional, as are the materials used. The exception is the structure of the boarding wing with its slender curved and tie-stiffened tubular ribs that act as the diaphragms of a lattice shell structure. Other significant aspects of the structure are the subordination of the shapes of its major elements to those of the outer skin (an inversion of the usual hierarchy), the differing kinds and amount of movement the structure must cope with, and the visual and empathetic role the structure plays in helping people relate to the building.

If the geometry is soft, then, in Okabe's words again, 'the structure is melting'. By this he means that its forms defer to the overriding geometric discipline. The main structural elements take their shape from those of the skin above and space below, though with no compromise to their structural effectiveness and integrity. This can be seen in the shaping of the main trusses of the main terminal building. These are asymmetrically arched and 4 metres at their deepest, where they span 82.8 metres between the sloping props that support them. The trusses then taper to lesser depths for the counter-curved spans beyond these props and the 6-metre cantilevers of the landside porch beyond the external vertical columns – which, in fact, only act in tension to prevent wind lift. (The ends of these cantilevers, with the last rows of tiles over-sailing them on exposed and tapering rafters, have been designed, again with little distortion of structural purpose, to evoke the eaves of Japan's traditional temples.) The structure can also be said to be melting because its principal members are fused together, specifically in the bottom chord of the main trusses now flowing seamlessly into each alternate arched rib of the boarding wing.

The trusses, which are at 14.4-metre centres, are welded from ordinary structural tubular steel and have an inverted triangular section, the angles of which remain constant no matter how the sides vary in length with the depth of the truss. So as not to interrupt the visual flow of these chords, they retain a constant external diameter (top chords, 267 millimetres; bottom chord, 406 millimetres), while the walls of the tubes vary in thickness as required structurally. For similar reasons, the 139-millimetre tubes of the diagonal webbing are welded to the top rather than sides of the bottom chord. These trusses are supported by splayed tubular legs, which are wider in diameter in their central portions than towards their ends, where they join either the bottom chord or the base plate that four of them share. (The actual structural element's rather clumsy form, which is necessary to resist bending moments, is concealed by elegant cigar-shaped, glass-reinforced cement fire-proof covers.) Along the gable ends of the main terminal building roof

171

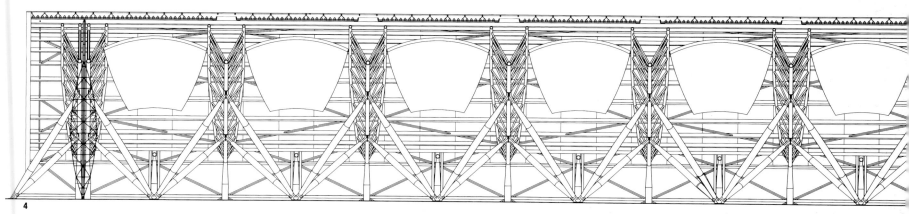

4

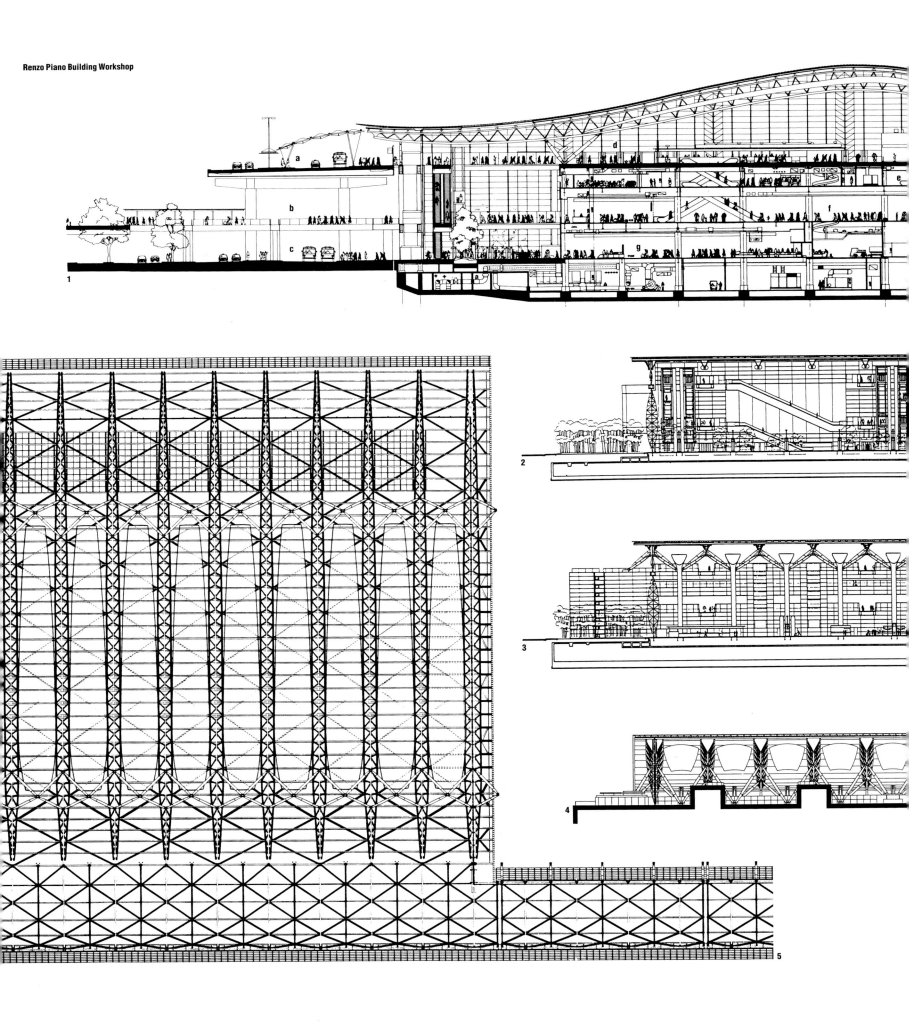

1

a

b

c

d

e

f

g

2

3

4

5

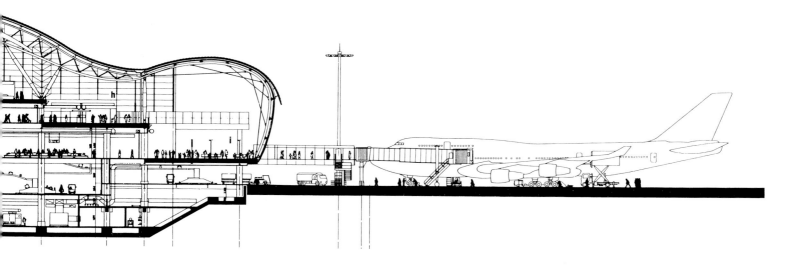

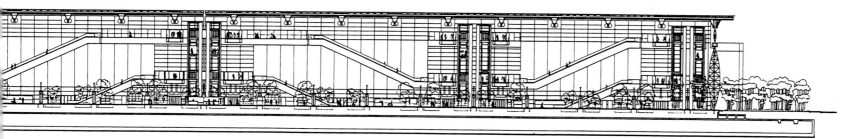

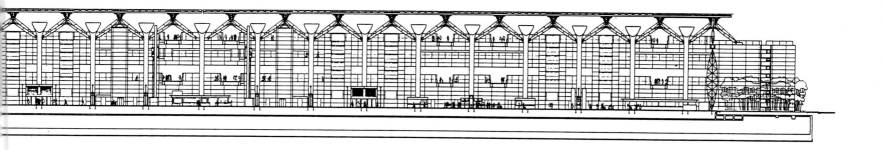

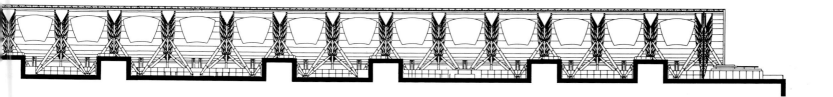

Kansai International Airport Terminal

1 Landside–airside section of main terminal block: **a** departures drop off **b** bridges from station **c** arrivals pick up **d** international departures hall **e** concessions and duty free **f** domestic arrivals and departures **g** international arrivals hall **h** transit lounge **i** domestic boarding lounge.

2 Portion of reflected ceiling plan.

3 Section of canyon looking to landside.

4 Section of canyon looking to airside.

5 Section of international departures lounge looking to airside.

Kansai International Airport Terminal

Details of structure and cladding of roof
of main terminal block and domestic
boarding lounge.

1 Plan and

2 elevation of landside end of main truss.

3 Landside eaves.

4 Canyon and landside of international
departures hall.

5 Airside of international departures hall.

6 Transit lounge.

7 Boarding wing.

8 Plan and **9** elevation of airside of main
truss where lower chord continues as
boarding-wing rib: **a** 1mm thick, dull-finished
stainless-steel tile **b** double-layer steel roof
(top layer 1mm thick and pvf2-coated, lower
layer 0.8mm thick) with 200mm rib and 16kg
per square metre glass wool insulation
between layers **c** 15mm rock wool acoustic-
absorbent ceiling board **d** 267.4mm diameter
tubular steel top chord **e** 406.4mm diameter
lower chord **f** 400 x 300mm purlin **g** 400 x
400mm purlin **h** steel gutter **i** 1.5mm thick
perforated and dull-finished stainless-steel
tile **j** 12mm laminated heat-absorbing glass
k 12mm glass **l** 250mm square hollow-
section secondary structure **m** 406.4 mm
diameter tubular rib **n** tension tie.

174

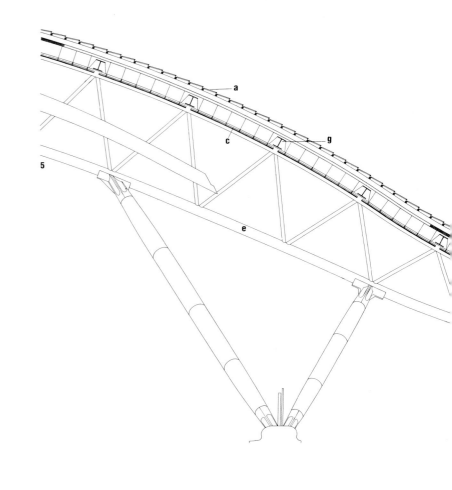

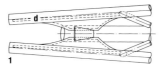

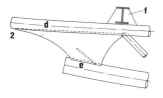

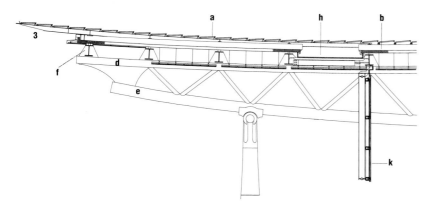

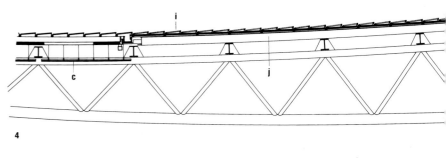

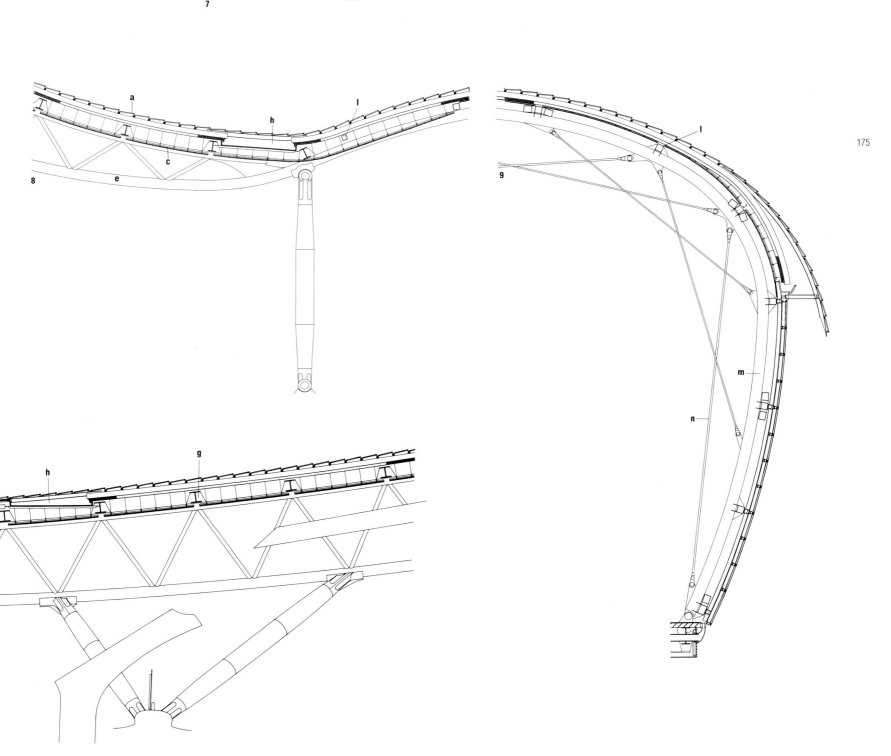

6

7

8

9

175

1

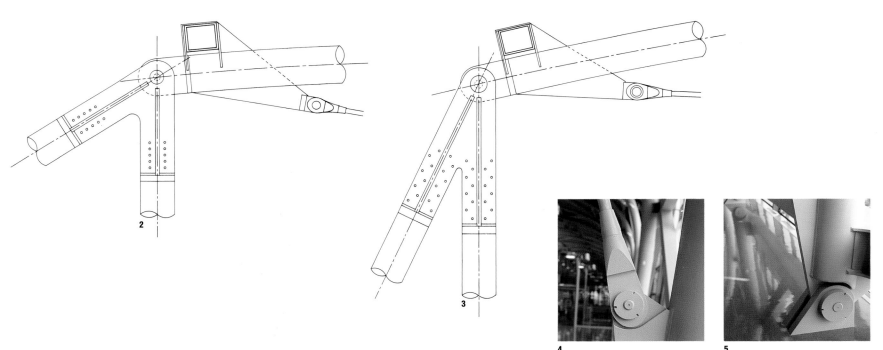

2

3

4

5

6

Instead of the cantilevered brackets of the competition design, which were too rigid, there is a continuous secondary structure that spans across the top chords of the trusses. This is designed to absorb the energy of the lateral forces that are characteristic of earthquakes. Until a fairly late stage, this secondary structure was to have been exposed and made up of box sections with extended

horizontal flanges. However, the subcontractors balked at the complexity of making these. To cut costs, standard I-sections have been used instead with additional cross-bracing and the whole secondary structure (apart from that between the top chords of the trusses) is hidden by a suspended ceiling. This is a solution that the architects now prefer as less busy and because it does not distract from the flow of the trusses.

Despite the loss of the rib-like brackets, the primary structure remains decidedly zoomorphic. This is fortuitous rather than intentional. Piano prefers the structural components of his buildings to have a strong identity of their own, and a sense of organic life that helps people to relate empathetically to them. Nevertheless, this does not imply that these structural elements should be recognizably organic in form.

The ribs of the boarding wing are also quite different from those of the competition design. If these were still to act as independent elements, they would have had to be up to

2 metres deep, and so utterly at odds with the intention that the wing be very light: as light in structure as it is abundantly lit. (If seen obliquely when looking along the length of the wing, these original deep ribs would have largely obscured a view of the glass.) If the final design of the main terminal block's roof is, apart from its zoomorphic shapes, conventional in structure, then the wing is the building's most sophisticated piece of structural engineering.

The structural elements of the boarding wing now work synergetically as a lattice shell. Loads are distributed through all elements of the structure and carried lengthwise along the wing rather than by each rib, which, with tension ties on each alternate one, now functions as a stiffening diaphragm for the shell. (The tie-bars were adjusted to length as the ribs lay on the ground prior to assembly,

Kansai International Airport Terminal
Boarding wing structure.

1 Curving ribs articulate space of boarding wing.

2, 3 Detail of junction of structural elements at head of landside of boarding wing. Here rib is pinned to external column and prop while tension tie is pinned to steel plate that extends through slot cut through rib to be welded also to rectangular secondary members. **2** shows condition at end of boarding wing and **3** condition beside main terminal block.

4 Detail of pinned junction of tension tie to rib.

5 Detail of junction of rib to floor of boarding wing.

6–8 Views up into boarding wing showing ribs, tension ties and secondary structure.

9–12 Details showing some of the sequence of angles at which ribs meet floor of boarding wing, **9** being at centre of building and **12** at end of boarding wing. Ribs also lean progressively in lateral direction to align radially with toroidal ring.

7

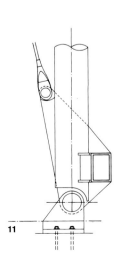
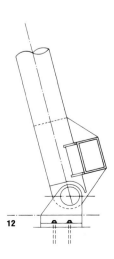

8

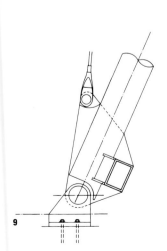

9

10

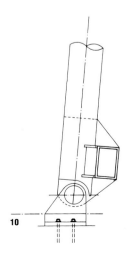

11

12

1

Kansai International Airport Terminal

Assembly of structure.

1 Foot of boarding-wing rib as test assembled.

2 Sloping props supporting main trusses before fire-proofing.

3 Stabilizing masts for gable-end glazing of main terminal block being manufactured in France.

4 Joint being secured in purlin of secondary structure close to where it passes over top chord of main truss.

3

2

and they only come into play as live loads deflect the structure.) The curve of these ribs is shaped both for the desired architectural form (with forward leaning, self-shading glazing and a sensual contrast between tight and less tightly curved portions) and to minimize bending moments within each rib. As a result the largest, central ribs could be made from the same 406-millimetre-diameter tube used for the bottom chords of the main terminal block's trusses.

As with the competition design, each of these ribs leans progressively away from the vertical, as its distance from the central main terminal block increases, so as to be radially aligned with the centre of the toroidal ring 16.8 kilometres below the earth. This allows each rib to follow an identical curve, and all to be manufactured on the same jig (though they are of different lengths, being progressively trimmed at top and bottom). The differing angles of inclination of each rib are achieved by changing the angles of the base plates to which they are pinned; and the diminishing length of the ribs with the tapering height of the wings allows the ribs to decrease in diameter to 355 millimetres and then 318 millimetres.

The toroidal geometry and leaning ribs allow the secondary elements also to be almost entirely identical. These are of 250-millimetre-square-sectioned hollow steel. As with the main terminal block, the secondary structure is not in the same plane as the primary elements. Although this solution results in considerable eccentric stresses on some members, as

well as more complex structural calculations, it brings ample visual rewards: it allows each rib to read clearly within the space and so articulate its immense length. Very thick (60 millimetre) steel plates secure the tie-bars, secondary structure and pin-joints at either ends of the ribs. Cutting the bent ribs and welding the plates in place without distorting the curvature was sufficient challenge as to bring very high tender prices from the Japanese steel fabricators. The ribs were eventually made in Britain by Robert Watson of Bolton. Each rib was transported in three pieces in containers to the site where the pieces were welded together, achieving a precision of within a 0.5 millimetre, with overall tolerances of only 1 millimetre.

In nearly all of Piano's buildings, structure is more than

4

5

Kansai International Airport Terminal

Boarding-wing structure.

5 Ribs lying on site prior to assembly.

6 Ribs in place awaiting completion of secondary structure.

7 Junction of rib and secondary structure.

8–10 Details of junctions of secondary structure.

7

a technical concern. It plays an architectural role that far exceeds merely making things stand up. Typically, structure is exposed and utterly intrinsic to the character of the spaces and the identity of the building. Many of the Building Workshop's designs can be identified by a glance at a structural component alone. Structure also serves in several ways as an intermediary between you and the building, not least by furnishing elements of graspable intermediate scale. This is especially essential in spaces as vast and fluid as those at Kansai.

Structure is also often shaped to elicit an empathetic response in the user. Sometimes, as with the arched main trusses and bowed boarding-wing ribs, the forms are so tensely sprung that you feel inside yourself the forces within them. Often this identification is intensified by using shapely components, such as the props with shared bases that support the main trusses, which you imagine, even if only subliminally, touching or caressing with pleasure. Piano talks a lot about tactility, by which he means an imagined sense of touch as much as an actual one. Sometimes these components are biomorphic, like the vaguely bone-like props, or the dinosaur skeletons these form together with the arched trusses, which extend over the canyon and then outside as tails, and in the other direction run into the boarding-wing ribs to bend down like the necks of grazing brontosauruses.

The combination of all these factors gives the structure a sense of organic life, so that it becomes an animate and companionable presence to

6

which the user relates at one level or another. You are greeted by the tail-like cantilevers supporting the eaves, guided inside and over a bridge to be welcomed by the portal formed by props. From here you are urged forward by the trusses and then led downwards by the boarding-wing ribs. Reaching the floor of this and turning to proceed along it you are almost passed from one rib to the next, each made clearly visible by the tapering geometry.

Although the structure at Kansai is especially effective in mediating scale and eliciting an empathetic response, these are strategies Piano has exploited often before. However, the sense of structure leading you through and between each space breaks new ground for him and the Building Workshop, if not indeed for architecture in general.

179

8

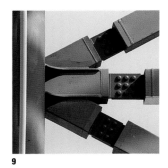

9

10

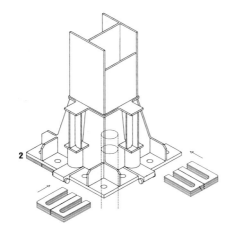

180 **Kansai International Airport Terminal**

Structural movement.

1 Foot of one of the 900 columns that can each be adjusted to cope with differential settlement.

2 Isometric of foot of column with shims used to adjust height.

3 Expansion joint in airside glazing and roof.

4,5 Details of expansion joint in: **4** airside glazing seen in plan; **5** roof seen in section.

6,7 Where bottom chord of truss penetrates canyon glazing, cover plate allows for 1.2 metres of movement.

8 Concertina gasket absorbs movement where landside wall of canyon meets gable wall.

8 Detail where props support double truss at gable and of main terminal block, showing how movement is absorbed at head of vertical truss that stabilizes the glazing that extends up between halves of truss.

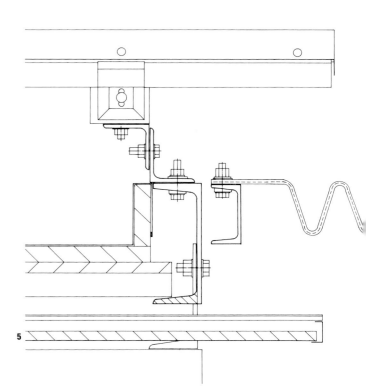

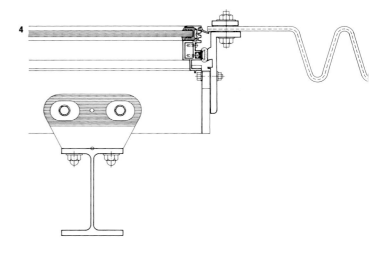

8

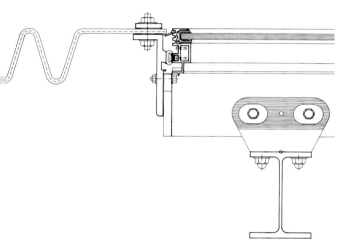

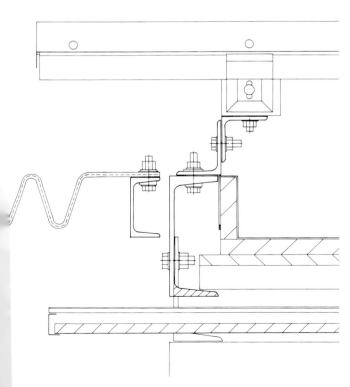

Structural movement

A key challenge in the design of both structure and cladding was the accommodation of different kinds and amounts of movement. Besides those due to dead weights, which are quite considerable, with spans up to 82.8 metres, structural deflections include those due to live loads such as typhoons, in which horizontal and up-lift wind loads are accompanied by huge weights of deluging rain, as well as frequent, and sometimes immense, seismic stresses. (Japanese building codes distinguish between two classes of earthquake: those of fairly frequent occurrence, which, though fairly strong, should cause the building no damage; and exceptional ones when limited damage to non-structural elements is allowed. The 1995 earthquake that destroyed so much of Kobe was a very strong one of the latter sort. Though the terminal was close to its epicentre, it suffered no damage whatever, except for a few external paving slabs being slightly misaligned.) The terminal's structural design also has to cope with a great deal of differential settlement.

Movement is absorbed in many ways and in many parts of the building. Dividing it into sections of 150–200 metres are expansion gaps of 450–600-millimetres width, which can absorb movement due to temperature change, earthquakes and uneven settlement. Where the expansion gaps interrupt the roof or glazing, they are made weathertight with concertina rubber elements. The head of the gable-end glazing, on the sides of the international departures hall, slides up and down between the double trusses that edge the main terminal block roof. Because the structure of the landside of the canyon is independent of that of the multi-level inner building, beams that span between them make allowance for horizontal movement of 0.5 metre. For the same reason, where the landside glazing is penetrated by the bottom chords of the main trusses, steel plates over a slot in the glass allow for horizontal movement of 1.2 metres.

As the island is so new, its whole surface and the buildings on it are settling. The terminal is lighter than the earth it displaces, so it is settling less than the runways. Because it floats on basements (housing air-conditioning and other plant), the multi-storey main terminal block (which is 8 tons per square metre lighter than the 17 tons per square metre excavated for these basements) sinks most slowly of all, despite an added ballast of 360,000 tons of dense iron ore. Piano's constant quest for structural lightness, which intuitively might seem correct when building on unstable soil, compounds the settlement problems here, though it does lessen the lateral earthquake loads.

To cope with this differential in settlement, the height of the base of all 900 columns is monitored by computer and adjusted (usually lowered) by jacks and the removal of spacing shims. This will need to continue for many years, if not indefinitely. Another technical constraint is that the levels cannot be aligned visually, by laser or other means. Over the building's immense length, the curvature of the earth becomes a significant factor. One end is about 70 millimetres below a straight horizontal extended from the other end, so heights have to be checked with interconnected water levels.

181

9

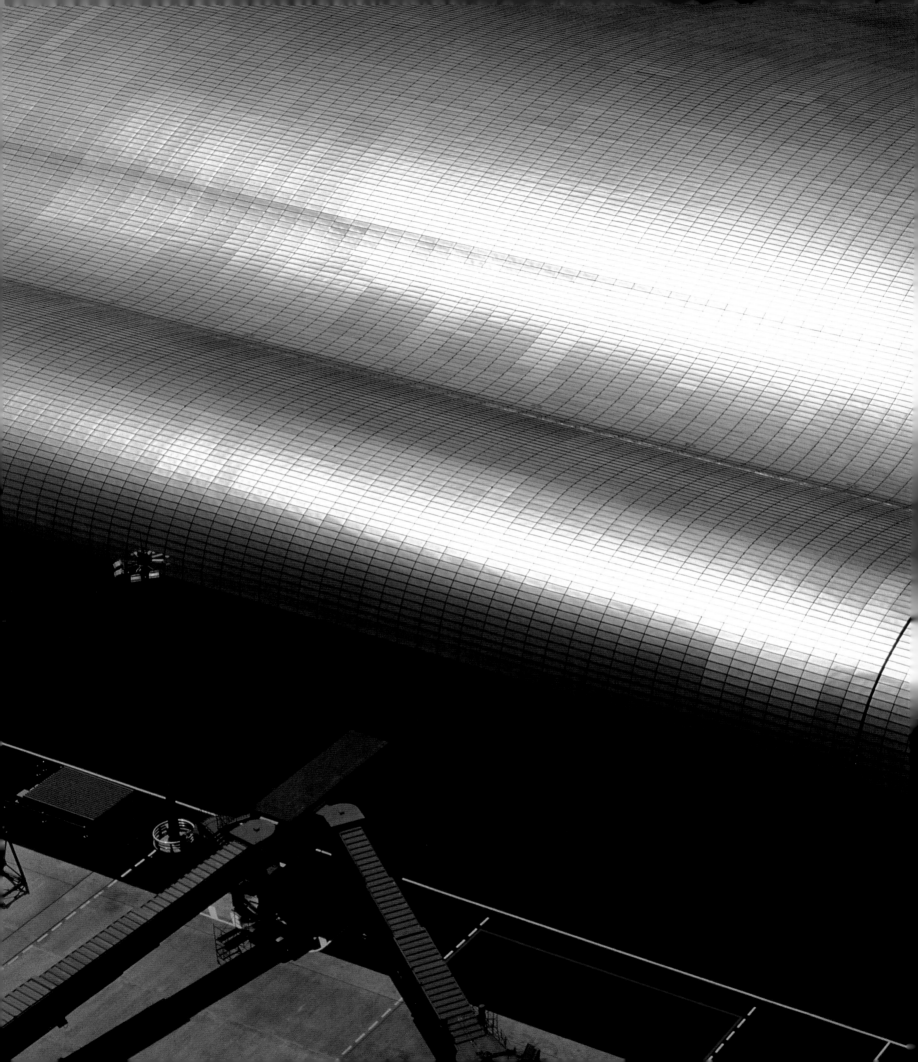

Cladding and glazing

A prime benefit of, and major reason for, adopting the geometric discipline that the building's outer envelope conforms to is that all the complex curves could be clad in repetitive rectangular units. All 82,000 stainless-steel roof tiles are identical, except those on either side of the expansion joints, as are the nearly 5,000 glass panes on the airside of the boarding wing, except those that meet the floor. Strictly speaking, the exact shape required for the roof tiles and glass panes on the toroidally curved parts was trapezoidal; but as the difference in length of

the top and bottom would not have exceeded 5 millimetres, this was absorbed easily in the joints.

The roof is one of a series of double-layered roofs developed by the Building Workshop, the first of which was used for the Bercy 2 Shopping Centre (Volume Two p 16). This also clad a double-curved roof in stainless-steel repetitive rectangular panels, though there the smaller scale had necessitated some thirty different panel sizes. With both roofs, the stainless-steel units are only an outer layer over an inner roof that is waterproof and insulated. The outer roof protects the inner one from abrasion by wind-borne particles (at Bercy, these come from the nearby TGV tracks and elevated motorway), while its shiny surface reflects the sun, and shades an airspace that is intermediate in temperature between that of the interior and exterior. This contributes to the thermal performance of the whole roof and to the longevity

of the inner layer. A further asset was that the inner roof could be laid quickly and early on to seal the building, while the outer roof was laid with precision later when it would sustain no accidental damage.

Besides these technical benefits there are aesthetic ones too, beyond the precision of the laying and the pristine condition of the roof on completion. Because water only washes over a single tile before draining behind that below it, there is less chance for staining, or for dirt to build up. (Remaining clean and shiny, the roof also retains its heat reflective capacity.) The repetitive pattern of the tiles gives a sense of scale and visual order that allows a better appreciation of the roof's size and shape.

The terminal's inner roof is made out of two layers of sheet steel folded into troughs and coated with polyvinylfluoridine (pvf2) (an outer layer of 1 millimetre and inner of 0.8 millimetre), with glass fibre insulation sandwiched between them. The outer roof's tiles are of a very high-grade ferrite-type stainless steel that can resist salt corrosion and abrasion from typhoon-borne grit. Folded from 1-millimetre-thick sheets,

specially rolled with a matt finish so that reflections do not dazzle pilots or the control tower, the tiles are held in place by brackets or clip tingles bolted to the ridges of the inner roof. (The consortia of contractors building the different halves of the building used slightly different concealed details, though what is visible is identical.) The size of the tiles, which are 1.8 x 0.6 metres, visually suits the huge scale of the roof. They comfortably accommodate the curves and geometric tolerances and, weighing 10 kilograms each, were easily carried by a single worker. In high winds, the uplift caused by the aerodynamic shape of the main terminal roof will cause the large thin tiles to flex and lift upwards at their middles.

Along the roof's air and landside edges, rafter-like elements are attached to the outside of the inner roof and cantilever beyond it. These carry a few rows of tiles, the underneath of which are exposed, to create delicate eaves on both of the building's long sides. On the boarding wing, these last rows of tiles overhang and shade the top of both the land and airside glazing. In the latter case, the projecting top flanges of the I-sectioned rafters provides a delicate punctuation to the shadow below them.

184 **Kansai International Airport Terminal**
The roof.

Previous pages The repetitive rectangular tiles help to give scale and define the form.

1 Fixing of roof tiles on northern half of building: **a** stainless-steel tile **b**, **c** clip tingle **d** sheet steel bracket **e** upper sheet of roof.

2 Folded steel bracket bridges between ribs of outer roof and secures clip tingle.

3 Row of fixing brackets and, to left, tiles secured to them.

4 Fixing of tiles to rafters of eaves on land- and airsides: **a** tile **b**, **c** clip tingle **d** rafter.

1

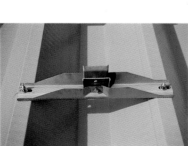

2

3

4

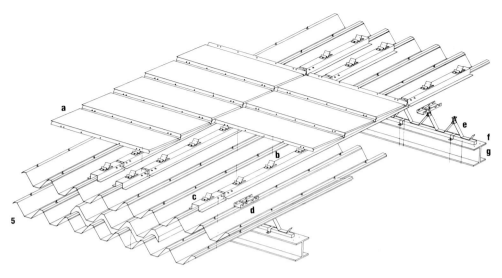

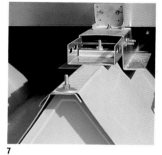

7

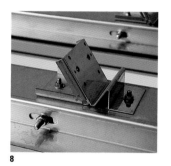

8

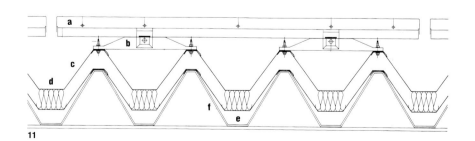

6

Roof.

5, **7**, **8** show details used on southern half of building; **6**, **9**, **10**, **11** shows system used on northern half.

5 Exploded isometric of roof construction: **a** tile **b** fixing cleat folded from 2mm stainless steel **c**, **d** folded from 2.5mm stainless steel **e** 50 x 4.5mm folded steel frame **f** 60mm square hollow section **g** 400 x 400mm purlin.

6 Fixing rafters and clip tingles for eaves overhang on landside of boarding wing.

7 Detail of roof assembly.

8 Cleat for fixing tiles.

9 Folded sheet steel roofing being laid and fixed to folded steel frames on top of purlins.

10, **11** Detail sections of double layer roof **a** 1 mm thick dull-finished stainless-steel tile **b** folded steel fixing bracket **c** 1 mm pvf2-coated folded sheet steel **d** 16kg/ square metre glass wool insulation **e** 0.8 mm folded sheet steel **f** folded steel supporting frame secured to purlin.

9

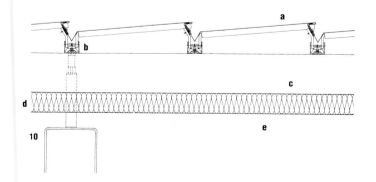

10

11

Renzo Piano Building Workshop

1

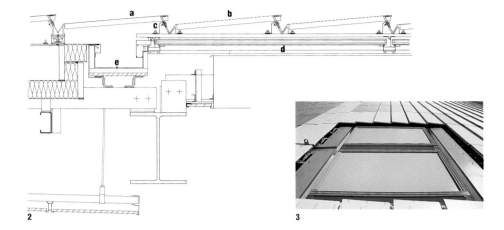

2

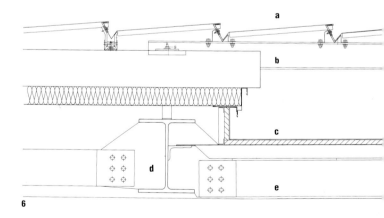

3

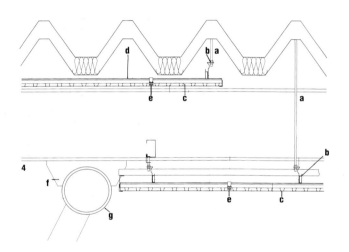

4

5

6

Kansai International Airport Terminal

Roof and ceiling details of central terminal block.

1 Except where interrupted by the main trusses, the canyon is lit by a continuous rooflight.

2 Section of landside edge of rooflight over canyon (scale 1:20): **a** 1mm stainless-steel tile **b** 1.5mm perforated stainless-steel tile **c** clip tingle **d** aluminium skylight **e** 0.6mm galvanized folded steel gutter.

3 Rooflight not yet covered by perforated tiles.

4 Detail of change in ceiling level over main truss (scale 1:20): **a** 9mm diameter suspension bolt **b** hanger **c** 15mm rock wool acoustic-absorbent board **d** aluminium T-bar **e** aluminium H-bar **f** gusset plate **g** top chord of truss.

5 Directly over the main trusses the ceiling is raised above of and exposing the secondary structure.

6 Gutter in valley between landside eaves and canyon (scale 1:20): **a** 1mm tile **b** 150 x 75 x 5 x 5mm pvf2-coated steel I-section **c** 0.6mm galvanized pressed steel gutter **d** 400 x 300 x 12 x 19mm purlin **e** 200 x 200mm brace.

7 Laying the folded sheet steel roofing with tubular rib visible through expansion gap.

8 Gutter on airside of canyon rooflight (scale 1:40): **a** 1mm tile **b** 1.5mm perforated tile **c** 150 x 75 x 5 x 7mm pvf2-coated I-section **d** 0.6mm pressed galvanized steel gutter **e** 400 x 400mm purlin **f** 200 x 200 x 6mm brace.

9 Landside eaves.

10 End of landside eaves (scale 1: 30): **a** 1mm tile **b** 2mm pressed stainless-steel trim **c** 175 x 90 x 5 x 8mm pvf2-coated steel I-section **d** 400 x 300mm purlin

11 Gable-end with overhanging eaves.

12, 13 Gable-end eaves (scale 1: 20): **a** tile **b** clip tingle **c** 2 mm pressed stainless-steel base for clip tingle **d** 60 x 40 x 3mm stainless steel L **e** 1 mm pvf2-coated pressed steel closer **f** 125 x 125 x 8mm square hollow section **g** 400 x 300mm purlin

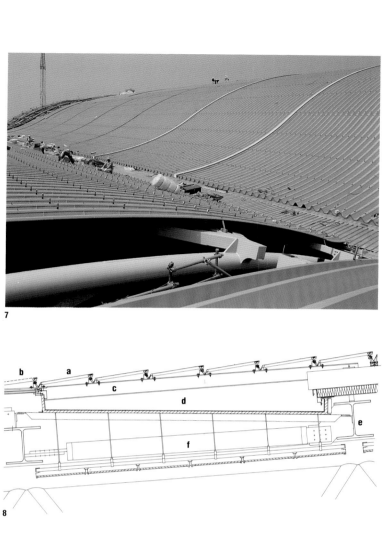

7

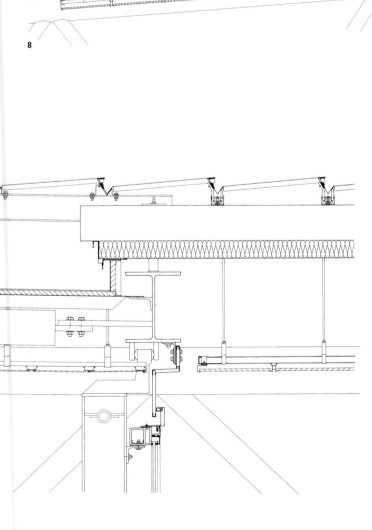

8

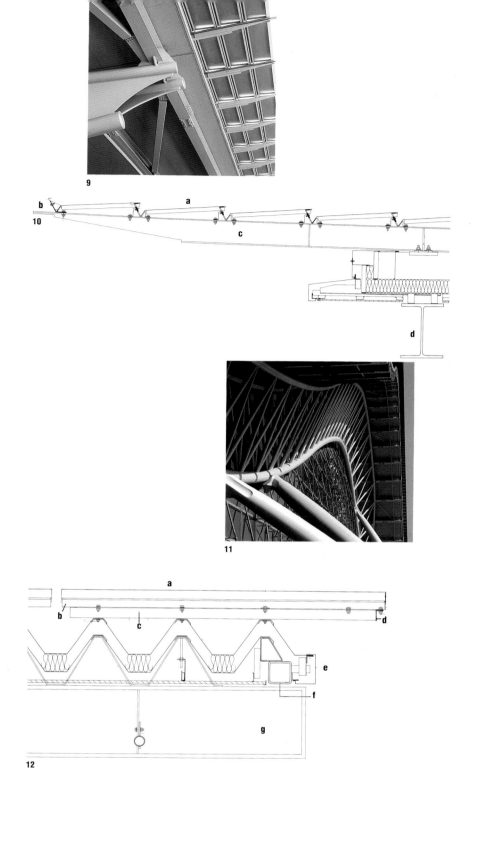

9

10

11

12

13

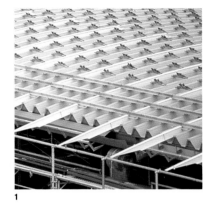

1

2

4

188 **Kansai International Airport Terminal**

Roof and glazing of boarding wing.

1 Fin-rafters project from troughs of ribbed roof to support eaves of tiles along landside.

2 Head of landside wall with overhanging eaves.

3 Detail section of head of landside wall: **a** 1mm stainless-steel tile **b** 150 x 75 x 5 x 7mm fin- rafter **c** 1mm pvf2-coated pressed steel fascia **d** 0.5mm pressed galvanized steel gutter **e** 300 x 250 x 12mm rectangular hollow section **f** neoprene skirt **g** 355.6mm diameter tubular rib **h** mullion.

4 Curved fin-rafters being attached to airside to support sun-shading overhang of tiles.

5, **6** Successive stages of application of roof and glazing.

7 Expansion gap is neatly accommodated in glazing and roof.

8 Close-up in-construction view of point where glazing and roof step up towards tip of boarding wing.

9 Detail section of airside eaves: **a** 1mm stainless-steel tile **b** 148 x 100 x 6 x 9mm pvf2-coated fin-rafter **c** 150 x 75 x 5 x 7mm pvf2-coated I-section **d** 148 x 100 x 6 x 9mm I-section **e** 250 x 250mm square hollow section **f** 148 x 100 x 6 x 9mm I-section mullion **g** 12 mm heat-absorbing glass.

10, **11** Views up under eaves before and after adding tiles and glazing.

3

5

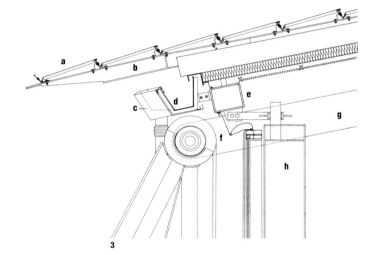

6

7

8

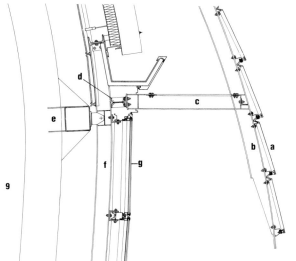

9

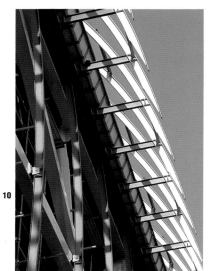

10

11

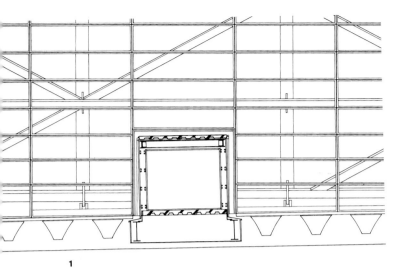

1

Kansai International Airport Terminal
Airside glazing of boarding wing.

Previous pages Lower tiles of roof extend
out to shade head of glazing made up of
rectangular flat panels of tinted glass. Through
the glass can be seen ribs and cross-bracing
of structure; below it are the 'fishtail' inlets that
admit conditioned air to boarding wing.

1 Section of boarding bridge showing how its
entrance is accommodated by glazing seen in
elevation.

2 Peeled-away isometric view showing
assembly of roof and glazing.

3–5 Installation of framed glazing units.

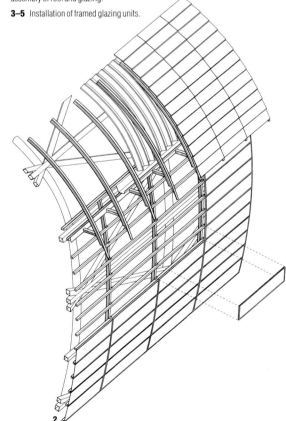

2

The terminal's vast expanses
of glazing presented formidable
problems of design and development. These were resolved in
collaboration with manufacturers in different parts of the
world, who in turn collaborated
with each other. The architects
wanted both the 1.7-kilometre-
long boarding wing and the
gable ends of the main terminal
building, which are up to
18 metres tall, to be glazed in
as smooth and continuous a
manner as possible. Yet, while
always remaining waterproof,
this glazing also has to be able
to deform under earthquake and
wind loads. On the long curved
stretch of airside glazing these
goals have been accomplished
by treating each glass pane as an
independent unit with its own
frame, with the curve taken up
in the joints between these flat
units thus eliminating all other
interruptive frames. On the
gable ends, where protruding
vertical trusses are necessary to
stabilize the large expanses of
glazing, the frames between
the trusses are kept minimal in
shape and size. Another design
constraint was that the airside
glazing of the boarding wing
also has to be an effective
acoustic barrier.

Though the boarding-
wing's glazing units, which are
3.6 x 1.008 metres, are twice
as long as the roof tiles, they
conform to the same geometric
disciplines as the tiles, with
tolerances absorbed in the joints
between units. Thus, these units
are only horizontal in the central
part of the boarding wing.
Elsewhere they follow the long
curves of the toroidal ring and
so meet the boarding-wing floor
at an increasingly steep angle as
they get closer to the wing tip.
The panes that meet the floor
are not rectangular, but specials
made to fit.

This glazing system was developed in collaboration with a
joint venture set up between YKK,
the leading Japanese curtain-
wall company, and Cupples, its
American counterpart. As part
of this process, a full-size prototype of a stretch of glazing was
extensively tested on a rig in
Japan. The Japanese-made,
grey-tinted heat-absorbing glass
is 12 millimetres thick so as to
provide acoustic isolation
from the planes outside. Each
pane came to site in its own
aluminium frame, which was
extruded in the USA, with
neoprene gaskets both securing
the glass and providing
waterproof seals between the
units. Every individual unit,
weighing about 210 kilograms, is
supported top and bottom by
extruded aluminium transoms,
in a way that both takes up the
curves and conceals the transom
from outside. These transoms
are held by brackets bolted to

steel I-section mullions, which
are in turn held by brackets
bolted to the hollow square-
sectioned secondary structure.
The mullions, which are at 3.6-
metre centres, are set so that the
primary structural ribs occur
midway between them.

The glazing of the gable ends
of the main terminal building
uses another system developed
with different manufacturers.
Here, there is no other structure
behind the glazing to use for
support or bracing. And as well
as the deflections in the glazing,
those of the huge truss along its
head also have to be accommodated. There are in fact two
separate stretches of glazing.
A glass wall, 26 metres wide by
17.5 metres high, closes the ends
of the canyon up to a beam that
ties an end of the canyon's landside wall to the floor of the international departures level. Above
this level and below the gable
beam is a second continuous
stretch of glazing 135 metres
long and varying between 6
and 18 metres in height.

The tinted heat-absorbing
glass used here was made in
Belgium by Saint Gobain.
Each pane is 3.6 x 1.16 metres,
weighs 146 kilograms and
is 15.5 millimetres thick (laminated from 8 millimetres of clear
glass and 6 millimetres of grey
solar control glass with four

3

4

5

interlayers of 0.38 millimetres polyvinylbutyl (pvb). In some crucial areas the glass is 17.5 millimetres (as above but with 10 millimetres clear glass). All the panes are held by heavy neoprene gaskets against steel transoms and mullions welded from simple rectangular steel bars.

Each mullion is the central element of, and stiffened by, a vertical bow-string truss. Though these look like masts, they do not function structurally as such, in that the bow-string chords are not tensioned out-riggers to a central compression member. Instead, the central mullion must allow the glass wall to deflect under earthquake loads, and also slide between the double truss at its head so as to accommodate the considerable deflections in this member. The bow-string chords, then, serve as both tension and compression elements. But so that this glass wall should seem as light

and open as possible, each chord is made of paired, machined-steel elements, none of which exceeds 35 millimetres in thickness. Yet the tallest of the vertical trusses along the international departures hall weighs 1.65 tons, and those that close the canyon weigh 2.1 tons.

These very delicate looking bow-string trusses were made, largely by hand, by Eiffel in France and shipped in containers via Antwerp to Kobe, from where they were delivered by barge. Before final manufacture, a prototyped section of the glazed wall had been tested in Italy.

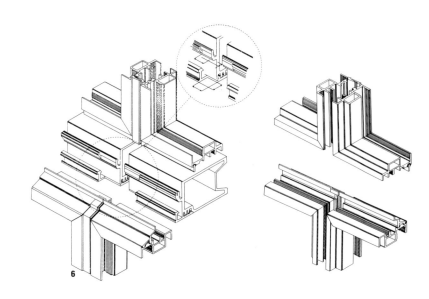

Kansai International Airport Terminal 193

Airside glazing of boarding wing.

6 Isometric views of extruded aluminium elements with EPDM gaskets installed.

7, **8** Close-up view of fixings of stiffening mullion to secondary structure and of transom to mullion.

9 Detail section at head and **10** foot of glazing (scale approximately 1:4).

11 Typical plan and **12** section detail (scale approximately 1:4): **a** 12mm heat-absorbent glass **b** extruded aluminium frame **c** silicone sealant **d**, **f** silicone gasket **e** EPDM gasket silicone gasket **g** extruded aluminium transom **h** extruded aluminium anchor bracket **i** 148 x 100 x 6 x 9mm steel I-section mullion.

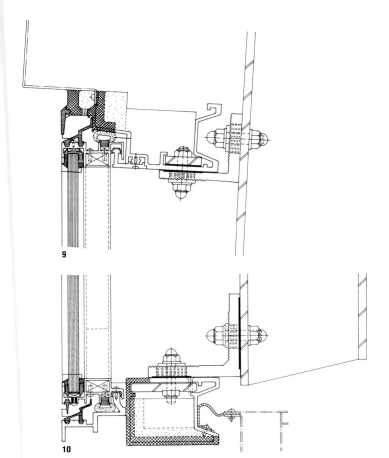

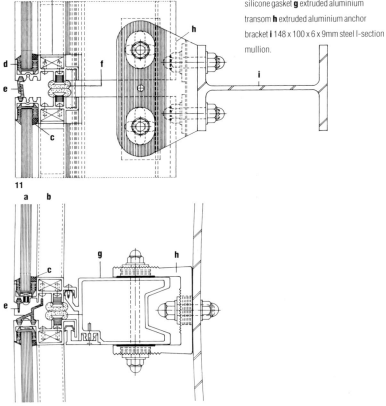

1

2

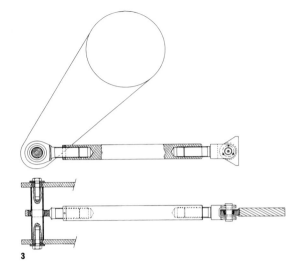

3

194 **Kansai International Airport Terminal**

Gable-end glazing of central terminal block.

1, **2** Views from inside of glazing and stabilizing trusses.

3 Detail of movement-absorbing arm at head of glazing.

4 Detail of movement-absorbing slotted junction where glazing passes between bottom chords of double truss.

5 Section detail of glazing gaskets.

6 Section: **a** pivoting joint (shown in detail **3**) **b** sliding joint (shown in detail **4**) **c** 12mm laminated heat-absorbing glass **d** vertical truss.

7, **8** Close-up views show delicacy achieved by doubling up machined steel elements of vertical trusses and using solid flat bars for glazing frame.

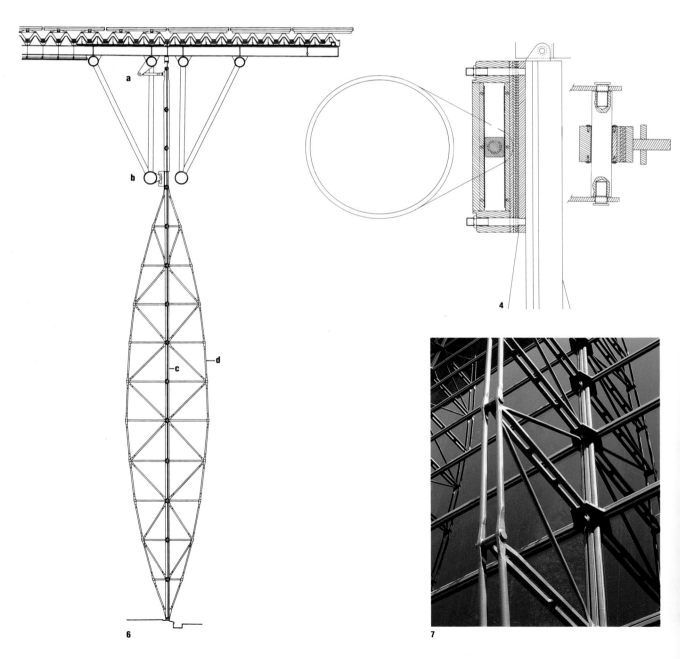

4

5

6

7

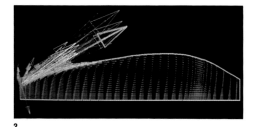

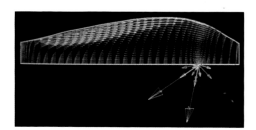

1

Kansai International Airport Terminal

Air-jets in international departures hall.

1 Computer studies seeking optimal angle of discharge of jet.

2–5 Computer studies of projected airflow under air-scoop.

6 Diagram shows derivation of shape of air-scoop and it suspended between main trusses.

7 Duct rises up canyon to nozzle, shaped to express its relationship with air-scoop.

8 Seen from international departures hall, broad mouth and shape of jet nozzle again make clear relationship with air-scoop that also reflects light from uplighter. Macro system of air-jet is complemented by local fine-tuning from fan-coil units in blue 'posts' just visible along base of gable-end glazing.

9 Section and **10** plan of jet-nozzle. External form does not correspond with that of duct within but is shaped to express functional relationships with air-scoops.

11 Transit lounge receives fresh air from international departures hall. This is fine-tuned locally by recycled air from blue horizontal tubular ducts similar to those above ceilings of check-in desks in hall above.

Services

The extraordinarily close match between the shapes of space, skin and structure, which is such a striking feature of the terminal's design, carries through to the way the services, particularly the air-conditioning, work with and determine some of these shapes. As in the competition design, the main terminal block roof is shaped according to the natural curve of a jet of air blown into the international departures hall from its landside, and the ceiling alone guides the air across the full length of the hall. This system (conceived of by Tom Barker and developed in collaboration with Alistair Guthrie, also of Ove Arup & Partners) not only obviates the need for the clutter of suspended ducts, but it also furnishes something of the fresh feeling of being outdoors rather than the stuffiness characteristic of many air-conditioned interiors.

The air-jet, though, only provides background conditions that are fine-tuned locally.

The concept of using a combination of what came to be called macro-systems, which deal with the whole space, and micro-systems, which fine-tune conditions locally, has been used throughout the building. All fresh and conditioned air is introduced by the macro-systems. The micro-systems only recycle air locally, simply heating or cooling it as required. In the international departures hall these micro-systems supply air through nozzles in tubular ducts that lie on the roofs of the check-in counters, redistributing the air drawn in by plant boxed in above the airside end of these roofs. At the foot of the huge expanses of single glazing along each side of the hall are rows of rectilinear 'posts' housing fan-coil units that compensate for heat gain or loss.

In the boarding wing, the distinction between macro- and micro-systems is not quite so clear. The macro-system is provided by air let in, via fishtail-shaped units visible from the outside, along the base of the airside glazing. The curve of the glazing and roof guides the air up and around the edge of the volume. The micro-system

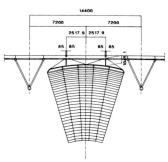

6

7

8

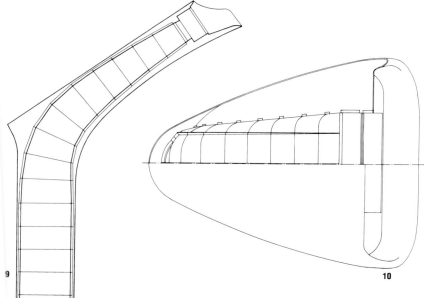

9

10

11

1

Kansai International Airport Terminal
Air-conditioning.
1, **2** In boarding wing, fresh conditioned air enters through grilles below glazing, **1**, from **2** external fishtail units.
3 Detail section through end of first floor slab and foot of airside glazing: **a** air inlet **b** fishtail unit **c** air duct **d** insulation.
4 Air-scoops seen above ducts that admit recycled air in transit lounge.
5 Posts in canyon admit fresh conditioned air.
6 Posts along gable-end glazing of international departures hall contain fan coil units for local fine-tuning of temperature.

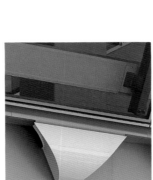

2

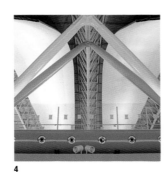

3

recycles air through units under the arrivals walkway that projects as an upper level gallery into this space. In the canyon, the macro-system of conditioned air is fed in through a row of large posts that rise from its floor close to the trees. Smaller posts, like those in the international departures hall, provide micro-system fine-tuning along the base of the gable end glazing.

The air-jet in the international departures hall is entrained by a scoop-like shell made from teflon-coated fabric. Condi-tioned air rises up the cylindrical ducts (of 1.2 metres in external diameter) in the canyon to leave the 4-metre-wide mouths of the jet-nozzles at 7 metres per second. The air then exactly follows, instead of being in any way deflected by, the shape of the shells, dragging other air with it, while some conditioned air descends into the space along the full length of the jets. Because the cantilevered brackets of the competition scheme were eliminated, the shells are no longer so intimately integrated with the structure but are merely suspended from the secondary structure. The fabric is now stretched taut to four aluminium supporting rails hidden above the shells. These were initially intended to be curved in cross section to a constant radius along their length, but they now conform in shape to part of the upper surface of a double-tapered rotated solid. A teflon-coated fabric was used because it is light in weight, offers little friction to impede airflow, is easy to wipe clean and, in any case, does not generate static electricity and so does not attract too much dirt.

The fibre-reinforced plastic covers of the jet nozzles, which terminate the cylindrical ducts rising through the canyon to supply the air, do not conform exactly to the steel ductwork within them. Instead they are shaped so as to read, especially from across the canyon, as terminating the tapering form of the air-shell, thus making clear their functional relationship. The shape they were given was in part inspired by the ogee curves of the wings of Concorde. Like all other elements that conduct air, with the exception of the suspended air-shells, they are painted a soft blue.

Computer modelling and testing with a 1:10 scale mock-up by Arups had shown that the air-shells, though contributing to the smooth efficiency of the system, were not absolutely necessary. However, they are crucial to the space in other ways. Their presence, together with the proximity of one end to the jet-nozzle, as well as the shape of the jet-nozzle itself, means that anyone who looks for a moment will understand how the system works. Brightly lit below the ceiling, the scoop-like forms of the shells emphasize the asymmetry of the roof and the forward flow of the space, while also helping to define the space. Last, but not least, the reason they are brighter than the ceiling is that they serve another main function as reflectors of the artificial lights.

4

5

6

Again, so as to keep the upper part of the space uncluttered (and also to reduce the weight on the roof and simplify maintenance), the hall is artificially lit not from the roof but by uplighters reflected off the airshells. For similar reasons, other services, such as emergency lighting and the public address system speakers, are mounted on posts – or what the architects called 'technical trees', a name that is a hangover from when their design was more complex. For cost reasons, light fittings, speakers and so on are now all off-the-peg items.

In the canyon and boarding wing, these posts also carry the artificial lights. In the canyon, in particular, they are meant to be seen as lampposts, and to enhance what is intended to be the street-like character of the space. To emphasize this character, it was originally intended that only the bottom of the canyon would be lit, with the floors of the bridges above locally illuminated from their handrails so as not to disturb the street-like impression. However, the health of the trees growing in the canyon depends on supplementary lighting, and because this has not been provided locally but by bright lights on the ceiling, the illusion has been spoiled. In the boarding wing, wall-mounted uplighters that reflect off the ceiling provide general lighting which is supplemented by the post-mounted downlighters. These, like all the artificial lighting units, are colour-coded yellow.

7

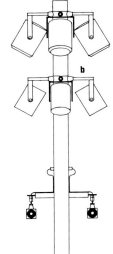

Kansai International Airport Terminal   199

Lighting and public address systems.
7 Post supporting uplighter and services pole in international departures hall.
8 Lighting and loudspeaker pole in domestic boarding lounge.
9–11 Typical configurations of services poles: **9** is in boarding wing, **10** in transit lounge and **11** in international departures hall.
a 110mm diameter aluminium pole **b** 28mm diameter arm **c** luminaire **d** emergency lighting **e** loudspeaker **f** cctv camera.
12 Emergency lighting and loudspeaker pole in international departures lounge. Above, airscoop acts as reflector for uplighters.

8

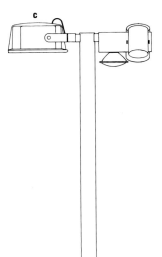

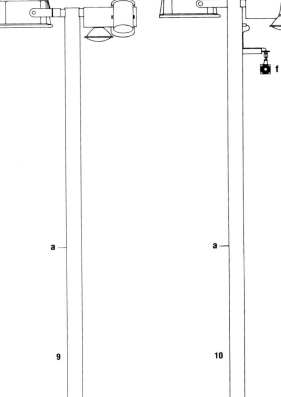

9

10

11

12

Fire

When considering the Kansai terminal, a question that will inevitably arise in the minds of most architects is: how was it possible to get approval from the fire authorities for a single un-subdivided space, which includes the 1.7-kilometre-long boarding wing and extends laterally from there to include the international departures hall and the canyon (and so is some 15 million cubic metres in volume)? Again, this was achieved with the assistance of Ove Arup & Partners, as well as with the cooperation of the very enlightened Japanese authorities. Though Japan has very stringent fire regulations with highly specific stipulations, the authorities were prepared to waive these in the face of an alternative approach convincingly based on engineering principles. Also crucial to success, according to Piano, was Okabe's persistent and

1

skilful negotiating, backed as it was by his immediate grasp of the consequences of, and alternatives to, options proposed in discussions.

A committee of experts was specially convened to judge the merits of the case put forward by the Building Workshop and Arups. Various factors favoured treating the terminal as an exceptional case: its spacious layout lets people move freely and see where they are going; potential fire hazards are clearly defined and easily isolated; high ceilings allow smoke to rise and collect far above the heads of people, and airports are intensively managed places where people are used to responding readily to public address-system announcements. Computer models and on-site tests confirmed that in all of the large spaces, huge amounts of smoke could collect and would remain high under the ceilings for long enough not to hinder evacuation of the building.

Two crucial aspects of the Building Workshop and Arup's approach, and the case they argued, are what came to be known as the cabin and the

island concepts. The cabin concept means that the main fire hazard areas, the concession floor, and to a lesser extent the check-in desks, are both contained and under sprinklers, as well as rapidly ventilated smoke hoods. The island concept means that the less hazardous elements, such as groups of seats (and again the check-in desks) are sufficiently far apart as to prevent fire spreading between them.

At the last moment, the local fire department (independently of the national authority with whose approval the above strategy was developed) asked for extra precautions to be taken in some spaces. So there are now a pair of infra-red sensitive, computer-guided water cannon mounted above check-in desks in the international departures hall that can each project a jet of water up to 80 metres. And as well as photo-electric smoke detectors in the canyon and boarding wing, there are sideways-spraying sprinklers on the walls and protruding from the tops of the air-conditioning posts in the canyon, and underneath the arrivals walkway in the boarding wing.

Throughout the building, conventional fire protection has been provided wherever it was possible without detriment to the basic design concept. As normally required, all structural steel is protected to a height of 4 metres. To achieve this, the props and columns supporting the steel trusses are clad in glass-reinforced cement covers that give at least an hour's protection. Even though the shell

structure of the boarding wing would redistribute loads and remain standing when some members were softened by heat, so rendering such precautions unnecessary, the ribs in the boarding wing are painted to a height of 4 metres with intumescent paint.

Immense care went into the design of the grc covers, which are not only prominent inside and outside, but also, as with the leaning props in the international departures hall, give crucial parts of the building a very particular 'organic' quality. These covers were designed as a family of related forms, that not only express the huge structural forces and different kinds of junctions within them, but also have a flowing, sensual softness of form.

After much sketching and modelling, the Building Workshop created CAD drawings from which the Japanese manufacturer made 1:5 scale clay models. After many versions of these had been made, full-size models were made in wood and styrofoam. These underwent yet further refinement before manufacture. Revisions in prototypes were immediately incorporated into the CAD program, which was essential for shaping the covers of all the slightly differently sized columns and props outside the landside of the boarding wing.

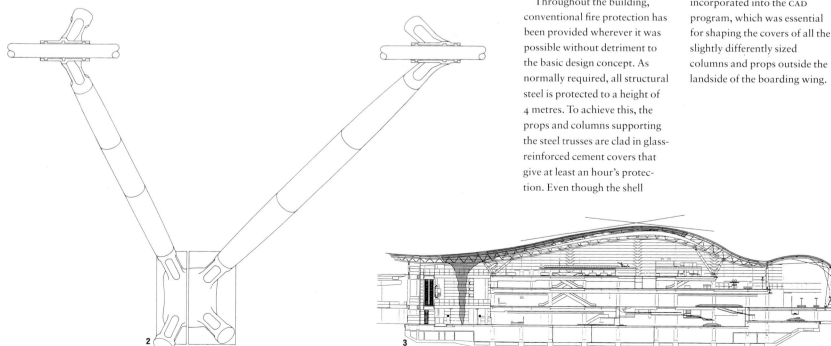

2

3

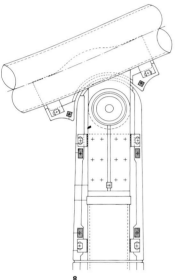

4

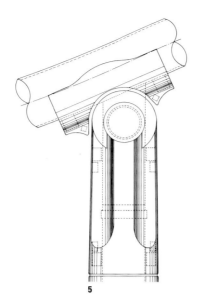

5

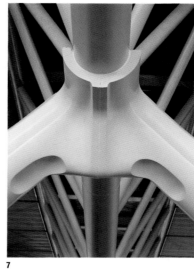

6

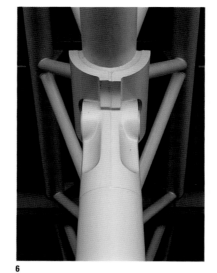

7

Kansai International Airport Terminal 201

Fire prevention.

1 Infra-red sensitive, computer-guided automatic water cannon in international departures hall.

2 Plan view of the grc fire cladding of sloping props to main trusses.

3 High ceilings provide emergency smoke reservoirs.

4–13 Details of fire-protective glass reinforced cement claddings. These are sculpted to express the structural functions of and forces acting on the members within them.

8

9

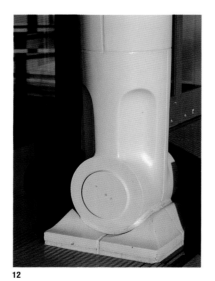

10

11

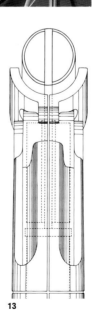

12

13

Renzo Piano Building Workshop

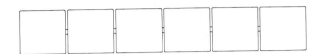

1

2

202

Kansai International Airport Terminal

Seating system.

1, **7** Six-seat backless version.

2 Early prototype with arms.

3 Cast aluminium legs as used to support single row of seats.

4, **5**, **6**, **9** Six-seat single-row configuration.

8 Four-seat version of basic back-to-back configuration. Together with six-seat version, this is the configuration used in most parts of terminal.

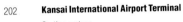

3

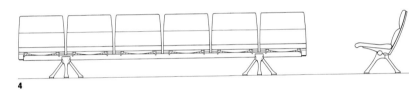

4

5

6

7

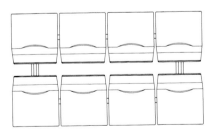

8

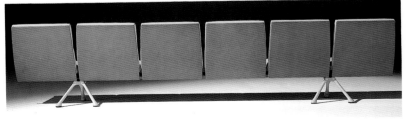

9

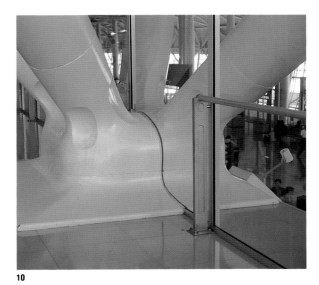

10

Kansai International Airport Terminal
Glass fences and balustrades.
10 Glass fence that edges land- and airsides
of international departures hall continues
uninterrupted over bases of sloping props.
11 Bridges across canyon, like edges of all
floors overlooking spaces below, is edged by
2.3 metre high glass fence. But here the
balustrade includes lights spanning between
the cast-aluminium balusters.
12 Stair landings projecting into canyon
support the glass shafts in which they are
sheathed.

11

Furniture and fitting out

There are nearly 9,000 seats in the terminal, 7,252 of them in the lounges of the boarding wing. Considerable research went into studying the off-the-peg systems available. Most of these proved to have some functional or aesthetic flaw (much the preferred one was an old system by Eames, but this was thought to stamp its own character too powerfully on its surroundings), and all were far too expensive. Eventually it proved much cheaper, despite the limited production run, for the Building Workshop to design its own thoroughly rationalized seating system (using standard steel tubes for structure and minimizing castings). This was conceived of as providing accents of bright colour, seemingly floating above the floor of the vast achromatic space of the boarding wing – the ceiling and structure, floor and walls of which are all in shades of grey.

To achieve this sense of floating, the cast-aluminium legs, which are recessive in colour and softly organic in form, are kept to a minimum. This also limits the number of expensive castings, the only other cast elements being the more cheaply made steel brackets that support each seat. Four such legs support two steel tubes on which up to twelve seats are ranged in back-to-back rows. Because of the limited production run, the seats and the backs are of plywood, which is curved and veneered in smooth, warm-toned beech. These support polyurethane padding covered in artificial leather, chosen because it is durable, easily cleaned and it breathes.

The five bright colours of the seats were chosen from a traditional French palette. About 200 seats of the same colour are arranged at right angles to the airside glazing in each boarding lounge. Seats in those few areas where smoking is permitted are marked in a sixth colour, purple. The system allows also for single rows of seats, which can be with or without backs.

The bright yellow-encased artificial lights supported on grey posts are also intended to be accents of colour floating in space. These posts and the lights, emergency lights and public address-system speakers that they support are meant to resemble street lamps punctuating the long space of the

boarding wing and the expanses of the international departures hall. Originally they were to have been more expressive in form, with the light fittings, as well as the posts with arms that supported them, all designed by the architects.

Another element extensively used in the boarding wing, and also along the edges of the international departures hall and elsewhere, are the glass fences that edge the upper level arrivals walkway and partition the routes by which arriving passengers pass between the departure lounges. Altogether there are 7 kilometres of this glass fence in the building. Where it separates arriving and departing passengers, the clear laminated glass is 3 metres high, and where it edges a floor it is 2.3 metres. The glass is held on its edges and along the bottom in extruded aluminium frames, and is unsupported at its head. The vertical frames are supported from cast aluminium uprights that also support the vivid green plastic-covered tubular handrails.

203

12

Walkthrough

Approach

Here, at last, is an airport designed to be seen from the air. The approach, from both the air and the mainland, offers thrilling views of the terminal's long, curved and silvery form. For those lucky enough to have a window seat in a landing plane, a particularly magical way to encounter the terminal is to arrive at sunset. With the curves of the roof highlighted by the glancing rays of the setting sun, the terminal's directional shape, shiny metal skin and lightness of poise together resemble some gigantic glider, its immensely long wings outstretched for all the planes to gather against, like progeny that have not yet acquired the mature form of the mother ship from which they are nurtured.

From above, you notice the contrasts between the wavy curve of the central block (the main terminal building) and the tighter curve of the boarding wing roof. Probably only when the plane has landed would you also notice that the boarding-wing roof curves slowly in the longitudinal direction as well; and even then you may wonder if it is not some trick of perspective, as it seems to whoosh across the island, seemingly from horizon to horizon. As the daylight fades, the dark glass beneath the curving carapace of stainless-steel panels suddenly becomes transparent as the lights inside come on to reveal an extraordinary vision of lofty curving ceilings, or brightly lit, splayed and sculpted props with swooping scoop-like forms above and beyond them, and everywhere masses of people en route to and from their planes.

Approaching the island by train or car affords a first view from the bridge, which is also enthralling. From here you can appreciate the immense silvery length and subtle curves, which together reflect the light in ever changing ways, so that it might sparkle in the sun, or loom mysteriously out of a grey sky and sea. However, for those who take the trouble to seek it out, perhaps the best view of all is from the public viewing terrace on the roof of the domestic cargo building, which is a little east of the tip of the northern boarding wing. (There is no viewing terrace on the main building itself; the smoothly curving envelope of the shell would not have lent itself easily to accommodating one. Besides, as the architects pointed out, such public terraces are usually closed nowadays for security reasons.)

Splendidly displayed from this observation point are not just the comings and goings of the planes but also the building itself. The curves of the boarding wing are compressed and emphasized by the very oblique angle of viewing, while those of the main terminal building roof can be seen rising gracefully from the trough behind the flat-topped mid-section of the wing. The contrast in the geometries between the two-directional toroidal curves of the boarding wing and the single-directional curve of its mid-section, which flows into the cylindrical arcs behind this, are revealed to be no mere expedient fudge. The flat-topped mid-section provides more than contrast and interest, it also provides a hiatus that introduces a certain ease in what would otherwise be a too relentlessly compelling geometry, and makes clear that the toroidal curves are no mere trick of perspective.

208 **Kansai International Airport Terminal**

Previous pages View from roof of cargo terminal show curves of roof to best effect.

Approaching the terminal.

1 The immense length of the glistening and curving roof is seen from the road descending from the bridge to the mainland.

2 Underside of roadbed.

3 The station designed by Nikken Sekkei.

4 From outside the station, bridges lead to the airport between the roads to the departures level above the arrivals level below.

3

Landside

Most of the people who are not flying into the airport arrive by train. After the thrilling glimpses of the terminal from above the sea and between the girders of the bridge, however, the initial impression on leaving the station is surprisingly mundane. Ahead are not sleek curves, panelled in steel and glass. Instead there are huge, but rather fussy elements of road engineering, which the Building Workshop are not responsible for, and beyond this is a

1

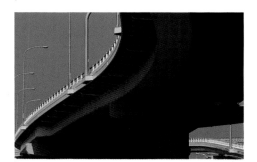

2

relatively nondescript facade.

As with most large airports, the landside entrance front is dominated by two levels of roadways and drop-offs. However, because of the multi-level organization which layers the domestic and international facilities in the one terminal, the two roads are separated further in height than usual. Therefore the columns supporting the roadway above are very tall, and passing between them are footbridges which span over the ground-level arrivals road to connect the station with the domestic flights level.

The basic forms of the cylindrical columns and the roadbed they support are fine, but the roadbed is made up of steel units small enough to be easily transported, which were then bolted together on site. The result is masses of boltheads and other distracting detail, such as service catwalks. Piano pleaded for some sort of canopy above the footbridges to hide all this, but was denied it on grounds of cost. Instead there are only little flat roofs over the beginnings of the footbridges, which are puny in the shadow of such road engineering.

The aspect the building offers those approaching from the upper, departures level road is much more distinctive, though

even this was compromised by cost cutting. Up here, the roof cantilevers forward to shelter and greet arriving travellers, and through the glass wall shaded by this overhang something of the drama of the interior can be glimpsed. Slightly distracting are the five little canopies which shelter people crossing the road and drop-off area until they get under the cover of the eaves. These canopies compensate for the narrowing of the cantilevering eave, which was a consequence of the cost cutting.

When approaching these eaves, or once underneath them, the elements of the structure and the roof it supports can be seen at close range. The ends of the three tubular chords of each truss are clearly expressed, as are the secondary structure and the last rows of the stainless-steel roof tiles. In their forms, scale and complexity, these details suggest the eaves of

4

5

Kansai International Airport Terminal
Departures drop-off.

5 Cost-cutting reduced eaves overhang so that independent canopies shelter people crossing road.

6 Under the eaves: stainless-steel tiles on fin-like rafters project beyond cantilevered ends of main trusses as a delicate termination of huge roof oversailing bus-stop canopies.

7 Exposure of structure of oversailing eaves and gradual peeling away of elements has affinities with Japanese temples.

8 Glazed gable-end of central terminal block offers dramatic night views of international departures hall with suspended air scoops.

6

7

traditional Japanese temples. This is deliberate, just as the colours of the hall immediately inside, which is known as the 'canyon', are chosen from the palette associated with traditional Japanese buildings. The terminal could be read as offering a trip from traditional Japan on the landside to the space age on the airside. This might sound a contrived and corny concept: in reality it is neither because, though the colours in the canyon are a bit of a surprise, nowhere does the design feel laboured. Instead, it unfolds before you with a remarkable sense of inevitability.

From the road up to this level there is also a fine view of the external half of the double, gable-end truss which supports the edge of the main terminal roof, and the huge wall of glazing below it stabilized by vertical bow-string trusses. Together these hint at the character of the space inside, and at night the glazing offers an extraordinarily dramatic view of the international departures hall. From up here you also get some glimpses of the landside of the boarding wing which is dominated by the tracks of the automated shuttle trains. The integration of architecture and transport engineering here is a little awkward: it is unclear, for instance, whether the track is meant to read as sitting on part of the building, or whether it is the latter which extends under the tracks and between its supports. The close proximity of the independent airline office buildings is disturbing also, though they do hide views of the boarding wing's landside from the lower levels. Designed by Nikken Sekkei, these offices, though understated, are too slickly styled to sit comfortably beside the terminal, whose forms seem devoid of anything gratuitous.

For all its considerable virtues, Aéroport de Paris's schematic solution, which was proposed by the competition brief and closely followed by the Building Workshop, also posed a formidable design challenge: how to make a suitable public face of the landside of the terminal when it is dominated by the engineering infrastructure of the roads and automated shuttles. However, this perhaps unresolvable conundrum is compensated for by the fact that, most unusually, the first view of the terminal on approaching it is the splendid airside aspect seen from the bridge from the mainland. Besides, masking the architecture by roads and shuttle tracks on the one side, and to a far lesser degree by planes, boarding bridges and tall lampposts on the other, is not only unavoidable, but expresses the nature of the building as an efficient interchange.

209

8

210 **Kansai International Airport Terminal**

The canyon.

1 View to landside from north end of domestic departures concourse. Outside and straight ahead is underside of departures level roadway. To right is glazing stiffened by vertical trusses.

2 View northwards. Those arriving from landside to left are immediately alerted to multi-level organization of terminal and can change levels by escalators and lifts. Those arriving from abroad are immediately confronted by trees indigenous to Japan and colours familiar from traditional architecture.

Canyon

From whichever of the three levels you arrive at the landside of the terminal, you enter the canyon: a hall extending the full width and height of the building, and so called both for its size and the trees that grow in it. Unspecified in the original brief, it was included by the Building Workshop as a crucial orientational element. It impresses immediately on all who enter the multi-level organization of the terminal, and puts on conspicuous display the escalators and lifts by which you might immediately change to the level you require.

Originally, the canyon was to have been entirely enclosed by glass on the landside. The intention was that as you approached from the station you would see directly into the canyon and so, even before entering, get some sense of the terminal's multi-level organiza-tion. You would notice especially the escalators aligned against the glass, and so be forewarned about changing levels. But last minute cost cutting substituted solid walls for much of the glazing. Now as you approach, the escalators are hidden by blank walls and glazing is restricted to panels above the automatic, opening, glass doors.

Inside the doors, you find that, even with the diminished glazing on the landside, the impressively scaled canyon is brightly lit through the roof it rises to and the fully glazed end walls it extends between. As well as the size and the trees, what rather takes you aback are the colours – the terracotta walls and escalators and ochre lift shafts. These soft earthy colours are consistent with the idea that this is a canyon, but they are rather surprising to find within the shiny metal shell of the building and above the emphatic datum of the artificial island's flat top. Along with the soft blue of the air-conditioning ducts, the colours were chosen as being familiar to, and perhaps associ-ated with, traditional Japanese architecture. Together with the presence of the indigenous trees in the canyon, these are intended to remind those arriving that while they have touched down on an artificial island they have also landed in Japan. (People waiting for passengers arriving from abroad do so on the floor of the canyon, which is adjacent the international baggage collection and customs.)

As things are arranged now, with the escalators hidden from outside, first time visitors are probably some way across the bridges or canyon floor before they fully register that they perhaps need to change level. They then have to return to the escalators along the landside wall, which were positioned correctly when this wall was to be entirely glass. Late and rushed exercises in cost cutting, without time to recall and reconsider the logic of early decisions, might save money only at the expense of the smooth efficiency of function. However, one benefit of replacing the glazing with a solid wall is that it hides the fiddly road engineering outside. Besides, it is still possible, having crossed the canyon, to change between the domestic and international departures levels by the escalators that connect both of these to the intermediate concessions level.

The semi-opaque landside wall and the stair shafts that protrude from the airside make the canyon seem in oblique views less transparent than it really is. In combination with the expanses of earth colours this makes the canyon appear literally more canyon-like. It has lost some of its intended light airiness. Nevertheless, it serves its original purpose of orien-tating you, both when arriving and as a visible reference behind you once you have crossed it and are proceeding to where the planes become clearly visible ahead. This works well when using the domestic level, in the inner building designed by Nikken Sekkei (which unavoid-ably lacks the light and lofty airiness of the rest of the build-ing), and brilliantly so on the international departures level.

1

International departures hall

The international departures hall is on the terminal's upper-most level, the third floor on top of the inner building for which Nikken Sekkei were responsible (and which contains the domestic and international arrivals facilities not shown here), and directly below the soaring asymmetrical curves of the roof. From the porch beneath the roof that cantilevers over the pavement of the upper road, bridges cross the deep canyon to land you under a portal dramatically framed by the props that slope up to support the huge main trusses. From a low point directly over the bridges, these trusses rise steadily upwards before swooping down more steeply to meet another set of splayed props on the far side of the hall. The asymmetrical curves of these arched trusses follow the tightening, decelerating curve of the jets of fresh conditioned air that ventilate this huge space and control its background temperature.

These jets are blown in from huge nozzles, terminating ducts that rise up through the canyon, that lean in over the bases of the sloping structural props. This air is then entrained by the scoop-like fabric shells which hang down below and between the trusses, and also act as reflectors for the uplighters which illuminate the space. If the trusses, and especially their conspicuous tubular lower chords, stress the continuous flow of space, then the more brightly lit shells give definition and even some intimacy to the international departures hall as a space in itself. Together, though, the trusses and shells seem to surge forward like a wave and almost tangibly tug you along in their undertow.

Resisting this surge for a moment allows you to look at and contemplate some details. The props, and the huge bases where four of them meet, are sensuously shaped in a way that clearly expresses their structural function. But, what look like cast-steel elements play no structural role and are only glass-reinforced cement covers to fireproof the real structural elements within. This solution, which has its precedent in the Pompidou Centre and many buildings since, is used elsewhere inside and outside the building. Some architects will feel a bit uneasy at what they see as a dishonest cover-up. However, the more realistic majority will recognize the inevitability of such a cover up and applaud one which so accurately expresses the structural realities they have to conceal.

The common bases shared by these splaying props achieve the beautiful and sensually inviting softness of form which Piano so often seeks in his current work. However, the way the bottom of the base flares to meet the floor somewhat distorts structural reality by suggesting that the loads of these props are dissipated in the floor slab which serves as a major structural element. In fact, these loads pass directly down through columns below, whose presence is suppressed instead of played up so that you can understand the structure at a glance (which is, after all, an obvious design theme everywhere else in the building). This inconsistency originates in (and perhaps aptly expresses) the division of the building's final execution between the two architects, with Nikken Sekkei's inner building forming a base for what has almost been treated as an autonomous structure above.

The sculpted form of the huge nozzles of the air-jets is also a cover-up (this time in fibre-reinforced plaster) in that it does not follow that of the duct inside. Nevertheless, it is beautifully judged in the way its shape and size relate to the structural props it leans between and to the suspended air-shells. Seen both from the side and from across the canyon, the form and its position make clear its functional relationship to the air-shell, which it seems to terminate visually in the most satisfying manner. Many people would probably notice this relationship and guess at the presence and purpose of the invisible air-jet. However, Piano decided to make their function unambiguous by having the client commission Susumu Shingu (the Japanese sculptor with whom Piano has collaborated on other projects) to suspend wind sculptures that spin and rock in the jet stream. Opinions might divide evenly as to whether this is a redundant gesture, and a few might also find the blue and yellow fabric 'sails' too emphatic in colour. For them, white sails, such as Shingu used for the wind sculptures at the Columbus International Exhibition in Genoa (Volume Two p 94), might have been more in keeping.

Turning away from inspecting these details and looking forward again, the air-jets and surging structure propel you to the check-in counters. Although otherwise neatly designed, these have distracting elements projecting above their ceilings. Held out on stalk-like spindly arms are public address-system speakers and emergency lighting (which in the open areas of the halls are supported on regularly spaced posts), both housed in cream cylindrical casings. The budget would not stretch to these being

212   **Kansai International Airport Terminal**

International departures hall

1 View across top of canyon. Relationship between nozzle of air-jet and air-scoop suspended between curving main trusses is immediately obvious.

2 Sloping props create dramatic portal welcoming those arriving across bridge from departures drop-off.

3 Nozzles of air-jets lean over glass wall along top of canyon that bisects bases of sloping props.

4 Sloping props and curving bottom chords of the main trusses dominate this view up from transit lounge into airside edge of hall.

1

2

3

4

resprayed grey. And atop both long edges of the ceiling are blue tubular ducts from which air is dispensed through nozzles, which are large versions of those found overhead the seats in aircraft. These recycle air from the plant boxed in above the far end of each check-in desk.

These blue tubes (like the exposed mechanisms of the lifts in the canyon and boarding wing) provoke a sense of déjà vu, belonging as they do to the Pompidou period of exposed and colour-coded services, and

of high-tech icons such as aircraft nozzles. They belong to a previous era when mechanical technology was not yet taken for granted, but naively celebrated and used to jolly up decoratively what might have been huge and characterless spaces. Here, though, together with the projecting lights and speakers and elevated plant rooms, they distract attention from the glorious forms of the structure and air-shells and the magnificent space these define. The ducts should probably have been hidden in the ceilings of the check-in desks, a solution Piano rejected lest the ceilings become too deep and prominent.

These distractions make it virtually impossible to decide what, if anything, this hall has suffered through the cost-cutting elimination of the rooflights which were to have been above each truss. Before the check-in counters were installed, the space had a

wonderful serenity, even a mystery, as the brightly lit air-shells seemed to float, between the trusses that loomed out of shadow, on the air and light they guide and reflect. Rooflights then would have created very different conditions, with the trusses well lit, and either dominant over the dark hovering presence of the air-shells or, if the latter were lit, as clutter-inducing elements competing for attention. Yet now that the building is fitted out, it seems that the rooflights might have been exactly the device to draw attention away from the clutter above the check-in desks and back to the roof, and so to an appreciation of the whole space.

As with one or two other elements of the building's design, the vertical bow-string trusses that stabilize the huge walls of glazing along both sides of this hall had already become rather familiar before the building had been completed. This is because the drawings had been seen in publications and imitated by other architects in smaller, more rapidly erected buildings. Nowhere, though, do they seem as at home as here. In part this is because, in Osaka's temperate climate, cold bridging is not a problem, and so the glazing does not have to bulge outside of the trusses. It is also partly due to the neat and delicate detailing of the machined-steel pieces. By doubling up the main roof truss at this point, movement at the head of this wall is absorbed with far less visual fuss than is usual in such cases.

As you walk across the departures hall, the eye is caught by the way the structure and ceiling beyond the props on the far side of the hall swoop up again and curve down once more. Proceeding further, you see where the ceiling gives way to

the glazing, and beyond that, under the overhanging tiles to the planes outside. Until late on during design, the glazing was intended to extend higher, so that the planes would be visible from all parts of this hall; but cost cutting forced the roof to be extended downwards. This is a considerable compromise to the original concept, yet in reality it does not seem such a great loss. The surge of the asymmetric roof makes it clear in what direction you must proceed, and you still see the planes before you leave this level. Besides, the architects prefer the way the exterior now looks: the boarding wing reads more clearly as a single volume than it would have done if the glazing stepped up at the same point as the roofline flattened out.

Eventually, as you near the far side of the hall, it becomes apparent that you are looking across the upper part of another magnificent space, and that the undulating ceiling causes the space you are standing in, again almost tangibly, to flow forward and down into that below. Directly below you two floor levels are visible. The upper of these is the transit lounge that is reached by descending to the concessions level and walking forward between the duty-free shops. The lower level is the boarding lounge for domestic flights, which occupies the central portion of the boarding wing.

216 **Kansai International Airport Terminal**
International departures hall.
Previous pages Passengers are led forward by the curves of structure and air-scoops. Sculptures by Shingu make visible the flow of the air-jets.
1, 2 Airside edge of hall overlooks transit lounge, domestic boarding lounge, and aircraft outside.
3 Southern gable-end of hall. Fan-coil units in rectilinear blue posts compensate for heat losses or gains through the truss-stiffened glazing.

1

2

Transit lounge and automatic shuttle

The transit lounge is on the second floor, the same floor as the concessions. On the airside of the duty free shops, it is open to the roof and is overlooked from above by the international departures hall; it in turn overlooks the domestic boarding lounge in the central portion of the boarding wing. Departing international passengers all pass through it on the way to their planes.

Although just a transitional space, it is one of the most exciting in the building. Here, the space of the international departures hall not only flows into that of the boarding wing, but the trusses over the former space merge with the ribs of the boarding wing. Reaching up from the edge of the floor above are the splayed props that support the trusses. At this point, these switch from the arched form which can be seen over the departures hall, with the brightly lit air-shells between them, to the sagging curve directly overhead as the trusses taper until only the bottom chord meets each alternate column along the airside edge of this space. Beyond these columns, the boarding-wing ribs sweep down in a complex concave curve to meet pin-jointed footings just inside the airside glazing. Through this glass can be seen parked planes, boarding bridges and planes taking off and landing. And beyond these are the sea and the mountains of the mainland.

Passengers proceeding to their planes walk to the ends of this space, past the bars and cafés that extend out into the lounge. The shuttle stations are on this level, and entered through the ends of this lounge. Because they are moving parts of the building, the outsides of the shuttle coaches are painted red, while their insides are treated as part of the building interior, in shades of grey with green hand-rails. Those passengers going to the closest gates cross to the elevated walkway that runs against the airside glazing of the boarding wing. This is part of the 'swing gate' system that gives flexibility in allocating the lounges and gates below for either international or domestic flights. Once past those gates being used for domestic flights, you take an escalator to the floor of the boarding wing below.

2

4

Transit lounge and shuttle.

1, 2 Transit lounge is, aptly, a transitional space, overlooked by the international departures hall, **1**, and overlooking the domestic boarding lounge, **2**. It is also where the main trusses swoop down and taper to meet a row of columns beyond which the bottom chord extends as the rib of the boarding wing.

3 Shuttle departing from central terminal block.

4 Shuttles on tracks alongside northern boarding wing.

Boarding wing

The boarding wing is a most extraordinarily impressive space. It is a single volume, which, from the ends of the domestic boarding lounge (itself an impressive 300 metres long and 20 metres high) stretches out in both directions to include the tapering volumes of the international boarding lounges. Scale is certainly part of its impact: at 1.7 kilometres long, it is probably the longest continuous internal volume ever built, even longer than the shed at the Boeing factory where so many of the planes outside were made. But a space of this length and narrowness could have appeared to be an interminable tunnel. What saves it are the beautifully judged curves in both cross and long section, and the forms of the structure and emphasis given to it, which together help to define and articulate the space visually.

The mixture of tight and more slack curves in cross section give a sprung tension to the form of the rib which a single radius curve would have lacked; and the longitudinal taper of the toroidal curve, the form and depth of which is clarified visually by the repetitive rhythm of the ribs, gives a satisfying finiteness of form. Crucial to the visual articulation is the way the tubular ribs project into the space from the square-sectioned elements of the secondary structure, which in turn are exposed inside the ceiling. Adopting the toroidal geometry has made it possible for all these ribs, though of differing length and diameter, to be of identical curve. However, to achieve this, the ribs progressively lean towards the ends of the boarding wing as they align with the radials of the toroid of which the roof is conceptually part. Particularly towards the centre of the boarding wing, these ribs seem extraordinarily light, a consequence of the whole structure functioning synergetically as a lattice shell.

Yet the precedent unavoidably called to mind by this advanced engineering is medieval. The protruding ribs articulate the space in a way reminiscent of the colonnettes and vault ribs of a Gothic cathedral. The lofty space with its long vistas, and the form and character given by a structure pushed to new limits of lightness, together achieve a grace and majesty equal to that of these great cathedrals.

Circulation, either to and from the main terminal building or nearest shuttle station, is along the landside edge of the boarding wing. Departing passengers promenade under the walkway that projects into the space until they reach the lounge beside their departure gate. The lounges are sparsely furnished with back-to-back banks of seating designed by the Building Workshop. Rising between the seats are posts supporting local and emergency lighting, and public address-system speakers. The volume of the space itself is lit by lights above the upper walkway which are reflected off the curved ceiling. All light fittings are off-the-peg items.

Passengers disembarking from planes are guided by 3-metre-high glass walls between the lounges and towards escalators and lifts. These deliver them to the upper level walkway by which they proceed to the nearest shuttle station or the main terminal block. The lifts and their shafts are glazed so as to minimize their intrusion on the space of the boarding wing.

The major obstruction to the spatial vistas, however, are the secondary elevated walkways necessitated by the 'swing gate' system that gives flexibility in allocating gates to domestic and international flights. These walkways, which extend from the airside corners of the transit lounge to carry departing international passengers over and beyond the lounges being

2

3

Kansai International Airport Terminal   223
Boarding wing.
Previous pages Domestic boarding lounge seen from beginning of walkway of 'swing gate' area. Roof of northern wing can be seen tapering down above 'swing gate' walkway at far end of lounge.
1 Domestic boarding lounge.
2 Walkway over 'swing gate' area.
3 International boarding lounges seen from head of station up to arrivals walkway that edges space on right.

224   **Kansai International Airport Terminal**

Boarding wing: international departures
lounges.

1 Lounges are very lofty towards central
terminal block.

2 Ceiling gradually tapers down in height
away from centre of terminal.

3 View from arrivals level walkway of
boarding lounges and aircraft. To right is end
of 'swing gate' walkway.

4 In wing tip, low ceiling and ribs leaning in
accordance with toroidal geometry can result
in unsettling optical illusions.

1

temporarily used for domestic
flights, run close to the airside
glazing for more than
200 metres. Though the
continuity of the ceiling can
always be seen, this intrusion
frustrates the natural urge to see
the entire length of the space.

Apart from this intrusion, the
space of the boarding wing, as
shaped by its enveloping ceiling
and glazing and articulated by
the structure, is truly splendid.
But although the structural rib
meets the pin-joint just inside
the foot of the airside glazing in
a particularly satisfying detail,
you do not see how its other
end is supported (which is by
columns and props outside,
along the shuttle tracks). Until
cost cutting at a late stage, the
landside wall was to have been
entirely glazed above the
arrivals walkway. Yet this
would have made the space feel
too open and the shuttles too
conspicuously intrusive, though

immediately alerting first-time
users of the airport to their presence would have been an asset.
Now this wall is glazed only
along its top. But the compromise proposed by the architects
would have been the best solution of all. This was to supple-
ment the present glazing with
vertical panes beside each
external column, bringing their
presence as well as glimpses
of the shuttles into the space
of the boarding wing.

Outside, the bases of these
columns and props are again
shaped to imply that their loads
are dispersed at this level rather
than being transferred to
columns below. This com-
pounds the ambiguities noted
from a distance as to whether
the shuttle tracks are part of the
building or not. Also, the wall
behind the columns would
have looked better if clearly
expressed as a cladding or infill
panelling. The architects were
always unhappy with this wall,
which is simply the cheapest
solution available, and proposed covering it with advertis-
ing hoardings, a pragmatic
solution that would have been
an improvement.

Out here also, the boxy
station at the end of the track
abuts uncomfortably the short
bit of curved and steel-tiled roof
on the landside of the wing tip.
Clearly, the roof should have
been extended to absorb this
station. This small refinement
would also have perfected the
proportions of the already
beautifully shaped outer shell,
particularly when seen from the
air from where the wing tip
looks a little insubstantial.

Although the toroidal curve
of the roof shell works wonder-
fully well everywhere else, it
results in the wing-tip ceiling
feeling a little low. This intensi-

fies the cramped impression
that already results from the
clustered gates and crowds of
passengers in these areas. Here,
the ribs, though of smaller
section than those which seem
so light in the taller parts of the
boarding wing here, feel
low and heavy. Moreover, their
appreciable lean, together with
the steepening slope of the airside glazing and the way the
ceiling bears down, produces
the somewhat unsettling optical
illusion of the floor tilting
upwards. This illusion might
also be compounded by the fact
that the arrivals walkway is not
quite horizontal here, but
climbs slowly from its end in
the wing-tip.

Throughout the boarding-
wing, the structure and airside
glazing are impeccably handled.
The pin-joint at the bottom of
each rib, the subtlety of rhythm
that comes from only every
second rib being stabilized by
ties, the interweaving of single
and double tie bars and the
connections of these with the
ribs are all just right. The varying slight slope in the longitudinal direction of the huge panes
of glazing is an added subtlety,
and the detailing of the frames
of these and the way they are
secured to the structure has a
beautiful simplicity and look
of effortless inevitability.

2

3

4

1

Kansai International Airport Terminal
Airside exterior.

1 On roadway below transparent part of boarding bridges, something of the immense length and height of boarding wing can be appreciated, as well as the gentle longitudinal curve.

2 Southern wing tip seen end-on with roof of central terminal curving away to left.

3 Boarding bridges await the arrival of aircraft.

Following pages Terminal with aircraft docked alongside.

Airside

The airside exterior of the boarding wing can be seen close up and obliquely from the glazed boarding bridges, though only in a tantalizingly brief glimpse before pressing on to board your plane. Apart from the distant vistas from the bridge to the mainland or the roof terrace of the domestic cargo building, views of the airside can only be had from the windows of taxi-ing planes, or from the airfield itself where no public are permitted.

Looking along the building from the boarding bridge shows that the glazing looks as nonchalantly straightforward as it does from inside. Further finely judged and enlivening touches include the way the last rows of tiles peel away and oversail the top of the glazing as a shading overhang, and the tiny punctuations of the projecting ends of the rafters to which they are secured. Even the single large step upwards, which the curving bottom edge of the roof takes towards each end (as it comes too low in relation to the space inside), works beautifully to clarify the form and enliven the ends of the roof.

Along the base of this glazing, there is a row of yellow fishtail-shaped elements, which are not always evenly spaced. These conduct fresh conditioned air to the inlets along the base of the glazing. Before the boarding bridges were installed, these were very distracting; but they are much less so now as it is impossible to see a long run of them. Nevertheless, it is a detail which still provokes some doubts, not least because it seems less derived from the internal logic of the design than resurrected, like some other dubious details, from Piano's past. (A similar detail was used for the IBM Travelling Pavilion, Volume One p 110, and Piano & Rogers' Patscentre building near Cambridge, England.) Also, as with the blue tubular ducts inside, the reason for introducing the eye-catching fishtails seems to be to jolly up this immensely long and understated facade. But such loss of nerve and resort to past solutions seems unwarranted, especially as following the logic of the design has worked elsewhere so brilliantly.

2

3

Kansai International Airport

Client Kansai International Airport Co Ltd

Competition-winning design
Architect Renzo Piano Building Workshop
Engineer Ove Arup & Partners
International Ltd

Basic design & detail design
Consortium for terminal building
Design architects & engineers
Renzo Piano Building Workshop Japan KK
in collaboration with Ove Arup & Partners
International Ltd, Nikken Sekkei Ltd
**Basic concept, functional analysis
and design of moving elements**
Aéroports de Paris (P Andreu, J-M Chevalier)
**Negotiation with government
departments, civil aviation authorities
and airside planning** Japan Airport
Consultants, Inc (M Matsumoto)

Competition team
Design team R Piano, N Okabe (associate
in charge), J-F Blassel, R Brennan, A Chaaya,
L Couton, R Keiser, L Koenig, K McBryde,
S Planchez, R Rolland, G Torre, O Touraine
Assisted by G le Breton, M Henry, J Lelay,
A O'Carrol, M Salerno, A H Téménidès,
N Westphal
Engineers Ove Arup & Partners
International Ltd (structure: P Rice; services:
T Barker)
Landscape architect M Desvigne

Basic design & detail design team
Design team R Piano, N Okabe
(associate in charge), J-F Blassel, A Chavela,
I Corte, K Fraser, R S Garlipp, M Goerdt,
G Hall, K Hirano, A Ikegami, S Ishida
(associate architect), A Johnson, C Kelly,
T Kimura, S Larsen, J Lelay, K McBryde,
T Miyazaki, S Nakaya, N Takata, T Tomuro,

O Touraine, M Turpin, M Yamada,
H Yamaguchi, T Yamaguchi
Assisted by A Autin, G Cohen, A Golzari,
B Gunning, G Hastrich, M Horie, I Kubo,
S Medio, K Miyake, S Montaldo, S Mukai,
K A Naderi, K Nyunt (landscape), S Oehler,
T O'Sullivan, P Persia, F Pierandrei,
M Rossato, R Shields, T Takagawa, T Ueno,
K Uezono, J M Weill, T Yamakoshi
Engineers Ove Arup & Partners International
Ltd (structure: P Rice, T Stevens, P Dilley;
services: A Guthrie; fire: P Beever)
Acoustics Peutz et Associés (Y Dekeyrel)
Endwall glazing study R Van Santen
Quantity surveyor Davis Langdon &
Everest (C Malby, T Gatehouse), Futaba
Quantity Surveying Co Ltd
Landscape Koung Nyunt

Site supervision team
Design team R Piano, N Okabe (associate
in charge), A Ikegami, T Kimura, T Tomuro,
Y Ueno
Assisted by S Kano, A Shimizu
Endwall glazing development RFR
(J-F Blassel)
Canyon planting Toshi Keikan Sekkei Inc
(S Okumura)

Contractors
North Passenger Terminal Building
Joint Venture (General manager: Shin'ichi
Ota) Obayashi Corporation, Shimuzu
Corporation, Fluor Daniel Japan, Toda
Corporation, Okumura Corporation, Konoike
Construction, Nishimatsu Construction,
Hazama Corporation, Sato Kogyo, Fudo
Construction

South Passenger Terminal Building
Joint Venture (General manager: Mitsuhiro
Onishi) Takenaka Corporation, Kajima
Corporation, Taisei Corporation, Overseas
Bechtel, Fujita Corporation, The Zenitaka
Corporation, Asanuma Corporation,
Matsumura-Gumi Corporation, Tokyu
Corporation, Tobishima Corporation

230 **Renzo Piano AIA, RIBA, BDA**

Born in Genoa on 14 September 1937, Renzo Piano studied architecture at the University of Florence and Milan Polytechnic, graduating from the latter in 1964. While studying he worked under Franco Albini and spent time on the construction sites of his father, a builder. In 1965 he set up Studio Piano and between then and 1970, with the support of his father, he experimented with lightweight structures, collaborating at various periods with Z S Makowsky in London, Marco Zanuso in Milan and Louis Kahn in Philadelphia. During this period he also met his friend and mentor Jean Prouvé.

Between 1971 and 1978 he was in partnership with Richard Rogers (Piano & Rogers) and between 1978 and 1980 with the engineer Peter Rice (Piano & Rice Associates), with whom he continued to collaborate until Rice's death in 1992. In 1981 he formed the Renzo Piano Building Workshop with offices in Genoa and Paris. From 1989 to 1994 the Building Workshop also had an office in Osaka, Japan, and now has another in Berlin.

Piano has been visiting professor at major universities around the world, including Columbia University in New York, University of Pennsylvania in Philadelphia, Oslo School of Architecture, Central London Polytechnic and the Architectural Association in London, and the universities of Stuttgart, Tokyo and Delft. Exhibitions of his work have been held in many cities worldwide, including Paris, London, Naples, Helsinki, Vicenza, Marseilles, Berlin, Madrid, Rotterdam, São Paulo, New York, Houston, Los Angeles, Philadelphia, Boston, Vancouver, Pittsburgh, Chicago, Tokyo, Osaka, Nagoya and Sapporo.

In 1978 he was awarded an Honorary Fellowship of the Union of International Architects and in 1981 the Compasso d'Oro in Italy and an AIA Honorary Fellowship in the USA. In 1984 he was awarded Commandeur des Arts et des Lettres in France and in 1985 the Legion d'Honneur and an RIBA Honorary Fellowship in London. In 1989 he was awarded the Royal Gold Medal of the RIBA and the Cavalieri di Gran Croce in Italy. In 1990 he received an Honorary Doctorate from Stuttgart University and the Inamori Foundation Prize in Kyoto, Japan. In 1991 he was awarded the Richard Neutra Prize in Pomona, California, and in 1992 was given an Honorary Doctorate from Delft University. In 1994 he was awarded an Honorary Fellowship of the American Academy of Arts and Letters, the Arnold W Brunner Memorial Prize and the Premio Michelangelo in Rome as well as being made an Officier dans l'Ordre Nationale du Mérite in France and UNESCO Goodwill Ambassador for Architecture. In 1995 he was awarded the Art Prize of the Akademie der Kunste in Berlin, the Praemium Imperiale in Tokyo and the Erasmus Prize in Amsterdam. In 1996 he received the Premio Capo Circeo and the Premio Simpatia in Rome.

Projects in progress that will be shown in future volumes include: the Lyon Internationale de Lyon multiplex cinema and hotel; a commercial and office centre in Lecco, Italy; Museum of Science and Technology in Amsterdam; Beyeler Museum near Basel, Switzerland; Padre Pio Pilgrimage Church near Foggia, Italy; Jean-Marie Tjibaou Cultural Centre in Noumea, New Caledonia; Mercedes-Benz Design Centre, Stuttgart; masterplan and several buildings in the Potsdamer Platz area of Berlin; Brancusi Atelier and rehabilitation of the Pompidou Centre, Paris; Rome Auditoria; Tiburtina Station, Rome; Ferrari Windtunnel, Maranello, Modena, Italy; an office tower in Sydney, Australia; and headquarters for Fila Corporation in Baltimore, USA and Seoul, Korea.

Acknowledgements

The development of the Building Workshop since its birth nearly 30 years ago is due to the efforts of those listed below; a list that includes those who have either worked with us or with whom we have had a close association. The list does not include the many more people who have contributed in some other way to our efforts over the years. We take this opportunity to express our gratitude to all.
Renzo Piano

Camilla Aasgard
Sebastien Abbado
Laurie Abbot
Maria Accardi
PeterAckermann
Naderi Kamran Afshar
Emilia Agazzi
Francesco Albini
Alessandra Alborghetti
Jean Philippe Allain
Michele Allevi
Michel Alluyn
Massimo Alvisi
Marco Amosso
Arianna Andidero
Sally Appleby
Andrea Arancio
Catherine Ardilley
Magda Arduino
Stefano Arecco
Eric Audoye
P Audran
Véronique Auger
Frank August
Alexandre Autin
Carmela Avagliano
Patrizio Avellino
Rita Avvenente

Carlo Bachschmidt
Jack Backus
Alessandro Badi
Susan Baggs
Emanuela Baglietto
Antonella Balassone
Nicolo Baldassini
François Barat
Henry Bardsley
Giulia Barone
Sonia Barone
Laura Bartolomei
Fabrizio Bartolomeo
Mario Bartylla
Christopher Bartz
Bruna Bassetti
Katy Bassière
Mario Bassignani
Sandro Battini
Roger Baumgarten
Paolo Beccio
Eva Belik
Annie Benzeno
Jan Berger
François Bertolero
Alessandro Bianchi
Giorgio Bianchi
Ptrizia Bianchini
Gianfranco Biggi
Grégoire Bignier

Germana Binelli
Judy Bing
Rosella Biondo
Jean François Blassel
A Blassone
William Blurock
Paolo Bodega
Marko Bojovic
Willaim Boley
Sara Bonati
Manuela Bonino
Gilles Bontemps
Gail Borden
Antonella Bordoni
Andrea Bosch
Pierre Botschi
Mariolijne Boudry
Sandrine Boulay
Bret Bowin
Carola Brammen
Ross Brennan
John Breshears
Gaëlle Breton
Flore Bringand
Maria Brizzolara
Cuno Brullmann
Michael Burckhardt
Christiane Bürklein
Mary Byrne
Hans-Peter Bysaeth

Federica Caccavale
Alessandro Calafati
Chrystelle Calafell
Benedetto Calcagno
Patrick Callegia
Maurizio Calosso
Michele Calvi
Stefan Camenzino
Nunzio Camerada
Daniele Campo
Florence Canal
Andrea Canepa
Stefania Canta
Vittorio Caponetto
Daniela Capuzzo
Alessandro Carisetto
Monica Carletti
Elena Carmignani
Isabella Carpiceci
Emanuele Carreri
Gilbert Carriera
Mark Carroll
Nicola Carta
Costanza Cartamantiglia
Elena Casali
Marta Castagna
Cristina Catino
Maria Cattaneo

Enrica Causa
Dante Cavagna
Simone Cecchi
Giorgio Celadon
Ottaviano Celadon
Massimo Cella
Alessandro Cereda
Antoine Chaaya
Patricia Chappell
Patrick Charles
Jean Luc Chassais
Pierre Chatelain
Hubert Chatenay
Ariel Chavela
Tina Chee
Laura Cherchi
Raimondo Chessa
Christopher Chevalier
Catherine Clarisse
Geoffrey Cohen
Franc Collect
Daniel Collin
Christophe Colson
Shelly Comer
Philippe Convercey
Guendalina Conti
Pier Luigi Copat
Michel Corajoud
Colman Corish
Cristian Cortto
Monica Corsilia
Ivan Corte
Giacomo Costa
Leopoldo Costa
Raffaella Costa
Loïc Couton
Rosa Coy
Paolo Crema
Raffaella Belmondi Croce
A Croxato
Mario Cucinella
Irene Cuppone
Catherine Cussoneau
Lorenzo Custer

Stefano D'Atri
Catherine D'Ovido
Isabelle Da Costa
Thomas Damisch
Michel Dananco
Paul Darmer
Lorenzo Dasso
K Matthew Daubman
Mike Davies
Daniela Defilla
S Degli Innocenti
Andreas Degn
Silvia De Leo
Valentina Delli Ponti

Alessandro De Luca
Dalia De Macina
Simona De Mattei
Alessio Demontis
Evelyne Delmoral
Michel Denancé
Olaf de Nooyer
Julien Descombes
Daria De Seta
Michel Desvigne
Laura Di Aichelburg
Carmelo Di Bartolo
Ottavio Di Blasi
Hélène Diebold
Maddalena Di Sopra
Brian Ditchburn
Vittorio Di Turi
John Doggart
Olivier Doizy
Eugenio Donato
François Doria
Michael Dowd
Mike Downs
Klaus Dreissigacker
Delphine Drouin
Serge Drouin
Giorgio Ducci
Frank Dubbers
Paul Du Mesnil Du Buisson
Susan Dunne
Jean Luc Dupanloup
Philippe Dupont
Susanne Durr
John Dutton

Mick Eekhout
Stacy Eisenberg
Birgit Eistert
Ahmed El Jerari
Kenneth Zammit Endrich
Lukas Epprecht
James Evans
Allison Ewing

Roberta Fambri
Roberto Faravelli
Giorgio Fascioli
Maxwell Fawcett
Monica Fea
David Felice
Alfonso Femia
Jacques Fendard
Ruben Prado Fernandez
Agostino Ferrari
Maurizio Filocca
Laurent Marc Fischer
Thomas Fisher
Richard Fitgerald
Eileen Fitzgerald

232

Peter Flack
Johannes Florin
Renato Foni
M Fordam
Gilles Fourel
Gianfranco Franchini
Kenneth Fraser
Nina Freedman
Marian Frezza
Enrico Frigerio
Junya Fujita
Pierre Furnemont

Rinaldo Gaggero
Sergio Gaggero
Alain Gallissian
Andrea Gallo
Antonio Gallo
Carla Garbato
Robert Garlipp
Maurizio Garrasi
G Gasbarri
Angelo Ghiotto
M Giacomelli
Davide Gibelli
Alain Gillette
Sonia Giordani
Alberto Giordano
Roberto Giordano
Antonella Giovannoni
Giovanna Giusto
Marion Goerdt
Marco Goldschmied
Enrico Gollo
Anahita Golzari
Alessandro Gortan
Philippe Goubet
Françoise Gouinguenet
Robert Grace
Giorgio Grandi
Cecil Granger
Walter Grasmug
Don Gray
Nigel Greenhill
Magali Grenier
Paolo Guerrini
Domenico Guerrisi
Alain Guèze
Barnaby Gunning
Ranjit Gupta

Antoine Hahne
Greg Hall
Donald L Hart
Thomas Hartman
Margrith Hartmann
Gunther Hastrich
Ulrike Hautsch
Adam Hayes

Christopher Hays
Eva Hegerl
Oliver Hempel
Pascal Hendier
Pierre Henneguier
Maire Henry
Gabriel Hernandez
Caroline Herrin
Christopher Hight
Kohji Hirano
Harry Hirsch
Andrew Holmes
Eric Holt
Abigal Hopkins
Masahiro Horie
Hélène Houizot
Michelle Howard
Bruno Hubert
Jean Huc
Ed Huckabi
Frank Hughes
Charles Hussey

Filippo Icardi
Frediano Iezzi
Akira Ikegami
Djénina Illoul
Luca Imberti
Paolo Insogna
Shunji Ishida

Charlotte Jackman
Angela Jackson
Tobias Jaklin
Robert Jan van Santen
Amanda Johnson
Luis Jose
Frédéric Joubert

Shin Kanoo
Jan Kaplicky
Elena Karitakis
Robert Keiser
Christopher Kelly
Paul Kelly
Werner Kestel
Irini Kilaiditi
Tetsuya Kimura
Laurent Koenig
Tomoko Komatsubara
Akira Komiyama
Misha Kramer
Jeff Krolicki
Eva Kruse
Betina Kurtz

Jean Baptiste Lacoudre
Antonio Lagorio
Giovanna Langasco

Frank La Riviere
Stig Larsen
Denis La Ville
François La Ville
Sojin Lee
Jean Lelay
Renata Lello
Claudia Leoncini
Laurent Le Voyer
Riccardo Librizzi
Olivier Lidon
Lorraine Lin
Bill Logan
Johanna Lohse
Federica Lombardo
François Lombardo
Steve Lopez
Riccardo Luccardini
Simonetta Lucci
Rolf Robert Ludewig
Claudine Luneberg
Massimiliano Lusetti

Paola Maggiora
Domenico Magnano
Nicholas Malby
Milena Mallamaci
Natalie Mallat
Claudio Manfreddo
Ester Manitto
Roberto Mantelli
Paolo Mantero
Flavio Marano
Andrea Marasso
Francesco Marconi
Massimo Mariani
Alberto Marre Brunenghi
Cristina Martinelli
Luca Massone
Daniela Mastragostino
Manuela Mattei
William Matthews
Marie Hélène Maurette
Gian Mauro Maurizio
Caroline Mahon Maxwell
Kathrin Mayer
Ken McBryde
Katherine McLone
Grainne McMahon
Jonathan McNeal
Nayla Mecattaf
Simone Medio
Barbara Mehren
Eveline Mercier
Benny Merello
Gabriella Merlo
Peter Metz

Jean C M'Fouara
Daniela Miccolis
Marcella Michelotti
Paolo Migone
Emanuela Minetti
Eduardo Miola
Takeshi Miyazaki
Gianni Modolo
Sandro Montaldo
Elisa Monti
Luca Mori
Julia Moser
Joost Moolhuijzen
Denise Morando
Nascimento
Gérard Mormina
Ingrid Morris
Jean Bernard Mothes
Farshid Moussavi
Mariette Müller
Philip Murphy
Andrea Musso

Hanne Nagel
Shinichi Nakaya
Hiroshi Naruse
Roberto Navarra
Pascale Nègre
Chi-Tam Nguyen
Andrew Nichols
Hiroko Nishikama
Susanne Lore Nobis
David Nock
Elizabeth Nodinot
Mojan Nouban
Marco Nouvion
Eric Novel
Koung Nyunt

Alphons Oberhoffer
Anna O'Carrol
Stefan Oehler
Noriaki Okabe
Antonella Oldani
Sonia Oldani
Grace Ong
Patrizia Orcamo
Stefania Orcamo
Roy Orengo
Carlos Osrej
Tim O'Sullivan
Piero Ottaggio
Mara Ottonello
Nedo Ottonello

Antonella Paci
Nicola Pacini
Filippo Pagliani
Michael Palmore

Roger Panduro
Giorgia Paraluppi
Chandra Patel
Pietro Pedrini
Roberto Pelagatti
Luigi Pellini
Danilo Peluffo
Gianluca Peluffo
Hembert Penaranda
Lionel Pénisson
Mauro Penna
Patrizia Persia
Morten Busk Petersen
Claire Petetin
Gil Petit
Ronan Phelan
Paul Phillips
Alberto Piancastelli
Carlo Piano
Daniele Piano
Lia Piano
Matteo Piano
Mario Piazza
Enrico Piazze
Gennaro Picardi
Alessandro Pierandrei
Fabrizio Pierandrei
M Pietrasanta
Claudia Pigionanti
Marie Pimmel
Alessandro Pisacane
Sandra Planchez
Bernard Plattner
Monica Poggi
Jean Alexandre Polette
Andrea Polleri
Antonio Porcile
Roberta Possanzini
Fabio Postani
Gabriella Primo
Nicolas Prouvé
Costanza Puglisi
Sophie Purnama

Gianfranco Queirolo

Michele Ras
Maria Cristina Rasero
Roberto Rasore
Dominique Rat
Neil Rawson
Judith Raymond
Antonella Recagno
Olaf Recktenwald
Philippe Reigner
Daniele Reimondo
Luis Renau
Tom Reynolds
Bryan Reynolds

Elena Ricciardi
Kieran Rice
Nemone Rice
Peter Rice
Jean Yves Richard
Gianni Robotti
Giuseppe Rocco
Richard Rogers
Renaud Rolland
Sylvie Romet Milanesi
Emilia Rossato
Paola Rossato
Stefano Rossi
Bernard Rouyer
Raffaella Rovani
Tammy Roy
Caroline Roux
Lucio Ruocco
Joachim Ruoff
Ken Rupard

Antonella Sacchi
Angela Sacco
Jean Gérard Saint
Riccardo Sala
Maria Salerno
Maurizio Santini
Francesca Santolini
Paulo Sanza
Carola Sapper
Paul Satchell
Alessandro Savioli
Susanna Scarabicchi
Maria Grazia Scavo
Stefan Schäfer
Helga Schlegel
Giuseppina Schmid
Jean François Schmit
Maren Schuessler
Andrea Schultz
C Segantini
Daniel Seibold
Ronnie Self
Barbara-Petra Sellwig
Mario Semino
Patrik Senné
Anna Serra
Kelly Shannon
Randy Shields
Aki Shimizu
Madoka Shimuzu
Cécile Simon
David Simonetti
Thibaud Simonin
Alessandro Sinagra
Luca Siracusa
Jan Sircus
Alan Smith
Stephanie Smith

Franc Somner
Richard Soundy
Claudette Spielmann
Susanne Stacher
Adrian Stadlmayer
Alan Stanton
Graham Stirk
Eric Stotts
David Summerfield
Franc Sumner
Jasmin Surti
Christian Susstrunk

José Luis Taborda
Barrientos
Hiroyuki Takahashi
Norio Takata
Noriko Takiguchi
Hélène Teboul
Anne Hélène Téménides
Carlo Teoldi
Peter Terbuchte
G L Terragna
David Thom
John Thornhill
Cinzia Tiberti
Luigi Tirelli
Elisabeth Tisseur
Vittorio Tolu
Taichi Tomuro
Bruno Tonfoni
Graciella Torre
Laura Torre
Olivier Touraine
Franco Trad
Alessandro Traldi
Renata Trapani
Renzo Venanzio Truffelli
Leland Turner
Mark Turpin

Yoshiko Ueno
Kiyomi Uezono
Joong-Yeun Uhr Sim
Peter Ullathorne

Colette Valensi
Maurizio Vallino
Harrie Van der Meijs
Mauritz Van der Staay
Michael Vaniscott
Antonia Van Oosten
Robert Jan Van Stanten
Arijan Van Timmeren
Maurizio Varratta
Paolo Varratta
Claudio Vaselli
William Vassal
Francesca Vattuone

Bernard Vaudeville
Martin Veith
Maria Veltcheva
Reiner Verbizh
Laura Vercelli
Maria Carla Verdona
Sonia Vernagen
Eric Verstrepen
Silvia Vignale
Antonella Vignoli
Mark Viktov
Alain Vincent
Paul Vincent
Patrick Virly
Marco Visconti
Lorenzo Viti
Bettina Volz
Erik Volz
Philippe Von Matt

Louis Waddell
Bashaar Wahab
Jean Marc Weill
Florian Wenz
Nicole Westermann
Nicolas Westphal
Chris Wilkinson
Neil Winder
Martin Wollensak
Jacob Woltjer
Sarah Wong

George Xydis

Masami Yamada
Sugako Yamada
Hiroshi Yamaguchi
Tatsuya Yamaguchi
Emi Yoshimura
John Young

Gianpaolo Zaccaria
Kenneth Endrich Zammit
Lorenzo Zamperetti
Antonio Zanuso
Martina Zappettini
Walter Zbinden
Maurizio Zepponi
Massimo Zero
Alessandro Zoppini
Ivana Zunino

Select bibliography

Listed below are publications that have appeared since the beginning of 1993. For a more complete bibliography the following should be read in conjunction with the bibliography in Volume Two.

Books

Renzo Piano, progetti e architetture, Vol 3, 1987–94, Milan, Electa, 1994 (English edition by Birkhäuser, Basel, 1994; German edition by D V A, Stuttgart, 1994)

The Making of Kansai International Airport, Osaka, Japan: Renzo Piano Building Workshop, Tokyo, Kodansha, 1994, by Renzo Piano Building Workshop

Monographic issues of journals

Japan Architect No 15, Autumn 1994: *Kansai International Airport Passenger Terminal Building*

Architectural Review November 1994: *Kansai* (Special issue edited and written by P Buchanan)

Process Architecture December 1994: *Kansai International Airport Passenger Terminal Building*

Articles

1993

Architectural Review January 1993, pp20–28: 'Crossroads Berlin' by D Cruikshank and pp36–41: 'Genoa Drama' by D Cruikshank

Arca January 1993, pp48–53: 'Un parco culturale per la città il Lingotto' by R Dorigati

Domus January 1993, pp52–59: 'Renzo Piano Aeroporto di Kansai, Osaka'

Costruire, January 1993, p48: 'Piano per tre' by Laura Rogliani

Werk, Bauen + Wohnen January/February 1993, pp41–48: 'Zwischen Seelandschaft und Piazza' by G Ullman

Architectural Design January/February 1993, pp18–23: 'Potsdamer Platz – Leipziger Platz, Berlin 1991' by C Sattler

Casabella January/February 1993, pp120–121: 'Sistemazione degli spazi esterni dell'industria Thomson a Guyancourt'

Interni January/February 1993, pp120–121: 'Crown Princess'

Architecture February 1993, pp22–23: 'Renzo Piano exhibit in NY' by D Albrecht

Progressive Architecture February 1993, pp19: 'Renzo Piano exhibit opens in NY' by P Arcidi

Detail February 1993, pp593–597: 'Elektronikfabrik in Guyancourt' and 'Das Experiment im Werk, Renzo Piano'

Rassenga March 1993, pp90–92: 'Lingotto: una completa gamma illuminotecnica ad alto contenuto tecnologico'

Arquitectura Viva March/April 1993, pp52–59: 'Mechanico e Organico' by P Buchanan

Domus April 1993, pp87–89: 'Renzo Piano' by E Morteo

Abitare April 1993, pp156–169: 'Unesco & Workshop' by E Regazzoni

Casabella May 1993, pp4–19: 'Il terminal passeggeri del Kansai International Airport nella baia di Osaka' by S Brandolini

Flare May 1993, pp26–28: 'La luce nell'architettura Hi-Tech' by N Baldessini

Le Moniteur May 1993, pp44–49: 'Aéroport International de Kansai' by O Touraine

Mwa Vee May 1993, pp48–53: 'Le Centre Cultural Jean-Marie Tjibaou'

Arquitectura Viva May/June 1993, pp96–97: 'Hipergeometrías, el ordenador en el studio de Renzo Piano' by J Sainz

Proporzione June 1993, pp32–40: 'Lingotto Fiere: montanti eccezionali per diaframmi luminosi'

234

Techniques et Architecture June/July 1993, pp114–121: 'La grande vague' by M Tardis

Japan Architect Summer 1993, pp212–217: 'Ushibuka fishing port connecting bridge'

Werk, Bauen + Wohnen July/August 1993, pp20–25: 'Solitärs in der periurbanen Würste' by R P Red

Detail August/September 1993, pp414–417: 'Haltestelle Brin in Genua'

GB Progetti September 1993, p4: 'Osaka: Aeroporto' and p16: 'Amsterdam: Musei' by F Premoli

Japan Architect Autumn 1993, pp54–69: 'Kansai International Airport, passenger terminal building'

GB Progetti November 1993, p10: 'Ushibuka – Giappone: Ponti'

Maiora December 1993, pp4–11: 'Un edificio residenziale a Parigi: rue de Meaux' by M Rognoni

Industria delle Costruzione December 1993, pp64–65: 'Progetti di Renzo Piano in mostra itinerante' by G Messina

Lapiz December 1993, pp45–49: 'Arquitectura en la confluencia de los límites' JM Alvarez Enjto

Casabella December 1993, p38: 'Nuovo Teatro Margherita'

Detail December 1993/January 1994, pp829–32: 'Stadium in Bari'

1994
Werk, Bauen + Wohnen No 567, January 1994, pp49–53: 'Flugzeugträger' by R Keiser

Kenchiku bunka No 567, January 1994, pp161–176: 'Kansai Airport'

Kenchiku bunka No 570, April 1994, pp21–74: 'Kansai Airport'

Costruire May 1994, pp125–128: 'Un Lingotto di tecnologia' by A Bugatti

Archis June 1994, pp5–7: 'Het juiste gebaar' by M Kloos

Kenchiku bunka No 572, June 1994, pp25–44: 'Kansai Airport'

Scroope No 6 94/95, pp28–29: 'Padre Pio Pilgrimage Church, Italy' by P Buchanan

GA July/August 1994, pp24–80: 'Special Feature: Kansai Airport'

AIT July/August 1994, pp26–35: 'Woge. Der Kansai-Airport in der Bucht von Osaka' by Dietmar Danner

Casabella July/August 1994, pp52–59: 'L'Auditorium al Lingotto di Torino'

Kenchiku bunka No 574, August 1994, pp89–118: 'Kansai Airport'

Kenchiku bunka No 575, September 1994, pp91–98: 'Kansai Airport'

Independent on Sunday 4 September 1994, pp18–21 of Sunday Review: 'Going with the Flow: Kansai International Airport' by P Buchanan

Domus Dossier No 2: 'Museum' September 1994, pp30–33: 'Museo Beyeler a Riehen, Basilea' by R Piano

Perspectives September 1994, pp34–37: 'Piano Forte' by D Cruikshank

Building Design September 1994, pp16–19: 'The hills are alive'

Modulo September 1994, pp284–291: 'Un nuovo Lingotto per Torino' by L Verdi

Progressive Architecture September 1994, p22: 'Kansai Airport artificial landscape'

Approach No 3, Autumn 1994, pp1–23: 'Special Report RPBW, Creating Harmony from Technology and Nature', by R Miyake

Domus October 1994, pp7–23: 'Renzo Piano Building Workshop, Aeroport Internazionale di Kansai, Osaka, Giappone' by L Gazzaniga

Arca October 1994, pp2–27: 'Kansai International Airport' by A Castellano

Bauwelt October 1994, pp60–61: 'Die Wochenschau – Neue Töne'

Costruire October 1994, pp46–49: 'Leggero come l'aria' by M C Clemente

GB Progetti October 1994, p16 : 'Auditorium Lingotto'

DBZ November 1994, pp67–70: 'Hafenanlage von Genua' by C F Kusch

Amadeus November 1994, pp43–45: 'Il nouvo Auditorium di Roma, una sfida urbanistica' by V Capelli

Lotus International November 1994, pp42–55: 'Noumea: Paris' by A Rocca

Werk, Bauen + Wohnen November 1994, pp6–17: 'Vorwärtsstrategien' by R Keiser

Arquitectura Viva November/December 1994, pp46–47: 'Dunas de metal: Kansai aeropuerto' by P Buchanan

Costruire December 1994, pp38–40: 'Luci della Cité' by G de Withy; and pp114–115: 'Le piazze perdute' by M P Belki

Industria delle Costruzione December 1994, pp40–42: 'Renzo Piano: un Auditorium per Roma' by G Messina

1995
Architecture January 1995, pp84–103: 'Plane Geometry' by P Buchanan and 'Ahead of the curve: technical aspects of Kansai' by P Buchanan

Arup Journal January 1995, pp14–23: 'Kansai International Airport terminal building' by P Dilley & A Guthrie

Building Design January 95, pp12–13: 'Best Fiat Forward' by J Melvin

Arca January 1995, pp4–9: 'Come casse armoniche' by A Castellano

Architecture d'Aujourd'hui February 1995, pp66–73: 'Potsdamer Platz'

Vetro Spazio March 1995, pp18–26: 'Appunti di volo per Kansai Airport' by N Okabe

Costruire March 1995, pp44–46: 'Il futuro in cantiere' by C A Bottigelli & M G Alessi

Domus March 1995, pp 68–69: 'Potsdamer Platz' by P Giordano

Architecture April 1995, p24: 'Cy Twombly Gallery' by D Dillon

Techniques et Architecture April/May 1995, pp72–77: 'Cité d'Avenir. Cité Internaionale de Lyon' by J F P

Costruire in Laterizio May/June 1995, pp162–167: 'IRCAM Parigi. Il terziario fra current architecture neotradizionalismo' by L Spagnoli

Finestra June 1995, pp176–185: 'Il Lingotto di Piano' by C Garbato

Modulo June 1995, pp494–495: 'Un Auditorium tutto in legno' by M Toffolon

Rassegna June 1995, pp 45–55: 'La città dei concorsi: Berlino del dopo muro' by P Rumpt

Ecclesia June 1995, pp48–57: 'Fede e tecnologia' by A Castellano

Idea July 1995, pp26–31: 'Crown Princess, il bianco delfino d'acciaio'

GB Progetti July/August 1995, p34–35: 'Al cantiere della Cité Internationale de Lyon' by L L Pirano & M Gatto

Architectural Review September 1995, pp76–80: 'Natural Workshop' by P Buchanan

Architektura–Murator September 1995, pp34–41: 'Organiczna maszyna (Kansai Airport)' by P Buchanan

Area September 1995, pp26–33: 'La conchiglia d'argento (Lyon)' by G Sgali

Abitare September 1995, pp85–86: 'Lione: la città internazionale'

GB Progetti September 1995, pp8–13: 'Saitama Arena competition'

A+U November 1995, pp6–17: 'Cy Twombly Annex at the Menil Collection' by S Ishida

At November 1995, pp44–49: 'Ushibuka Bridge' by N Okabe

Architektur Aktuell December 1995, pp40–45: 'Kompaß' by V V de Raulino

Casabella December 1995, pp8–23: 'Lione: la politica degli spazi' by M Bedarida

1996

Architectural Review January 1996, pp50–57: 'The key to the city (Lyon)' by P Buchanan

Arkitekten January 1996, pp8–11: 'Auditorium Roma' by L L Sorensen

Costruire January 1996, pp30–31: 'San Nicola: Bari-Soltanto per Bari' by R Laera

Domus January 1996, p96: 'Renzo Piano'

Casabella January/February 1996, p84: 'Kanak' by R Piano and pp 126–127: 'The International of the Tourist' by R Ingersoll

Grap Casa January/February 1996, pp96–101: 'Berlino-cantiere laboratorio' by A Dominoni

Culture Zones Spring 1996, pp16–19: 'The Twombly and the making of place' by W F Stern

Archis March 1996, pp38–45: 'La Cité Internationale de Lyon' by C A Boyer

Bauwelt March 1996, p424: 'Cité Internationale in Lyon'

Häuser March 1996, pp51–62: 'Renzo Piano' by I Maisch

Parcours April 1996, pp66–69: 'Lyon: une eurocité' by D Chetrit

Detail April/May 1996, pp280–290: 'Alt und New. Ein interview mit Renzo Piano' by C Schittich and pp 331–337: 'Centre for Business and Art in Turin'

Mercedes April/May 1996, pp20–27: 'La configurazione dello spazio' by C Garbato

DBZ May 1996, pp83–90: 'Eine Architektur der ortsbezogenen Technologie' by V C F Kush

Domus May 1996, pp4–8: 'Universalismo e Regionalismo' by K Frampton

Micromega May/June 1996, pp107–109: 'Il mestiere piu antico del mondo' by R Piano

Domus June 1996, pp84–88: 'Susumu Shingu, poeta e filosofo dello spazio' by P Restany

Building Design June 1996, pp16–19: 'The craft of diversity'

Abitare June 1996, pp104–105: 'Germania, da Berlino verso Est' by I Lupi

Architektura-Murator June 1996, pp32–37: 'Ray uczestnictwa' by P Buchanan

Ottagono June/August 1996, p43: 'Luce, spazio e visione' by L Pagani & A Perversi; pp50–53: 'Un luminoso rigore' by C Garbato

DBZ July 1996, pp26–27: 'Urbane Zukunftsvision'

Abitare July/August 1996, p34: 'La Ferrari e Maranello, Maranello e la Ferrari'

Domus July/August 1996, pp16–25: 'Cité Internationale: Lyon' by C A Boyer

Bauwelt August 1996, pp 1752–1753: 'Stuttgart 21'

Architecture Intérieure-crée August/September 1996, pp50–55: 'Noumea, Centre Jean-Marie Tjibaou'; pp66–69: 'Lyon. Batiment pour installations'; and pp74–77: 'L'IRCAM en trois actes et quatre batiments'

Architects' Journal 19 September 1996, pp28–30: 'Freedom of ideas under fire' by P Buchanan

Arca October 1996, pp6–9: 'Ferrovia e città' by G Muratore

Abitare October 1996, p96: 'Al Lingotto'

Jaaverslag October 1996, pp1–25: 'Technologie Museum NINT/Impuls Science and Technology Centre' by D Elco

Eden rivista dell'architettura nel paesaggio Autumn 1996, pp15–26: 'L'Aeroporto internazionale di Kansai, Osaka, Giappone 1988–1994'; pp27–32: 'La trasfomazione della fabrica Fiat, Lingotto, Italia, 1991–'; and pp33–38: 'Il centro culturale Kanak Jean-Marie Tjibaou, Noumea, Nuova Caledonia', all by B Camerana

Atrium Haus und Wohnen International November/December 1996, pp84–91: 'Renzo Piano: Kolumbus der neuen Architektur' by C Wolf and pp126–129: 'B & B. Innovative Technik und zeitgemäßes Design' by I Meier

236   **Index**

Page numbers in *italic* refer to the illustrations

acoustics
  Lingotto Factory Renovation, Turin **48–52**
  Rome Auditoria **108**, **109**, *109*
  Saitama Arena **125**
Aéroport de Paris **140**, **143**, **149**, **150**, **151**,
  162, **209**
air-conditioning
  Cy Twombly Gallery, Houston 60
  Kansai International Airport, Osaka **147–8**,
  154, **196–8**, **196–8**, **212**, **216**
  Saitama Arena **125**
airports *see* Kansai International Airport, Osaka
Albini, Franco **23**
aluminium *32*, *70*, *72*, **156**, **192**, **198**, **201**,
  203, *186*, *193*, *202*, *203*
Amsterdam *see* National Centre for Science
  and Technology
Andreu, Paul **140**
art galleries **22**
  see also Bankside Power Station, London;
  Cité Internationale de Lyon; Cy Twombly
  Gallery, Houston; Lingotto Factory
  Renovation, Turin
Art Nouveau *12*, **133**
Arup, Ove & Partners **9**
  Cité Internationale de Lyon **33**
  Cy Twombly Gallery, Houston **59–60**
  Grand Stade, Paris **118**
  Kansai International Airport, Osaka **130**, **138**,
  141, **149**, **150**, **151**, **152**, **154**, **155**,
  196, **198**, **200**
  Lingotto Factory Renovation, Turin **52**, **53**
  Sydney Opera House **168**
Arup Acoustics **48**, **108**
Awaji Island **138**, *138*

Banca Popolare di Lodi, **17–21**, *18–19*, **28**,
  77
Bankside Power Station, London **22**, **23**, *23*,
  24, **34**, **54**, *54–5*

plan *55*
Bari *see* San Nicola Stadium
Barker, Tom **9**, **130**, **141**, **147**, **196**
Barnstone, Howard **56**
Bas Meudon, Paris *32*, **98–100**, *99–101*
  plan *99*
Basle *see* Beyeler Foundation Museum
Battersea Power Station, London **22**
Bechtel contractors **156**
Bercy 2 Shopping Centre, Paris *17*, **38**, **141**,
  147, **184**
Berlin *see* Potsdamer Platz project
Beyeler Foundation Museum, Basle **60**
bio-mechanical tradition *12*, **133**
biomorphic components **179**
Blassel, Jean-François **141**, **148**, **149**, **150**,
  150, **151**
bleacher seats
  Grand Stade, Paris *116*, **118**
  Saitama Arena **123**
blinds
  Cy Twombly Gallery, Houston **59**
Brancusi, Constantin **34**, **35**, **168**
Brancusi Studio, Paris **34**, **35–8**, *36*
  plan *36*

ceilings
  Kansai International Airport, Osaka **128**,
  131, **216**
  Saitama Arena **123**, **125**, *125*
Charenton *see* Bercy 2 Shopping Centre, Paris
Chavela, Ariel **150**, *150*
cinemas, Rome Auditoria **112**
  Cité Internationale de Lyon **77**, **84**, **86**, **94**
  Saitama Arena **125**
Cité Internationale de Lyon **21**, *21*, **28**, **32–3**,
  32, **74–81**, *74–97*, **140**
  Atrium museum **76–7**, *94*
  plans **77**, *79*, **84**, **88**, *96*
cities

poly-nucleated **16**, **29–32**
urban reconstruction schemes **16–17**,
  21–2
cladding, clapboard
  Menil Collection, Houston **26**, **29**
cladding, copper
  Saitama Arena **122**
cladding, stainless-steel tiles
  Bercy 2 Shopping Centre, Paris **184**
  Kansai International Airport, Osaka **184**,
  184–6
cladding, stone
  Cy Twombly Gallery, Houston **29**, **56**, **58**
  plan *62*
cladding, terracotta
  Banca Popolare di Lodi, Genoa *18–19*, **21**,
  77
  Bas Meudon, Paris *32*
  Cité Internationale de Lyon **21**, *21*, **32–4**,
  32, **74**, **77–9**, *93*
  Columbus International Exposition, Genoa
  17, *17*, **21**
  Harbour Master's Office, Genoa *21*, **77**
  Ile Seguin, Paris *32*
  IRCAM Extension, Paris *32*, **77**
  Potsdamer Platz project, Berlin *32*, **33**, **77**
  Rue de Meaux Housing, Paris *32*
Colosseum, Rome **24**, **25**, **114**
colour, Kansai International Airport, Osaka
  203, **209**, **210**, **219**
Columbus International Exposition, Genoa
  17, *17*, **21**, **212**
computers **13–14**
  Kansai International Airport, Osaka **132–3**,
  200
concert–congress hall
  Lingotto Factory Renovation, Turin **40–2**, *40*,
  48-52, *48*, *51*, *53*, **80**, **108**
concert hall
  Rome Auditoria, **16**, **28**, *29*, **32**, **102–12**,

102–13
  conference centre
  Cité Internationale de Lyon **79–81**, *81*, *96*
  Lingotto Factory Renovation *34*, *48*
copper cladding *see* cladding
Corajoud, Michel **74**, **76**
Corte, Ivan **150**, *150*
Cowell, Richard **52**
Cy Twombly Gallery, Houston **26**, **28–9**, *28*,
  56–60, *56–73*

Davis Langdon Everest **155–6**
Dilley, Philip **52**
dome, Lingotto Factory Renovation, Turin
  42–4, *44*
Drees & Sommer **33**

Eames, Charles **28**, **203**
earthquakes **181**, **192**, **193**
Eiffel **155**, **193**
energy efficiency **32–3**
  Cité Internationale de Lyon **78**
  Cy Twombly Gallery, Houston **60**
European Union **33**, **34**
expansion gaps, Kansai International Airport,
  Osaka **181**
Expo 1970, Osaka *9*

Fiat *see* Lingotto Factory Renovation, Turin
Fiat Engineering **52**
fire prevention, Kansai International Airport,
  Osaka **200**, *201*
Flaminio soccer stadium, Rome **102**
floors
  Cy Twombly Gallery, Houston **59–60**
  Kansai International Airport, Osaka **156**
Fluor Daniel **156**
Foster, Sir Norman **132**
Foster Associates **146**
fractals **168**

Fraser, Kenny **108**, **149**, **150**, *150*

Genoa *see* Columbus International Exposition;
 Harbour Master's Office
geometry
 fractals **168**
 Kansai International Airport, Osaka **132–3**,
  143, *146–7*, **147**, **166–8**, *167–8*
 toroidal geometry **109**, **132–3**, *143*, **147**,
  167–8
glass fences, Kansai International Airport,
 Osaka **203**, *203*
glazing
 Cité Internationale de Lyon **32–3**, *32*, **74**,
  76, **77**, **78–9**, *82*, **90**
 Cy Twombly Gallery, Houston **58**, **59**, *70*,
  73
 Kansai International Airport, Osaka **148**,
  154–5, *158*, **181**, **184**, *188*, **192–3**,
  192–4, **224**
 Lingotto Factory Renovation, Turin **44**
 Saitama Arena **122–3**
Grand Stade, Paris **24**, *24*, **25–6**, *25*,
 114–18, *114–19*, **123**
 plans *116*, *118*
Grenoble Synchroton **140**
Guthrie, Alistair **52**, **196**

Harbour Master's Office, Genoa **21**, *21*, **77**
heliport, Lingotto Factory Renovation, Turin
 40, **42**, *42*
Hirano, Kohji *150*, *151*
hotels, Lingotto Factory Renovation, Turin **42**
housing, Bas Meudon, Paris *100*
Houston *see* Cy Twombly Gallery; Menil
 Collection

IBM Travelling Pavilion **9**, *14*, **15**, **168**, **226**
Ikegami, Akira **150**, *151*
Île Seguin, Paris **28**, **32**, *32*, **98–100**,

99–101
 plan *99*
Inakura, Takayuki *150*
industrial buildings, converting **21–3**
Industrial Revolution **22**
International Style **10**
IRCAM extension, Paris *9*, **15**, *17*, **21**, **26**,
 28, *32*, **77**, **108**
Ishida, Shunji *9*, **108**, **140**, **149–50**, *150*
island, Kansai International Airport, Osaka
 136–9, *138*
Italian Industry Pavilion, Expo 1970, Osaka *9*
Itami Airport, Osaka **136**

Japan Airports Consultants Inc **149**, **150**
Japan Railways West **138**
Johnson, Philip **28**, **56**
Joule II research programme **33**
Jourda & Perraudin **24**, **116**

Kansai Academic City **136**
Kansai International Airport, Osaka **6**, *9*,
 11–14, *13*, *14*, **16**, **17**, *38*, **109**,
 128–227, *128–227*
 airside exterior **143**, **147–9**, **152**, *156*,
  158, **166–9**, *171*, *172*, *174*, **180**, **184**,
  188, **192**, *192*, *193*, **198**, *203*, **209**,
  210, **226**, *226*
 approach **155**, **204**, *208*
 background and design development
  136–58
 boarding wing **130**, **132**, **140**, *140*, *143*,
  146–9, *146*, *147*, **151–6**, *154*, *158*,
  160, **162**, *166*, *168*, *170*, **171**, **177**,
  185, **188**, **192**, *193*, **196**, **199**, *199*, **200**,
  203, **204**, **209**, **216**, *219*, **223–4**,
  223–5
 canyon **130**, **131**, *140*, **146**, **148**, *149*,
  151–2, **154**, *163*, *164*, **167**, *173*, *174*,
  179, *180*, **181**, *186*, **192–3**, *196*,

198–201, *203*, **209–12**, *210*, *212*, **216**
 circulation **160–2**
 cladding **184**, *184–8*
 competition **140–8**
 cost cutting and construction **154–6**
 detail design **152**
 development of final design **149–51**
 fire prevention **200**, *201*
 furniture and fitting out *202–3*, **203**
 geometry **132–3**, *143*, *146–7*, **147**,
  166–8, *167–8*
 glazing **148**, **154–5**, *158*, **181**, **184**, *188*,
  192–3, *192–4*, **224**
 international departures hall **212–16**,
  212–17
 island **136–9**, *138*
 landside exterior **208–9**, *209*
 plans *164*, *174*
 services **196–9**, *196*
 structural movement *180*, **181**
 structure **171–9**, *171–9*
 transit lounge and shuttle **219**, *219*
Kansai International Airport Company **151**
Kawasaki Steel Corporation **155**
Kobe **136**, **138**, **181**
Kyoto **136**, **138**

lighting, Kansai International Airport, Osaka
 199, *199*, **203**
Lingotto Factory Renovation, Turin **22**, **23–4**,
 23, **34**, *34*, **40–52**, *40–53*, **80**
 concert hall/congress hall **40–2**, *40*,
  48–52, *48*, *51*, *53*, **80**, **108**
  conference auditoria **40**, **48**
  conference bubble **40–4**, *40*, *42–4*
  plan *48*
Lodi *see* Banco Popolare di Lodi
London *see* Bankside Power Station; Battersea
 Power Station
Lyon *see* Cité International de Lyon

McBryde, Ken **141**, **149**, **150**, *150*
Maison de Publicité, Paris **10**
Maison du Peuple, Paris **10**
Maison Suspendue, Paris **10**
mall
 Cité Internationale de Lyon **74**, **81**, *79*, *86*,
  94, *96*
Mandelbrot, Benoît **168**
Matté-Trucco, Giacomo **22**
Menil Collection, Houston *9*, **10**, **15**, *26*,
 28–9, *28*, **56**, **58**
Mercedes-Benz Design Centre, Stuttgart **16**,
 26, **28**, **29**, *29–31*, **109**
 plan *30*
Michigan, University of **60**
Mikami, Uzo **168**
Milan Triennale (1967) *9*
Mobile Structure for Sulphur Extraction,
 Pomezia, Rome *9*
Montaldo, Alessandro *150*
Müller Bbm **52**, **53**, **108**
Museum of Modern Art, New York **22**
museums *see* Beyeler Foundation Museum;
 Cité Internationale de Lyon; Menil
 Collection; Museum of Modern Art, New
 York; National Centre for Science and
 Technology, Amsterdam

Nankai railway company **138**
Narita Airport, Tokyo **138**
National Academy of Santa Cecilia **108**
National Centre for Science and Technology,
 Amsterdam *14*, **16**
Nelson, Paul **10**
Neo-Gothic **12**, **133**
neoprene *188*, **192**, *193*
Nervi, Pier Luigi **102**, *104*
New York *see* Museum of Modern Art
Nikken Sekkei **128**, **140**, **149**, **150**, **152**,
 208, **209**, **210**, **212**

Nippon Steel **155**

offices, Cité Internationale de Lyon **79**, *81*,
 86, *88*, *90*
Okabe, Noriaki *9*, **130**, **140**, **141**, **148**, **149**,
 150, *150*, *151*, **168**, **171**, **200**
organic architecture, Kansai International
 Airport, Osaka **12**, **14**, **130**, **131**, **132–3**,
 168, **177**, **179**
Osaka *see* Expo 1970; Kansai International
 Airport
Otranto *see* UNESCO Neighbourhood
 Workshop
Ove Arup *see* Arup, Ove & Partners

Palazzetto della Sport, Rome **102**, *104*
Paris *see* Bas Meudon; Bercy 2 Shopping
 Centre; Brancusi Studio; Grand Stade; Ile
 Seguin; IRCAM extension; Pompidou
 Centre; Rue de Meaux Housing;
 Schlumberger Renovation
Piano, Renzo, photographs of *150*, *151*
Piano & Fitzgerald
 Menil Collection, Houston *9*, **10**, **15**, *26*,
  28–9, *28*, **56**, **58**
Piano & Rogers
 Patscentre building, Cambridge **226**
 Pompidou Centre, Paris **6**, *9*, *9*, **10–11**,
  10, *12*, **14**, **15–16**, **22**, **34–5**, *36*, *38*
Piano Rice Associates
 UNESCO Neighbourhood Workshop,
  Otranto *9*, **10**, *10*, **15**
piazzas
 Bankside Power Station **23**, **24**, **52**, *53*
 Île Seguin and Bas Meudon, Paris **98**
 Lingotto Factory Renovation **23**, **24**, **40**,
  42, **46**, *51*
 Rome Auditoria **104**, **109**, *110*, **112**
Place Beaubourg, Paris **116**
Plattner, Bernard *9*

238 'pointillist' effect **32**, **78**, *82*
Pompidou Centre, Paris **6**, **9**, *9*, **10–11**, *10*, *12*, **14**, **15–16**, **22**, **34–5**, *36*, *38*
plan *36*
Potsdamer Platz project, Berlin **16**, **17**, *32*, **33**, **77**, *78*, **81**
promenade, Île Seguin and Bas Meudon, Paris **98**, *100*
Prouvé, Jean **10**
public address systems, Kansai International Airport, Osaka **199**, *199*, **203**

Reinforced Polyester Space Frame, Genoa *9*
Renaissance **132**, **133**
Renzo Piano Building Workshop **8**, **9–10**, **15**
Renzo Piano Building Workshop Japan **149**
Rice, Peter **9**, **15**, **130**, **141–2**, **146**, **147**, **148**, *150*, **168**
Rogers, Richard **9**, **34**, **81**
Rome Auditoria **16**, **28**, **29**, *29*, **32**, **102–12**, *102–13*
plans *104–7*
roofs
Banca Popolare di Lodi, Genoa *19*
Bercy 2 Shopping Centre, Paris **184**
Cy Twombly Gallery, Houston **59**, **60**, *60*, *70*, *73*
Grand Stade, Paris **25**, *25*, **118**
Ile Seguin and Bas Meudon, Paris **100**
Kansai International Airport, Osaka **109**, **131**, **143**, *143*, **146–7**, *146–7*, **148**, **151**, *158*, **166–7**, *167–8*, *174*, **184**, *184–92*, *208*
Mercedes-Benz Design Centre, Stuttgart **29**, *30–1*, **109**
Rome Auditoria **104–8**, *108*, **109**
Saitama Arena **25**, *25*, **122**, *122*, **125**
Rothko Chapel, Houston **56**, *60*
Rue de Meaux Housing, Paris **9**, *17*, *32*

Saint Gobain **192**
Saint Quentin-en-Yvelines *see* Thomson Optronics Factory
Saitama Arena **24**, **25–6**, *25*, **120–5**, *120–7*
plan *122*
San Nicola Stadium, Bari **9**, *14*, **15**, **25**, **114**
Schlumberger Renovation, Paris **15**, *17*, **23**
sculpture
Constantin Brancusi **35**
wind sculptures, Susumu Shigu **212**, *216*
seating, Kansai International Airport, Osaka *202*, **203**
seismic stresses **12**, **129**, **133**, **139**, **142**, **149**, **181**
shell structural system *9*
shell principle
Kansai International Airport, Osaka **132**, **171**, **177–8**
Shingu, Susumu *42*, **212**, *216*
sports stadia **24–6**
Grand Stade, Paris **24**, *24*, **25–6**, *25*, **114–18**, *114–19*, **123**
Saitama Arena **24**, **25–6**, *25*, **120–5**, *120–7*
San Nicola Stadium, Bari *14*, **15**, **25**, **114**
stainless-steel cladding *see* cladding
Stansted Airport **132**, **146**
Strasbourg *see* University Hospital
Structural-Rationalism **10**
structure
concrete structures **25**, **46**, **58**, *92*, **118**
steel structures **28**, *43*, **44**, **48**, **80**, **118**, **144**, **152**, **193**, **200**
wood structures **38**, **32**
Studio Piano **8**, *9*
Stuttgart *see* Mercedes-Benz Design Centre
Sydney Opera House **168**, *168*

Takenaka Corporation **156**
Tate Gallery, London *see* Bankside

Power Station
terracotta cladding *see* cladding
Thomson Optronics Factory, Saint Quentin-en- Yvelines **16**, *17*
tidal waves **138**
Tomuro, Taichi **150**, *151*
toroidal geometry **109**, **132–3**, *143*, **147**, **167–8**
Touraine, Olivier **141**, **143**, **149**, **150**, *150*
trees, Kansai International Airport, Osaka *140*, **142–3**, **146**, **148**, **156**, **199**
Turin *see* Lingotto Factory Renovation
Twombly, Cy **56**, **59**, *66*
typhoons **181**

UNESCO Laboratory-workshop, Vesima **9**, **26–8**, **38**, *38*
UNESCO Neighbourhood Workshop, Otranto **9**, **10**, *10*, **15**
University Hospital, Strasbourg **17–21**, *27*, **28**
plan *27*
urban reconstruction schemes **16–17**, **21–2**
Utzon, Jørn **168**, *168*

ventilation
Cité Internationale de Lyon **32–3**, **78**
Kansai International Airport, Osaka **131**
Saitama Arena **125**
see also air-conditioning
Vesima *see* UNESCO Laboratory-workshop
Viollet-le-Duc, Eugène **12**

Watson, Robert **155**, **178**
Wernick, Jane **118**
wind sculptures **212**, *216*
windows *see* glazing
Woodwork Shop, Genoa *9*

zinc, Rome Auditoria **109**

239

Renzo Piano Building Workshop

Volume 1 contents

Aluminium Research Institute, Novara **166–73**
B&B Italia Offices, Como **50**
Calder Retrospective **80–3**
Contemporary Art Museum, Newport Harbour **164**
European Synchrotron Radiation Facility, Grenoble **200**
Fiat VSS Experimental Car **64**
'Flying Carpet' Basic Vehicle **65**
Free-plan Houses, Cusago **51**
Genoa office–workshop **44**
IBM Ladybird Pavilion **132–3**
IBM Travelling Pavilion **110–30**
IRCAM Extension, Paris **202–13**
Italian Industry Pavilion, Expo 1970 **49**
Kansai International Airport Terminal **20–5**
Lowara Offices, Montecchio Maggiore **134–9**
Menil Collection gallery, Houston **140–63**
Mobile Structure for Sulphur Extraction **47**
'The Open Site' **66–7**
Palladio Basilica Rehabilitation, Vicenza **177**

Piano & Rice Associates **64–77**
Piano & Rogers **50–63**
Pompidou Centre, Paris **52–63**
Prometeo opera, setting for **84–9**
QB Housing, Genoa **44**
Reinforced Polyester Space Frame **47**
Rhodes Moat Development **176**
Il Rigo Housing, Corciano **18–19**
Rue de Meaux Housing, Paris **214–27**
San Nicola Stadium, Bari **179–99**
Schlumberger Renovation, Paris **90–109**
Shell Structural System for the Fourteenth Milan Triennale **48**
Sistiana Tourist Resort, Trieste **201**
Studio Piano **46–9**
Tensile Steel and Reinforced-Polyester Structure **48**
Twombly (Cy) Pavilion, Houston **165**
UNESCO Neighbourhood Workshop, Otranto **68–77**
Valletta City Gate **174–5**
Woodwork Shop, Genoa **47**

Volume 2 contents

'Automobiles in Milan' Exhibition, Milan **168–169**
Bercy 2 Shopping Centre, Paris **16–33**
Beyeler Foundation Museum, near Basle **170–179**
Columbus International Exposition, Genoa **94–129**
Credito Industriale Sardo, Cagliari **140–149**
Cruise Ships and Yacht **58–63**
'Further Dimensions of the Organic', introductory essay **6–15**
'Galileo in Padua' Exhibition Project, Padua **130–131**
Glass Furniture **92–93**
Interview with Renzo Piano **64–75**

Kansai International Airport, Osaka **220–227**
Lingotto Factory Renovation, Turin **150–167**
Metro Stations, Genoa **46–57**
National Centre for Science and Technology, Amsterdam **132–139**
Padre Pio Pilgrimage Church, San Giovanni Rotondo **180–189**
Potsdamer Platz, Berlin **210–219**
Thomson Optronics Factory, Saint Quentin-en-Yvelines **34–45**
J M Tjibaou Cultural Centre, Nouméa **190–209**
UNESCO Laboratory-workshop, Vesima **76–91**